Job's Body and the Dı
Comedy of Moralising

This book focuses on the expressions used to describe Job's body in pain and on the reactions of his friends to explore the moral and social world reflected in the language and the values that their speeches betray.

A key contribution of this monograph is to highlight how the perspective of illness as retribution is powerfully refuted in Job's speeches and, in particular, to show how this is achieved through comedy. Comedy in Job is a powerful weapon used to expose and ridicule the idea of retribution. Rejecting the approach of retrospective diagnosis, this monograph carefully analyses the expression of pain in Job, focusing specifically on somatic language used in the deity attack metaphors, in the deity surveillance metaphors, and in the language connected to the body and social status. These metaphors are analysed in a comparative way using research from medical anthropology and sociology which focuses on illness narratives and expressions of pain.

Job's Body and the Dramatised Comedy of Moralising will be of interest to anyone working on the Book of Job, as well as those with an interest in suffering and pain in the Hebrew Bible more broadly.

Katherine E. Southwood is Associate Professor in the Faculty of Theology and Religion at the University of Oxford, UK, and Tutorial Fellow in Theology and Religion and Fellow for Women at St John's College, Oxford. She is author of *Marriage by Capture in Judges 21: An Anthropological Approach* (2017) and *Ethnicity and the Mixed Marriage Crisis in Ezra 9–10: An Anthropological Approach* (2012).

Routledge Studies in the Biblical World

A Commentary on Numbers
Narrative, Ritual, and Colonialism
Pekka Pitkänen

Masculinities in the Court Tales of Daniel
Advancing Gender Studies in the Hebrew Bible
Brian Charles DiPalma

Religion, Ethnicity, and Xenophobia in the Bible
A Theoretical, Exegetical and Theological Survey
Brian Rainey

Job's Body and the Dramatised Comedy of Moralising
Katherine E. Southwood

www.routledge.com/classicalstudies/series/BIBWORLD

Job's Body and the Dramatised Comedy of Moralising

Katherine E. Southwood

LONDON AND NEW YORK

First published 2021
by Routledge
2 Park Square, Milton Park, Abingdon, Oxon OX14 4RN

and by Routledge
52 Vanderbilt Avenue, New York, NY 10017

Routledge is an imprint of the Taylor & Francis Group, an informa business

British Library Cataloguing-in-Publication Data
A catalogue record for this book is available from the British Library

Library of Congress Cataloging-in-Publication Data
Names: Southwood, Katherine, 1982– author.
Title: Job's Body and the Dramatised Comedy of Moralising/Katherine E. Southwood.
Description: Milton Park, Abingdon, Oxon; New York, NY: Routledge, [2021] | Series: Routledge studies in the biblical world | Includes bibliographical references and index.
Identifiers: LCCN 2020012128 (print) | LCCN 2020012129 (ebook) | ISBN 9780367462574 (hardback) | ISBN 9781003029489 (ebook)
Subjects: LCSH: Bible. Job – Socio-rhetorical criticism. | Suffering in the Bible. | Metaphor in the Bible.
Classification: LCC BS1415.52. S58 2021 (print) | LCC BS1415.52 (ebook) |DDC 223/.1066 – dc23
LC record available at https://lccn.loc.gov/2020012128
LC ebook record available at https://lccn.loc.gov/2020012129

ISBN: 978-0-367-46257-4 (hbk)
ISBN: 978-0-367-53311-3 (pbk)
ISBN: 978-1-003-02948-9 (ebk)

DOI: 10.4324/9781003029489

To James.

Contents

Preface ix

1 **Introduction and methods** 1
Introduction 1
'Illness', 'sickness', 'disease' and the perils of retrospective diagnosis 16
Illness narratives and the quest for meaning: pain resists language? 24
Avoiding pitfalls: using illness and pain narratives to analyse Job's speeches 28
Outline 38

2 **Methinks the Job, he doth protest too much** 50
Introduction 50
'The arrows of Shaddai': Job's body and the deity attack metaphor in Job 6 50
'He multiplies my wounds rashly': Job 9:17–19 and the metaphor of deity attack 60
'He seized me by the scruff and shattered me': Job's body and the deity attack metaphor in Job 16 66
A further deity attack metaphor in Job 16 80
Who can but moralise?: Job's body and the supernatural attack in Job 19 86
'By night he chews at my bones within me': the deity attack metaphor in Job 30 92
Summary 99

3 **The tyranny of tradition** 111
Introduction 111
'Am I Yam?! Or Tannin': creation and the deity surveillance metaphor in Job 7 112

Watch and pounce: the deity surveillance and attack metaphor in Job 10 127
'Do you fix your eyes on such a one?': deity surveillance in Job 13 and 14 135
Summary 140

4 Pride comes before a fool: Job's loss of social status 148
Introduction 148
'My wind is repulsive to my wife': Job 19 and how not to win friends and influence people 149
'Look at my body, ye mighty friends, and despair!': the body and powerlessness in Job 21 156
Summary 160

5 Is the answer for Job blowin' in the wind? 163
Job as a dramatised comedy of advice 163
Job's responses to Yahweh 168

Name index 176
Subject index 178
Job's body*: index of scriptural references* 182

Preface

The dialogues form the major corpus of the book of Job. However, in the dialogues, the entrenched and unrelenting positions of all of the characters result in the conversation seeming to have a somewhat circular, almost pointless, character. Perhaps this is why when many readers first encounter the book of Job, they often tend to focus on, and prioritise, the prologue, Job's curse (Job 3), Job's sarcastic doxology (Job 7), the quest for wisdom (Job 28), the whirlwind speeches, and Job's responses to Yahweh. This monograph, in contrast, has sought to prioritise the speeches. Far from being irrelevant, perhaps dare we suggest even rather dull at first glance, this monograph understands speeches as the central core of Job. In particular, this monograph focuses on Job's body within his own speeches, suggesting that it is a device through which the author/s can explore some of the ethical and epistemological aspects of Yahwism at the time of writing and for early audiences. In order to try and contextualise and understand the way Job's body functioned in the speeches, this monograph has used research concerning illness narratives and expressions of pain from medical anthropology. However, the serious topics that Job and his friends discuss are portrayed in a light-hearted way in Job, which we have imagined as a play to be performed before audiences. Rethinking Job in this way brings the dialogues to life. Far from being dull and repetitive, they regularly move from the tragic to the comic and vice versa. They are full of parody, sarcasm, hyperbole, misdirection, word plays, absurdity, and anticlimaxes. Indeed, the entire surreal premise upon which the play is set (that the Satan can touch Job's body, but not kill him), is a grandiose piece of dramatic irony. This allows audiences to be privy to information that the baffled Job struggles to explain and ferociously argues about. It also allows the audiences to observe the friends' advice to Job and the irony of their self-assured moralising. In addition to this monograph, I have several articles that use a similar method. These include 'Metaphor, Illness, and Identity in Psalm 88 and 102'. *Journal for the Study of the Old Testament* (2) 2019, 228–246. Also 'You Are All Quacks; If Only You Would Shut Up' (Job 13:4b-5a): Sin and Illness in the Sacred and Secular. *Theology* 121(2) 2018, 84–91; and, 'The "Innards" in the Psalms and Job as Metaphors for Illness' in *Horizons in Biblical Literature* (forthcoming).

I imagine that very few, if any, monographs could ever be published without support of other people who surround authors. Too often this help is assumed, invisible, and unrecognised. I seize the opportunity here publicly to recognise, acknowledge, and thank all those who have made it possible for me to produce this research. I owe Elisabeth Hsu, professor of anthropology and a specialist in medical anthropology, a tremendous debt of gratitude for having allowed me to attend her lectures. I also owe her my thanks for working together with me to co-convene an international seminar series from January to March 2019 on 'The Personification of Pain in Different Religions: Engaging with Religious Texts through Medical Anthropology'. Working with Elisabeth has been an absolute privilege and a pleasure: she has been patient, supportive, and kind, and I could not have produced this monograph without her guidance. As a result of Elisabeth's inspiration, and as chair of the Society of Biblical Literature programme unit 'Social Sciences and the Interpretation of Hebrew Scripture', I ran a successful panel on medical anthropology entitled 'How Can Medical Anthropology Be Used in Biblical Studies?' for November 2019. I was excited by this and am glad to see so much high-quality interdisciplinary work emerging in biblical studies.

I am keen to acknowledge the Revd Canon Dr Margaret Whipp who, until recently, was the lead chaplain for Oxford University Hospitals. Margaret and I successfully applied for funding from the Wellcome Institutional Strategic Support Public Engagement with Research Fund and ran a project entitled 'Illness as a Moral Event'. The project included three large conferences designed to bring together hospital chaplains and academics focusing on illness and language and the nuances of 'meaning' and 'value' when it comes to caring for those who are ill. I cannot emphasise enough how useful it was for me to participate in and organise these events. I learned a lot from listening to the experiences of the hospital chaplains: it is a role that I deeply admire and respect. On a related note, I am also grateful for the Medical Humanities Award that I received from The Oxford Centre for Research in the Humanities that enabled me to run a further interdisciplinary conference, 'Accounts of Illness in Historical and Modern Texts: Exploring Methods in Medical Humanities Research Across Disciplines'. I am also grateful to my colleague Professor Joshua Hordern and also to Dr Andrew Papanikitas for allowing me to participate in many of the events run through, and in relation to, the Arts and Humanities Research Council-funded 'Healthcare Values Partnership'.

The results of the research in this monograph are perhaps suggestive in terms of healthism, the wellness industry, and the medicalisation of everyday life. The National Health Service (NHS) Constitution for England suggests that people 'recognise that you can make a significant contribution to your own, and your family's, good health and wellbeing, and take personal responsibility for it', and there is an increasing movement towards 'responsibilisation' in UK healthcare policy, as demonstrated in Her Majesty's government publication *Healthy Lives, Healthy People* (Great Britain Department of Health, 2010). It is perhaps worth remembering that responsibility may be used in a positive and empowering sense, but when it is used in a more negative, moralising way, it only adds to the burden of health complications.

I consider myself to be truly fortunate to have successfully gained funding for two research assistants (Eleanor Vivian, whose help with the editing of the monograph was invaluable, and Susy Rees, who helped with the impact work related to this monograph). Although I consciously tried hard not to lean too much on Ellie, I am grateful for her eagle-eyed attention to detail in the work that she put into proofreading and editing my material into style. Finally, I am grateful to my colleagues in Oxford, in particular, John Barton, Sue Gillingham, Laura Quick, and Sarah Foot, for their support of my research whether through references or through listening to me continually whinge about this monograph. Similarly, I thank my husband Bruce Forman for putting up with what became affectionately known as "grant-application hell" through this monograph project, and I especially thank our daughters Abigail and Samantha for making me laugh at the absurdity of all the toil that I put into academic work. Nevertheless, I dedicate this monograph to my brother, Dr James Southwood. Perhaps this is fitting given that he is a clinical psychologist? Thankfully for his patients, however, his advice is only ever professional and never, ever 'moralising'!

1 Introduction and methods

Introduction

Eskenazi comments 'nowhere else in the Bible is the face of the other in utterly uncontainable pain so carefully and relentlessly attended to than in the book of Job' (Eskenazi 2003:68). More dramatically phrased, Duhm suggested that Job 'wrote with his own blood' (Duhm 1897:ix). A key feature of Job is the persistent focus on the protagonist's body in pain and how this changes the social dynamic between Job and his friends. As will be demonstrated, the book reveals little to nothing about disease. Nevertheless, this monograph argues that there is a clear case to be made for Job's contribution to our understanding of how pain and illness were imagined and contextualised socially at the time of writing and for early audiences. In the book of Job, illness and pain are presented as moral events that provoke profound introspection but also, more importantly, as culturally salient events which cause the community to question its meaning and significance as well as their own values. This is achieved in the book of Job through tragedy but also, importantly, through comedy. The entire scenario is rather surreal, the one-dimensional characters Eliphaz, Bildad, and Zophar (and Elihu) are overflowing with moralising advice, and the main protagonist is a pompous, self-aggrandising windbag. We should note here that by 'moralising' language and advice, what is meant is judgemental communication – speech emphasising personal responsibility and incriminating assumptions embedded within advice. Moralising is specifically embedded within language and interaction. This is because, as Newsom observes, 'every way of talking implies a moral and a social world' so that 'all sorts of values are built into talk, not only in what is explicitly affirmed or criticized but also in the structure and texture of the talk and what it requires of one who hears and responds to it' (Newsom 1993:119).

One interesting critical niche concerning the body in Job can be found through using modern research focusing on illness and pain experiences and behaviours from medical anthropology and sociology comparatively with the dialogues in Job.[1] This body of research enables us to assess critically the social

1 Although throughout this monograph we refer regularly to the research as coming from medical anthropology, there are also numerous references to research beyond this specific field. Therefore, it is acknowledged that although a lot of the comparative research is drawn from medical anthropology, we have not ruled out other relevant research simply for the benefit of remaining strictly within the limits of this discipline.

DOI: 10.4324/9781003029489-1

dynamics between Job and his friends in a comparative way. There is a case to be made that the Hebrew Bible is far from irrelevant for the study of the social aspects of illness and pain. The book of Job, which can be dated to approximately the late exilic period, at the very earliest, or more likely, later in the post-exilic period,[2] asks some of the most pertinent questions about community and provides a rich and fertile resource for examining the social ramifications of suffering. A key contribution of this monograph is to highlight the nuances of how the perspective of illness as retribution is powerfully refuted in Job's speeches and, in particular, to show how this is achieved through satirical comedy. Comedy in Job is a weapon used to expose and ridicule the idea that suffering is punishment for some wrongdoing. A particular site upon which this exposure plays out is on Job's body. The book, despite its many genres, and therefore its regular description as a 'polyphonic', 'multivalent', and less regular designation as a 'contrapuntal' text, is treated here as a coherent whole (Jones 2010; Newsom 2002). Indeed, the book of Job is imagined in this monograph as a drama to be performed with an audience, perhaps with some similarities to Aristophanes and the Athenian theatre. Therefore, perhaps like Aristophanes, 'comic elements' are used 'to support serious points concerning his audience's world and ideals' (Lazarus 2014:47), Job is, we therefore argue, a dramatised comedy of 'advice'.

In much of the Hebrew Bible we find a persistent stance on illness which aligns well with theories and arguments concerning retribution.[3] A suitable example of this is the presence of illness in curses which come with not observing the covenant in Deuteronomy 28:[4]

> The Lord will make the pestilence[5] cling to you until it has consumed you . . . The Lord will afflict you with consumption, fever, inflammation,

2 A date in the exilic period would be, more specifically, to the very late sixth and the first half of the fifth century BCE, at the very earliest. This is partly on account of the resonance between parts of Job and Deutero-Isaiah, Lamentations, Psalms, Proverbs, and Jeremiah (although given their dating is also a matter of debate, the reasoning here is admittedly somewhat circular). The mention of 'The Adversary' is also a possible clue to quite a late dating, given the adversary appears only elsewhere in Zechariah and Chronicles. The matter is made more complex by the rather wide range of nonbiblical primary material that exhibits similarities with Job (refer to note 11).

3 For a helpful summary of this and especially in terms of the nuances of the idea of retribution, which is not to be dismissed as 'simplistic', refer to Kaminsky's article (Kaminsky 2015). Refer also to Dell 2000:32; Adamiak 1982. The treatment of the idea of retribution in this monograph is limited to a focus on the body.

4 This is often viewed as stereotypical curse language which accompanies the breaking of a treaty, as is found in comparative material such as the Vassal Treaties of Esarhaddon, the Syrian and Assyrian Treaties, Hittite Treaties, and the Code of Hammurabi, as well as the Sefire Inscriptions and the Tel Fakhariyah inscription (refer to Quick 2017; *pace* Crouch 2014). The grouping of curses into the different categories which Hillers suggests is helpful, and these would be considered divine curses (Hillers 1964; refer also to the discussion of curses in Kitz 2014).

5 The term translated here as "pestilence" (דֶּבֶר) is possibly 'an infectious disease of epidemic proportions' which the LXX 'translates with θάνατον (death)' (Lundbom 2013:770; cf. Jer. 21:6; Hos. 13:14). However, given the perils of retrospective diagnosis, which we will later discuss, Lundbom is correct to exercise caution through vagueness.

> with fiery heat[6] and drought, and with blight and mildew . . . The LORD will afflict you with the boils of Egypt,[7] with ulcers, scurvy, and itch,[8] *of which you cannot be healed.* The LORD will afflict you with madness, blindness, and confusion of mind.[9]
>
> (Deuteronomy 28:21–22, 27–28)

Here the implication is that if you fail to uphold your side of the covenant that is tantamount to bringing the listed conditions upon yourself. These ailments can simply be avoided through human agency: to live in an upright manner in accordance with the covenant will, after all, mean that the god YHWH will 'turn away from you every illness; all the dread diseases of Egypt . . . he will not inflict on you' (Deut. 7:15). Such reasoning also appears in other sources which compare with Job (Magdalene 2007). To use an Akkadian example, in the *Dialogue Between a Man and His God* the young man is 'sickened with his burden' and admits 'I have blasphemed you' after which the god orders restoration of health,[10] stating:

> Your disease is under control, let your heart not be despondent! The years and days you were filled with misery are over. How could you have lasted the whole of this grievous illness? You have seen distress . . . is (now) held back. You have borne its massive load to the end.
>
> (Hallo and Younger 1997:485)[11]

6 'Consumption' (שחפת), 'fever' (קדחת), 'fiery heat' (חרחר + דלקת). It is not clear what these terms refer to. The term קדחת is a *hapax legomenon* which the LXX translates with πυρετῷ ('fever'). Various theories about what these conditions might mean exist (Lundbom 2013:770; Nelson 2002:331; Mayes 1979:354; Driver 1902:208).

7 It is not clear what 'boils' (שחין) of Egypt means. The same term is used in the prologue of Job (Job 2:7–8). The term is sometimes linked to the unknown condition צרעת on account of the link between them in Leviticus (Lev. 13:20). Refer to note 35 for a discussion of צרעת.

8 עפל is usually translated 'tumour' or 'haemorrhoid' (NRSV 'ulcer'). The *qere* has טחרים also meaning 'haemorrhoids' (but a perpetual *qere*, euphemistically replacing potentially offensive terms), as BHQ notes. The LXX reads 'an Egyptian boil in the seats' (ἐν ἕλκει Αἰγυπτίῳ ἐν ταῖς ἕδραις) which combines the first two afflictions. The term translated by NRSV as 'scurvy' (גרב) seems to affect both humans and animals in Lev. 21:20 and 22:22 and is understood by the LXX as 'a severe itch' (ψώρᾳ ἀγρίᾳ). Similarly, the *hapax legomenon* חֶרֶס seems to mean 'itch'. Again, it is best to be vague here, given the perils of retrospective diagnosis, which will be discussed later.

9 The conditions 'madness, blindness, and confusion of mind' could be understood in an atomistic way as separate problems or could be understood as a three-fold description of the same problem seemingly related to some kind of physical, mental, or emotional disorientation.

10 The focus of this monograph is on illness rather than healing. However, it is appropriate to point out that in much of the Hebrew Bible and comparative literature, as in this example, healing is often the responsibility of the deity (Pilch 2000:62).

11 Refer also to Lambert's translation: Lambert 1987:187–202. Numerous parallels to the book of Job exist. For example, in Egyptian material The *Admonitions of Ipuwer* cites the conventional belief 'He [God] is the herdsman of all; there is no evil in his heart . . . only lament the wickedness that the deity allowed to stand'. Because of the social upheaval, the author denies the existence of a providential deity guiding human affairs. He asks: 'Where is he today? Is he asleep?' Similarly, the *Dispute*

Essentially, as Brown argues, the logic follows that 'if one lost one's health . . . one became a burden to both family and society, apparently suffering from divine disfavour as well' (Brown 1995:54). A similar line of reasoning is taken in the Sumerian *Man and His God* wherein the sufferer complains that 'Asag, [a demon of sickness] the evil one, bathes in my body' and acknowledges the cause '[n]ever has a sinless child been born to its mother . . . a sinless man has never existed' (Hallo and Younger 1997:574).[12]

To develop the point, it is possible in many of the so-called exemplary sufferer texts which compare with Job to trace a cyclical idea of a deity or demon that physically punishes humans for moral and cultic violations but then restores health. For example, in a prayer to Ishtar, Assurbanipal 'attributes his illness to an unknown sin against Ishtar' (Bosworth 2015:691).[13] Similarly, in *Ludlul Bēl Nēmequ*, we have the dialectical couplets possibly translated 'His beatings are

---

Between a Man and His Ba describes a miserable person who tries to persuade his soul to join him in a pact to commit suicide. The man longs for death which is 'like a sick man's recovery'. Likewise, the *Eloquent Peasant* welcomes death 'a thirsty man's approach to water, an infant's mouth reaching for milk, thus is a longed-for death seen coming thus does his death arrive at last'. Like the book of Job, these texts have prose frameworks enclosing poetic complaints. In Mesopotamian material we have *I Will Praise the Lord of Wisdom* wherein the sufferer believes in compassion: 'I will praise the Lord of wisdom . . . whose heart is merciful . . . whose gentle hand sustains the dying'. Also relevant is the *Babylonian Theodicy* which resembles Job in that a sufferer engages in a dispute with a learned friend. Finally, *The Dialogue Between a Master and His Slave* has similarities with Job. Also similar is the Canaanite *Epic of Keret* wherein the hero loses his wife and sons but eventually finds favour with the gods and acquires a new wife and additional children (Crenshaw 1992:858–868). Various similarities in style and genre, which Newsom and van der Toorn point out, are particularly helpful (Newsom 2003:72–89; van der Toorn 1991). There are several helpful overviews of Mesopotamian sources that compare with Job (Müller 1995; Mattingly 1990; Weinfeld 1988). On the basis of several similarities, Schmid suggests it is plausible to interpret the author as an intellectual supporter of Job's social class. The high degree of scholarly knowledge regarding especially Israelite, but also Egyptian, Mesopotamian and Greek texts and the numerous subjects examined and presented, appear to indicate that the composer of the dialogues was a scribal professional from the Jerusalem temple (Schmid 2008:150).

However, although it is sensible to accept that there are significant similarities, we should question the depth and significance of the similarities while also acknowledge that there are substantial differences between these writings and Job.

12 Similarly, to take a Greek example, Lloyd notes that Herodotus also on occasion endorses 'the traditional belief that being afflicted with disease – physical or mental – may be the gods' doing, the retribution they exact for some offence to them or other wrongdoing' (Lloyd 2003:119). However, Lloyd also notes that even if a lot of Greeks diagnosed divine punishment, 'they certainly did not agree about what that punishment was for exactly' (Lloyd 2003:119).

13 A significant body of scholarship exists on ancient Mesopotamian medicine wherein several distinct kinds of healers exist (the *āšipu*, a magician and exorcist as well as a priest, and the *asû* were closer to what we might call a physician, and in addition the *bārû*, or diviner), with medical and magical texts, although there is not a sharp divide between the two, given that some medical texts have rituals and prayers, and some magical texts include medical recipes, (Steinert 2018; Geller 2015; Lenzi 2010, 2011; Scheyhing 2011; Abusch 2007). Unfortunately, significant engagement with this material is beyond the parameters of the current monograph. Nevertheless, there is much potential for engagement with the material using medical anthropology, as demonstrated by Lilly's exciting approach to 'Spirit' in the Ancient Near East (Lilly 2016).

painful (lit.: sting)[14] and pierce the body/(but) his (healing) plasters are *soothing* and bring the *dead man* (lit.: Namtar, the god of death) to life' (Oshima 2014:78–79; cf. Annus and Lenzi 2010; Lambert 1960; Job 5:18).[15] However, it must also be acknowledged that the cause of afflictions are not always clear: 'a deity may inflict what seems to be unjustified punishment on a devotee' (Lambert 2013:480). Indeed, in many of the descriptions of suffering, the focus is dominated simply by the complaint itself expressed in somatic terms. For example, in a prayer to an unknown deity we are informed that

> Torment [lit., alû-demon] draws near, and distress, an[xiety and depression] disease [mursụ], oath, and curse, overwhelm me. My whole body they afflict. I am clothed in them as if with a garment.
>
> (Lenzi 2011:690)

Similarly, in the Babylonian Theodicy, we are told 'My body is a wreck, emaciation darkens [me]. . . . My strength is enfeebled. . . . Moaning and grief have blackened my features' (Lambert 1960:63–89).[16] An interesting nuance is created through the focus on so-called "juste souffrant"[17] and the body of the main protagonist. This, at once, emphasises the need to identify wrongdoing and appease the deity yet at the same time, paradoxically, it also serves to distance the deity from the scene. Nevertheless, both the biblical and non-biblical evidence suggests that there is a connection between human responsibility and bodily distress.

One productive means through which to examine this connection has emerged through the excellent scholarship produced by the thriving field of disability studies (Bengtsson 2014; Moss and Schipper 2011; Olyan 2008; Avalos *et al.* 2007; Raphael 2008; Schipper 2006). As Avalos, Melcher, and Schipper argue, 'Job reflects a theodicy that is different from that of Deuteronomy. In Deut 28, illness is the inevitable result of the violation of the covenant, and health is the inevitable reward for keeping the covenant'; however, 'Job provides an alternative moral universe, in which people are not sick because of any transgression (Avalos *et al.* 2007:57–58).[18] Similarly, as Claassens suggests,

14 The term *zaqta* is the accusative form of the adjective *zaqtu* 'pointed'. CAD notes that a sufferer of *ziqtu* disease was 'barbed (of a whip)'. The 'barbed whip' metaphor, which is not a unique metaphor to *Ludlul*, is used in other descriptions of illness.

15 Also, regarding the body in *Ludlul Bēl Nēmequ,* refer to Piccin and Worthington 2015; Lenzi 2015.

16 Refer also to Foster's translation (Foster 1996). For further recent discussions of the Babylonian Theodicy and Job also refer to the essays in Krüger 2007.

17 Nougayrol 1968.

18 However, it must also be acknowledged that the character Job sometimes adheres to the logic of retributive suffering. As Witte argues, the character sometimes 'takes up the juridical explanatory option, owed both to the sapiental and the deuteronomic-deuteronomistic traditions to account for his situation' (Witte 2013:86). It is not clear what Wittte means by 'deuteronomic-deuteronomistic', however. These terms are, as Keil has argued, 'too imprecise and speculative to be helpful' (Kiel 2012:3).

the rationale of connecting pain and human agency is 'representative of the numerous texts in the Hebrew Bible that draw a link between disability[19] and sin, viewing disability as a punishment' (Claassens 2013:171).[20] The uncomfortable connection between illness and responsibility is not new. As Gotto points out, '[t]hroughout history people have viewed and understood disease in religious terms' (Gotto 2012:421).[21] However, one awkward implication

19 There is a lot of existing literature which addresses the Hebrew Bible from the perspective of disability studies, and Claassens may be understood within this model of interpretation.

20 Other examples of the link between illness and sin in the Old Testament include the diseases on Pharaoh and his household on account of Abram's wife-sister deception (Gen 12:17); the striking blind of the men threatening Lot's house (Gen. 19:11); the closing of wombs in Abimelech's household again because of Abraham's wife-sister trickery (Gen 20:17–18); plagues and death of the Egyptian first-born on account of the genocide and forced labour of Hebrews (Exod. 7–11); Miriam's infection of צרעת on account of her and Aaron's speaking out against Moses's intermarriage with an Ethiopian woman (Num. 12:9–10); various occasions in Numbers when Yahweh threatened the Israelites with illness during their rebellions against Moses and Aaron (Num. 14:11–12, 36–37; 17:12–15; 25:3–9, 17–18; 31:16); the Philistines' tumours upon capturing in the ark (1 Sam. 5:6–6:12); the unfaithful king Jeroboam's child dies in Yahweh's manoeuvre to wipe his house out (1 Kgs 14:10–14); Yahweh refuses to heal Ahaziah because he consulted with Beelzebub (2 Kgs 1:16); greed incites צרעת in Gehazi as punishment (2 Kgs 5:26–27); the pride of King Uzziah causes him to get2) צרעת Chr. 26:16–20); Jehoram gets an incurable illness on account of deserting Yahweh (2 Chr. 21:14–15); and David's census annoys Yahweh, so he is punished with a plague resulting in the death of 70,000 people (2 Sam. 24:10–15; 1 Chr. 21:7–14). To use a poetic example, the psalmist explicitly connects God's anger and his body's dysfunction, stating: 'There is no soundness in my flesh because of your indignation; there is no health in my bones because of my sin' and 'my wounds grow foul and fester because of my foolishness' (Ps. 38:3, 5). This idea continues in the New Testament material, wherein it is epitomised by the question the disciplines ask in reaction to a man born blind 'Rabbi, who sinned, this man or his parents, that he was born blind?' (John 9:2).

21 Gotto gives a range of examples, including:

> The ancient Egyptians believed that illness was sent to earth by gods or demons, by the dead, or even by one's enemies. . . . Treatment involved a supernatural element, such as magical rituals to remove bad spirits. . . . The ancient Greeks interpreted disease to be a punishment by the gods. . . . Some of the gods were believed to be temperamental, and they would indiscriminately wreak havoc on humanity, whether as punishment or just for random mischief. Zeus, for example, threw thunderbolts when he was angry. Poseidon, the god of the sea, caused storms. When the gods caused a disease to occur, it became necessary to appease them through some form of purification or by sacrifice.
>
> (Gotto 2012:421)

However, as Gotto also notes, despite being a very ancient line of reasoning, this 'magical' thinking about illness and disease has been present in modern times and in present-day situations. For example,

> in the mid-19th century, outbreaks of cholera were blamed on Irish immigrants in England and the United States, particularly in New York City. In the early 20th century, epidemics of plague in California were blamed on Chinese and Mexican immigrants. Epidemics of venereal disease have historically been attributed to "loose women." At the beginning of the 1980s, the spread of AIDS was blamed on gay men, Haitians, and haemophiliacs. Today, certain behaviours can indeed increase the risk for chronic disease and other illnesses. For example, alcohol and drug consumption, obesity, smoking, an unhealthy diet, physical inactivity, and unsafe sex – these behaviours can place individuals at increased risk for developing heart disease, diabetes, cancer,

emerging as a consequence of the connection is that anybody experiencing any of the conditions mentioned is experiencing punishment for some wrongdoing either known or unknown to them. Put more forcefully, the internal reasoning might be understood to suggest that illness is always deserved and it betrays some form of moral turpitude. As will be demonstrated, it is this perspective that the book of Job powerfully undermines through comedy, tragedy, and parody, perhaps with some similarities to Tobit.[22] There are various generalised explanations of suffering aside from the idea of retribution. Explanations also understand suffering as something disciplinary which promotes character; something probative that is a test; something eschatological with a future beyond death; something redemptive as modelled on the sacrificial system; something revelatory; or simply a learning curve. It is also explained as being ineffable (the reason is unknown but a reason exists), or as incidental or just 'happens'.[23] However, it is remarkable that when there is the more specific focus of the body in suffering, the retribution explanation regularly persists. As Magdalene suggests,

> The theological idea that human disability, disease, and disaster stem from human sin is very ancient and continues to hold sway in some theological circles. . . . Such theology remains highly problematic to those who experience disability, illness, or any kind of trauma . . . because of the predominance of such a theology.
>
> (Magdalene 2007:23)

Throughout Job, the character relentlessly wrestles with the arguments of his friends, who adopt this retribution model in response to his complaints about

---

> sexually transmitted diseases, and other conditions. Not everyone who has these risk factors actually becomes ill, and not everyone who contracts a disease does so because of their lifestyle. However, the tendency to associate disease with blame or punishment persists to this day.
>
> (Gotto 2012:423)

22 A similar juxtaposition of comedy and tragedy wherein the body is the site of dialogue and wherein there is, to an extent, an undermining of the theology of divine retribution might be traced within the book of Tobit. The exaggerated piety of the character Tobit who at the beginning of the book, like Job, moves from one catastrophe to another, is matched by his blindness which 'appears to the reader as both symptom and symbol of his internal blindness' (Portier-Young 2001:41–42). Although we note the ablest position Portier-Young takes here, there is also a degree of dark parody and intense irony running through the book through which simplistic retribution theology is mimicked and undermined. This is particularly evident within Tobit's exaggerated, pious death wish, which bears some similarities with Job's wishes for God to end his life. Like Jonah, Tobit cannot cope with a world wherein his perspectives (simplistic retributive theology) are challenged (Tob. 3:6; Jonah 4:3, 8). For both characters, and for Job's friends, we find that there is more to life than their philosophy would have allowed. In Tobit as in Job, we see 'the transformation of suffering into something laughable' (Lazarus 2014:224).

23 The abundance of theories here is reminiscent of the Peanuts comic strip wherein Charlie Brown is left without a 'ball team' (which has been replaced by a 'theological seminary') because everybody has descended into theorising.

his body. This is highly problematic, given that audiences are informed from the outset that the character is 'blameless' (תם) and 'upright' (ישר) (Job 1:1).[24] This is a key device within the play. It functions by letting the audience know that Job is innocent, while the characters themselves as they pontificate – at vast length – on the various reasons for Job's problems are seemingly unaware of it. As Meshel argues, 'dramatic irony' serves as 'an organising principle' in Job which allows for 'two simultaneous, incompatible readings to coexist – one from the limited perspective of one or more of the characters; the other from the privileged perspective of the reader' (Meshel 2015:48).[25] Likewise, Sharp comments that dramatic irony 'throbs beneath the poetry because the audience knows, as none of the human characters in the book do, that everything that has befallen Job has been the result of a capricious heavenly wager' (Sharp 2009:190). This creates a sense of superiority within the audience, enabling tragedy to turn to comedy, as the advice given to Job by his friends is continually undermined by the very premise of the entire play: that the audience is aware from the start of Job's innocence. The audience is aware that the entire scenario rests on a gamble between Yahweh and the Satan wherein Job is the butt of the joke, reducing the entire speeches to the level of mere melodrama. Therefore the text might loosely be described using the overarching category 'dramatised comedy'.[26] It is a dramatised comedy, however, which is set up in a

24 Ironically, Job's friends use these very words to defend their arguments about Job's responsibility for his situation. Eliphaz asks 'who that was innocent (נקי) ever perished, and where were the upright (ישר) cut off?' (Job 4:7). Similarly, Bildad asserts that 'if you were pure (זך) and upright (ישר), then surely he would cause himself to wake for you' and suggests that 'God will not reject a blameless תם man' (Job 8:6, 20). Zophar goes even further, suggesting that although Job says his 'insights are pure (זך)' he must be wrong about that: How could Job possibly know, given the magnitude of the Almighty? Therefore, Zophar advises Job to 'prepare his heart and stretch out his hand towards Shaddai' (Job 11:4, 13). It should be acknowledged, though, that the way Job is characterised leaves some readers pitying him as an innocent victim of a smug gambling game by a God 'who causes human suffering for no other reason than to win a bet with someone whose job is to pick quarrels' (Raphael 2004:423). Although, as Krüger notes, unjustified suffering 'is not without analogies' in the Old Testament, '[t]he story of Cain and Abel, for example. . . [does not supply] reasonable cause' (Krüger 2007:228). At other times, however, the character seems more pompous and arrogant than 'blameless' or 'upright'. As Clines points out,

> Is this a perfect man? We see him in the town council, acting the authoritarian patriarch (29.7–10, 12–25) . . . . This is a man so concerned for his honour that he can wish for the disgrace of his wife (31.9–10), a man who was convinced himself that his slaves are treated fairly, while discounting the fact that they remain slaves (31.13–15), a man who congratulates himself on his support of the underprivileged (31.16–22) while never questioning the system.
>
> (Clines 1998:799)

25 Another useful way of describing this dual perspective (audience and characters) that exists throughout the dialogues is to suggest that 'the use of paradox' is 'central to the author's argument' (Aaron 2001:197).

26 There is no evidence whether or not the book of Job was dramatised or intended as a play or even originally a play. This monograph simply acknowledges this as a possibility. However, given the 'disproportionately print-orientated hermeneutic in our study of the bible' and the importance of taking orality seriously, it should not be entirely beyond our imagination to conceive of it as a

way that keeps audiences on the knife edge between the tragic and the comical, and this tension is maintained throughout the dialogues.[27] It is a play potentially evoking the 'laughtears' of the audience.

Imagining Job as a performance aligns well with the way that comedy was understood in ancient Greece. As Jackson points out, the traditional, formal meaning of comedy refers narrowly to a dramatic performance of this particular Greek form (Jackson 2012:10). Similarly, Dell notes that 'in relation to Greek tragedy . . . there are some fascinating parallels, especially with Aeschylus' *Prometheus Bound* but ultimately cross-dependence is unlikely' (Dell 2007:19). Indeed, in many ways Job aligns quite well with Aeschylus's *Prometheus Bound*. Like Job, Prometheus is surrounded by three characters – Kratus, Bia, and Caucasus – who moralise in detail about the reasons why Prometheus deserves his punishment. Like Job, Prometheus calls on nature to witness his suffering, and like Job the theme of the body needing healing emerges. In light of this observation, Whedbee's remark 'as far back as Theodore of Mopsuestia, scholars have observed affinities of Job with Greek drama' is particularly fitting (Whedbee 1977:2). The link between Job and Prometheus is not particularly new, however (Pachmuss 1979; Irwin 1950; Sparks 1903). It is also worth recognising the similarities with Aristophanes wherein there is regularly a central character who constructs his own society despite strong opposition, driving away all the people who come to challenge him and eventually achieving a heroic triumph. The plays, characteristic of Old Comedy, result in a catharsis of sympathy and ridicule: comic heroism and comic irony. Furthermore, the plays demonstrate 'a recurring tendency . . . to ridicule and scold an audience assumed to be hankering after sentiment, solemnity, and the triumph of fidelity and approved moral standards' (Frye and Bloom 2000:48).

---

performance (Ong 1988:174; cf. Vayntrub 2019; Kelber 1997). After all, as Niditch argues, 'Biblical literature, is traditional literature having more in common with Homer's Odyssey than a Faulkner novel' (Niditch 1996:xvii).

27 The connection between comedy and tragedy is well established. As Jackson argues,

> In ancient Greece, comedy, as a form, developed as the dramatic companion to tragedy. The tragic form was given official standing in 535 BCE, the comic form later in 486 BCE. These forms are believed to have emerged out of the religious rituals associated with Dionysus, and the first known, fully developed comedy is Aristophanes' *The Acharnians* from *c.*25 BCE.
>
> (Jackson 2012:13)

It should be noted, however, that in Old Comedy, not all subjects could be given the comic treatment; for example, higher gods such as Zeus and Athena and certain aspects of Greek religion had to be given due respect. Perhaps this is why the tetragrammaton is almost absent from the dialogues and the character is cast as a foreigner in a distant, almost mythical, land (refer to note 75). Having noted this, it is interesting also to acknowledge that some comic treatment was, nevertheless, allotted to the gods. As Revermann notes, 'religious matters are featured in it [Greek comedy] very frequently indeed', so much so that 'the material provided by Aristophanes and the scholiasts on the Aristophanic plays constitutes a principal and absolutely indispensable source of evidence pertaining to religious life in Athens' (Revermann 2012:266–277; cf. Parker 2007).

The fact that all is restored at the end of Job is another reason not to take the material too seriously. The plot, like many comic scenarios, is a U-shaped one: as Jackson demonstrates,

> comedy's opening scenario is a harmonious one; society is in a state of integration. Enter into this situation some challenge or test that jeopardizes the harmony, and the plot begins a downward movement. Then, as the plot is descending to its lowest point, something or someone acts on it, changes its direction and causes it to swing upwards. At comedy's ending, a new situation of harmony and integration is established, a harmony that typically includes the integration or reintegration into society of the 'not hero'. Importantly, this re-established society is not merely a reproduction of the old one, but is instead a new and rejuvenated one. This newness is proclaimed in the comic 'happy ending' and frequently marked with celebration, 'festivals of freedom and hope': marriage, birth, feast, carnival.
> (Jackson 2012:17–18)

This U-shape fits neatly with the book of Job, with the prologue and epilogue forming the tops of the curves. The exaggerated length of the bottom of the U-shape, the dialogues, also contributes to the comical nature of the play. The prolonged speeches are infinitely repetitive, and this augmented level of exaggeration creates a sense of ludicrous absurdity.[28] The length of the dialogues is matched by an increasing sense of irritation on the parts of all the characters. Moving through the dialogues, as the puffed-up, self-righteous Job becomes ever more frustrated, the friends also increase their moralising until, after 30 chapters, the character Elihu emerges on the scene stating that he is 'full of words' and offering little more than the same moralising that Eliphaz, Bildad, and Zophar had already plenteously provided Job with.[29] Jackson also com-

28 It is interesting to note that exaggeration's comic counterpart, understatement, is almost entirely absent from Job.

29 Some commentators prefer to make distinctions between the friends and note recurrent themes in their speeches. For example, Clines suggests that 'Eliphaz argues from the piety of Job in order to offer consolation; Bildad argues from the contrast between the fates of Job and Job's children in order to offer warning; Zophar argues from the suffering of Job in order to denounce Job' (Clines 1998:731; cf. Engljähringer 2003; Perdue 1991). This monograph does not make distinctions between the arguments of the three friends, but instead views their number as representative of the weight of tradition. As Driver commented,

> It is unnecessary to review in detail here all the speeches of the friends and Job's replies to them: they cover the same ground again and again. So far as the friends are concerned it is of the very essence of the writer's purpose that they should one and all say essentially the same thing: they are not introduced to represent many existing theories; but the three of them, expounding the same theory, represent that as the unchallenged judgement of ancient and still current opinion.
> (Driver and Gray 1986:lvi)

Driver's argument here, that the friends represent the same unopposed theory, is persuasive, given the similarities of assumptions of wrongdoing behind their advice to the character Job. Furthermore,

ments that comedy's repetition being a 'repetition overdone or not going anywhere' (Jackson 2012:19). This is certainly a good way to describe the dialogue. As Brown observes, they 'seem interminable, particularly since the speakers often talk past each other, running around in circles, as they become firmly entrenched in their positions' (Brown 1999:228). For an audience, knowing all along that Job is deemed innocent by God, the experience of watching the frustration of all the characters as they move through the dialogues creates a sense of superiority which gives way quickly to humour.

Another crucial device which allows for a certain comic licence is that of introducing the character Job as an 'Other'. Unlike the probable 'us' of the audience watching, Job is not a Yahwist, but instead a foreigner, perhaps an Edomite, from the land of 'Uz' somewhere in the 'east' (Job 1:1, 3).[30] The mention of Job as among 'the people of the east' gives the setting an obscure and distant character, as does the lack of the tetragrammaton throughout the dialogues.[31] Indeed, the east could be associated with the past or with the unknown, perhaps giving the setting a sense of mystery and antiquity, which is in many ways similar to the setting of the Eden narrative (Gen. 2:8). The audience can freely be amused by Job, since he is not quite like them: the unknown Other, and implied Edomite, can be laughed at while a character closer to the audience might more readily promote sympathy.

In addition, it should be noted that this monograph is not the first to suggest that Job may be viewed as comedy. Several smaller treatments of Job suggest that it may be viewed through the lens of comedy. For example, Whedbee used Frye's outline of comedy to argue for 'the comedy of Job' (Whedbee 1977; cf. Frye and

---

Albertz describes the wisdom of Job's friends as 'a conscious synthesis of the sapiential mastering of life and piety, or as reason's permeation of personal piety, fashioned by the perspective of the upper class' (Albertz 1990:260).

30 In Lam. 4:21, Uz appears in parallel with Edom. The Hebrew Bible seems to reflect a widespread anti-Edom tradition. The Edomites are supposedly descendants of Esau (Num. 20:14; Deut. 2:4–5; Amos 1:11; Obad. 1:10) and are depicted as complicit in the destruction leading to the Babylonian exile (Ps. 137:7; Ezek. 35:1–5; Obad. 1:10–14). Two detailed monographs are worthy of mention with regard to Edom: Bartlett 1989; Anderson 2011. If we are to take the suggestive mention of 'Uz' as a link to Edomites, the audience may even assume that by implication Job is more deserving of punishment.

Day puts forward four arguments to explain why Job is cast as an Edomite: first, because Wisdom writers 'were more internationally minded'; second, 'because it was so fixed in tradition that it could not be altered'; third because 'to make the figure of an Edomite Job acceptable' as mitigation he 'is represented as a Yahweh worshipper'; fourth, because 'Job is set in ancient times, when relations with Edomites were less hostile than they were to become after 586 BCE' (Day 1994:397–398). Day's third and fourth points here are interesting especially if we are assuming that Job is written at the end of the exilic or post-exilic period. A good Yahwist might still read or listen to Job, despite the fact that it is about an Edomite, given the mitigation that he is, at least, a Yahwist. However, we are arguing that what the good Yahwist might find in the figure of Job is an undermining of the various traditions at the heart of Yahwism at the time. What better way to question authoritative traditions than to do so through an Edomite who, if the questioning becomes too risky, can be dismissed as merely an outsider?

31 Refer to note 75.

Bloom 2000). Similarly, Keller argues that Job is a 'tehomic' comedy, or a comedy of creation. Keller's focus is on the whirlwind speeches in which she suggests that the 'the joke is on Job' so that a 'suicidal anti-cosmogony turns suddenly comicosmic . . . the epiphany pulses between impatience at human anthropocentrism, and unabashed glee in a complex, undomesticated universe' (Keller 2003:129–130). Furthermore, the comic nature of Job is later played out in the Testament of Job, which draws heavily on the Septuagint of Job and is sometimes linked with the Therapeutae. The Testament of Job is also humorous at times, with exaggeratedly long speeches and Job's exaggerated generosity and piety. Indeed, the testament goes from absurd, nature-defying wealth to extravagant charity:

> Those who milked the cows grew weary, since milk flowed in the mountains. Butter spread over my roads, and from its abundance my herds bedded down in the rocks and mountains because of the births. So the mountains were washed over with milk and became as congealed butter. And my servants who prepared the meals for the widows and the poor, grew tired and would curse me in contempt, saying "who will give us some of his meat cuts to be satisfied?" Nevertheless, I was quite kind.
>
> (Testament of Job 13:1–6)

Here the servants are the victims of Job's hospitality, and the exaggerated wealth is almost diametrically opposite to the type of futility curses that emerge in treaty language (Hillers 1964). For Job's servants, his generosity is a curse of abundance. As such, they curse him who in all his elevated charity has completely forgotten the human needs of the very ones delivering it (cf. Job 31:13). Ironically, through his great acts of charity Job oppresses the hired servant who is poor and needy (cf. Deut. 24:14). Unlike the book of Job, the Testament of Job focuses less on Job's body and has many more characters. Nevertheless, even the portrayal of Job's body in the Testament of Job is ironic and comical. Once upon the dunghill, Job claims that 'many worms were in my body and if a worm ever sprang off, I would take it up and return it to its original place, saying, "Stay in the same place you were put until you are directed otherwise by your commander"' (Testament of Job 20:9). Job is depicted here as the big commander of the little worm. Ironically, through his insistence on forcing the worm's compliance with its ordained role, Job actively encourages the destruction of his body. Although our focus for this monograph is on Job's body and the comedy of advice in the book of Job, the retelling of Job in the Testament of Job suggests traces of a tradition of reading wherein the main character is painted as ridiculous partly (in the Testament of Job) and largely (in the book of Job), using by his body as a medium through which to locate the satire.

Finally, when considering the possibility of Job as a dramatised comedy, it is important to recall the argument first coined by Todorov that no genre exists in isolation (Ducrot and Todorov 1972:193–197). Rather, every genre is:

> always defined against a constellation of neighbouring forms, and exists in a dynamic tension with them. What is more, these forms are not given a

> priori, but emerge historically; nor do such forms reach a stable or final condition, what Aristotle called their *telos*, at which point they are no longer subject to further evolution. Rather, every new composition in the genre produces an alteration in it, with the result that it is constantly subject to change and deformation, and at a certain point may lose its identity and come to constitute a new form.
>
> (Konstan 2012:29)

The advantage of thinking about genre in Job using Todorov's approach to genre is that it emphasises the profound connectedness that exists between the play, or book, and more traditional forms found within the Hebrew Bible, such as lament. However paradoxically, it is the combination of connectedness to other forms but also the *dynamic tension* between Job and other forms that produces the possibility of reframing the way we think about Job to include the idea of a dramatised comedy. Through imagining Job in this way, our horizon of expectation shifts dramatically with the concurrent effect that so, too, do interpretive possibilities. Through imagining Job as a comedy wherein melodramatic metaphors are used to symbolically protest against moralising advice, the centrality of the work's objections to the idea of retribution in Yahwism are thrown into sharper relief. Through using Todorov's approach to genre, wherein it is more than a set of rules or forms, a high degree of critical competence is assumed of Job's author/s who both conform to but at the same time modify traditional forms in order to produce a highly socially coded dramatised comedy. Todorov's approach to genre allows us to leave behind constraining, fixed, and two-dimensional ideas about what material might, and might not, be possible to interpret as comedy and about what type of material comedy is, such as as 'jests and vulgar knockabout (βωμολοχία)' (Hunter 1985, 2012). It allows us to refocus and reconsider how Job transforms traditional forms and to trace the possible effects the transformations have. Through enabling us to think about the connections between ideas and forms, Todorov's approach to genre also opens up the possibility of considering comedy as presented in Job as, albeit on the surface light-hearted, something which is used to make profoundly serious points about Yahwism at the time of composition and for early audiences.

A further detailed discussion of Job as dramatised comedy will follow in the conclusion, and the case will be sustained throughout the monograph. However, before simplistically assuming that Job can be read as comedy, it is important to acknowledge the barriers to doing so, noting also that a longer discussion of the difficulties emerges in the conclusion. Radday cautions against approaching any of the Bible as comedy on account of anachronism and cultural distance, arguing that we should focus on 'what ancient writers . . . meant to be humorous rather than with what a . . . reader . . . conceives of as such' (Radday 1990:25). A similar point is made in the first issue of the *Journal of Humor* [sic.] *Research* wherein it is noted that humour occurs in all human cultures but it occurs in an infinite variety of forms (Handelman and Raskin

1990).[32] We should be aware that there is a potential problem arising from a mismatch in terms of what original audiences might have experienced as amusing and what we might find funny. As Whedbee notes, 'we do not exactly know what might have elicited laughter from the ancient Israelites or any of their contemporaries in the Near East' (Whedbee 1977:4). Nevertheless, we can make the claim that humour is a global and timeless phenomenon and that comic phenomenon are 'the ubiquitous, universal, pervasive nature of the comic experience'; therefore, while the 'subjectivity of comedy cannot and never should be denied . . . the urge to create, experience, and appreciate the comic in some form has existed across all known contexts' (Jackson 2012:7; cf. Berger 1997). Indeed, several publications have emerged which address the matter in terms of cross-cultural comparison. These include Apte's indispensable survey of anthropological approaches to humour and Sciama's more recent volume, which also takes an anthropological approach (Apte 1985; Sciama 2016). Therefore, while the temporal and cultural distance between us and Job means that caution should, of course, be exercised when arguing that the play

32 Further research is in this area would certainly be welcome. It is worth noting that 'the First International Conference on Humour and Laughter in Cardiff, Wales, already had a symposium on cross-cultural aspects' of humour in the 1970s (Ruch 2008:73). As Oring observes,

> The problem that anthropologists and folklorists jointly share is the effort to document, analyze, and interpret the great diversity of humorous speech and behavior that exists in societies around the world. Their focus on humor in real social situations in different cultures often keeps their interpretations local and rooted in the life and lore of particular groups and particular societies. This attention to the diversity of humorous expression is perhaps the greatest contribution of these disciplines. Humor researchers need to confront the range of phenomena they are called to analyze and explain. They must determine whether they truly understand what others are laughing at. . . . Theories must account for an extraordinary variety of data spread across a great range of peoples and historical periods.
>
> (Oring 2008:204)

However, it is noted that while a systematic statement defining comedy is not available, we can be a little more confident on certain 'identifying characteristics, styles, motifs, devices, approaches, and so on that *contribute* to comedy' (Jackson 2012:16). These include but are not restricted to examples such as incongruence theory, relief theory, superiority theory, misdirection, benign violations of norms both practical (e.g. social inversion) and linguistic (e.g. wordplay, puns, double entendre, sound-play), buffoonery, confronting taboo topics playfully, satire, parody, and irony.

It should be noted further that may of the classic theories are not uncontested. For example, Eagleton suggests that superiority theory is 'vastly implausible' because 'it is motivated by a malign urge to do others down' (Eagleton 2019:39). In some tribal societies joking relationships do not create divides, but instead illustrate the strength of bonds through being 'able to withstand such barbs' (Eagleton 2019:62; cf. Douglas 1968). Similarly, Eagleton argues that the incongruity theory is not particularly helpful because it is largely descriptive, telling us *what* we laugh at, rather than *why* we laugh. These difficulties are acknowledged. However, they haven't stopped some from contributing very usefully to the anthropological study of humour (Apte 1985; Sciama 2016). If we are to work with the idea that Job may be a dramatised comedy, we have to at least use what theories are available, while acknowledging that said theories are not flawless or complete. Likewise, the genre comedy in relation to the Hebrew Bible is not comprehensive and static, as Todorov's approach to genre may help to explain.

is comedy, it is nevertheless not impossible to imagine it as comedy. Doing so does not diminish Job's serious subject matter in any way. As Whedbee argues, 'comedy can be profoundly serious; in fact, it has often served as one of the most compelling strategies for dealing with chaos and suffering' (Whedbee 1977:4).[33] As will be demonstrated, comedy is an excellent way of dealing with the problems that emerge in the simplistic concept of retribution that Job's friends regularly seem to espouse. Introducing a problem with material assuming the authority of ideas about retribution may have been taboo at an early period, given the weight of tradition, and comedy provides the perfect tool for addressing difficulties and undermining authority and tradition. Indeed, comedy seems to have been the ideal tool of choice for the author of Tobit, who has his main character whose 'charity', paradoxically, does not appear to extend to his own wife (Tob. 2:13–14). In the midst of accomplishing deeds that serve his petty piety Tobit is arbitrarily blinded by bird droppings, a scatological misfortune perhaps rather enjoyable for readers who notice the main character's small-minded simplicity, and he struggles to explain the reasons for this (Tob. 2:7–10). However, all the various straightforward expressions of retribution that Tobit espouses are restricted to the main character, and his high estimation of himself appears not quite to be shared by the other characters. This style of retribution, which as Kiel shows totally lacks nuance, is perhaps what Job also questions (Kiel 2012:59–78). Comedy seems to work quite well to undermine the superficial and self-righteous piety of Tobit here, and, as with Job, dramatic irony is used throughout the work continually to undermine the authority of the character's ideas about retribution (McCracken 1995; Portier-Young 2001). Why does comedy work so well as a serious means of questioning ethically dubious or insincere piety? Perhaps it is because comedy can be iconoclastic in nature: it 'is not committed to following a set of rules'; instead '[i]t prefers "situation ethics" because "unique situations may require [a] unique response"' (Jackson 2012:23). This is key for the book of Job because the way the play is set up reveals that the character Job is in a unique situation, and his suffering cannot be theorised away by a committee of friends who are learned in the art of reducing life's complexity to a set of maxims.

This monograph seeks to expose the ways in which the book of Job undermines the retribution model by specifically focusing on Job's body. Job is overly keen to share his interpretations of his body's demise and his expressions of pain with his friends, almost like Argan in Molière's *Le malade imaginaire* (Barnwell 1982). Significant quantities of the book of Job are devoted to this. This monograph will explore the social significance of the body in Job in a way that probes comparatively into the modern prevalence

33 Whedbee and Pelham provide helpful analysis of the character Elihu as a particularly comical figure (Pelham 2010; Whedbee 1977). Refer also to Heinlein's novel, based on Job, which satirises American evangelical Christianity, making Heaven seem like a bit of a bore and Hell far more attractive (Heinlein 1984).

of the retribution model and that also draws out the tragic and comic elements of the play. In order to do so, it is important to be clear about how specific terms are defined. Clarity is also required to pre-empt any potential confusion; therefore, it is necessary to describe what we *are* and what we *are not* trying to achieve. The following sections will critique the widespread tendency in recent scholarship to 'diagnose' Job retrospectively, after which we will explore some of the research from medical anthropology on illness narratives and expressions of pain.

'Illness', 'sickness', 'disease' and the perils of retrospective diagnosis

A surprising amount of scholarship focusing on the theme of the body in Job seems, sometimes rather peculiarly, to 'diagnose' the character retrospectively. For example, Gorman and Kaplan suggest that when Job's 'signs and symptoms are viewed as a whole, poisoning appears to be the most plausible, heuristic etiology. . . . Arsenic, one of the most available poisons in his time, can readily account for Job's complaints' (Gorman and Kaplan 1999:127). A wide range of other diagnoses have been suggested. As Rowley notes,

> Job's disease is commonly identified with the form of leprosy known as elephantiasis. . . . Koehler . . . calls it smallpox and S. L. Terrien suggests the skin disorder known as *pemphicus foliaceus*. G. N. Münch . . . proposes the identification with chronic eczema. Dhorme thinks it is going too far to identify Job's disease with leprosy . . . but notes that Syriac and Green tradition saw in the disease malignant ulcers.
>
> (Rowley 1976:35–36)

The sheer range of suggestions in this relatively small quotation may be seen as evidence of the problems of attempting a retrospective diagnosis.[34] One scholar may choose to prioritise certain parts of the text, while, for another, other parts are more important. Problems also emerge here, given the very wide range of suggestions: it is impossible to pin down a condition, and it is not clear what doing so actually achieves exegetically.

A slightly more familiar way of approaching the theme of the body in the book of Job is to examine the statement in the prologue in light of other texts which use similar language or phrases 'Satan went out from the presence of the LORD, and inflicted loathsome sores (שחין) on Job from the sole of his foot to the crown of his head. Job took a potsherd with which to scrape himself, and sat among the ashes' (Job 2:7). First, the term 'sore' or 'boil' (שחין) is mentioned

34 For an extended methodological discussion concerning applying medical anthropology to the Hebrew Bible, refer to Southwood: 'The "innards" in the Psalms and Job as Metaphors for Illness' in *Horizons in Biblical Literature* (forthcoming).

in Leviticus 13:18–23 as the first sign of the condition known as צרעת.[35] Second, those who take this approach often note the merismus 'from the sole of his foot to the crown of his head' indicating the entirety of the human body (cf. Dt. 28:35; 2 Sam 14:25). However, as Glasby sensibly notes, the term צרעת is 'nowhere to be found in that book [Job]' (Glasby 2017:276).[36] It also seems that the focus on the description of the 'disease' in the prologue of Job puts a lot of weight on that specific part of the text and ignores other descriptions of bodily and mental suffering (of which there are plenty) in the rest of the material. Furthermore, looking to other texts which contain descriptions of צרעת in order to ascertain what condition the character Job might have had potentially risks homogenising attitudes towards the condition. Therefore, attempting to 'diagnose' the character Job through using inner-biblical evidence is also a problematic venture.

Unfortunately, however, an abundance of retrospective diagnoses of Job exists.[37] One common suggestion is that Job is suffering from some sort of a

35 צרעת is traditionally translated 'leprosy', but we should be clear that whatever the strange condition, which apparently even a house can catch, is (Lev. 13:49), it appears to be associated with the term טמא which, according to Erbele-Küster, indicates 'unsuitable for the cult', 'unclean in a ritual respect', 'compromising the cult', 'cult-abstinent', 'cult-disabled', 'ritual noncompliance', 'cultic disqualification', 'in conflict with the cult' (Erbele-Küster 2017:142). This does not correlate with modern medical definitions of leprosy (Douglas 1999:183; Milgrom 1991:768–889). As Pilch notes, 'Medically "Absurd!" That's how Arthur Johnson, leprologist and director of the Regional Hansen's Disease Center for Florida and Georgia, evaluated the biblical reports of leprosy' (Pilch 2000:39). The condition is also said to be what Hezekiah suffered from (2 Kgs 20:7; Isa. 38:21) and what Miriam was struck with as punishment. Both Miriam and Elisha's servant are described as being 'white as snow' as a consequence (Num. 12:10; 2 Kgs 5:27). Interestingly, Leviticus takes a contrasting attitude, as Douglas notes:

> There is no attempt to identify a sin that caused the disease. This is very striking. Nowhere does Leviticus say that the disease can be attributed to sin of the victim. In the sweep of comparison with other religions this is noteworthy. In Africa leprosy is widely associated with incest. Deuteronomy uses the idea that such diseases as 'the boils of Egypt' are caused by sin. Typically Leviticus avoids blaming and accusations. . . . Leviticus is not at all inclined to search out causes of disasters or attribute blame. . . . Like the animals, and like the tabernacle, no sin has caused the impurity, leprosy is not a punishment any more than a nocturnal emission is a sin.
>
> (Douglas 1999:185, 188)

The lack of a link between illness and wrongdoing is, as Douglas describes it, 'striking' indeed. In many ways this observation is more interesting than the question about what the 'disease', if it can be called a disease, actually might have been because the text illustrates how the condition was imagined and situated socially. The victim is socially ostracised (Lev. 13:45–46) but, strangely, no human explanation for the condition is provided nor sought.

36 Glasby, a distinguished consultant clinical neurophysiologist, focuses on Leviticus in his monograph, which contains several warnings about trying to 'to make precise diagnoses from the biblical symptomatology. This is the so-called *hyperdiagnostic* approach whose very significant limitations have taken far too long to be recognized in scholarship' (Glasby 2017:39).

37 We should note here that retrospective diagnosis is not unique to the book of Job. Indeed, there are some similarities to the trend of diagnosing Ezekiel using psychology. Such diagnosis displays a 'marked tendency to go beyond the evidence. . . . The scant personal details found in this ancient

mental health problem (de Villiers 2004). Venter, for example, discusses in very general terms Job's apparent psychological transformation, claiming that 'Job underwent a change or transformation of ego' (Venter 2015:6). Similarly, Kahn and Solomon provide a psychological analysis of Job arguing that the illness which Job suffers from should be 'envisaged as having depressive, obsessional, and paranoid features' (Kahn and Solomon 1975:54; cf. Jung 1979). For Kahn and Solomon, the reason dialogue between Job and his friends[38] is so fraught is because '[t]hose around him tell him that he is deluded, and the fault is within him' (Kahn and Solomon 1975:60). Glasby similarly suggests that Job's 'symptomatology progresses through *psychosomatic* → *psychoneurotic* → *psychotic* phases to which *obsessional neurosis, reactive depression* and *paranoia* become super-added' (Glasby 2017:277). Similarly, Houck-Loomis argues that Job's being terrified by night visions indicates 'deep psychological splits' in the character's psyche

text are an insufficient basis for a project as bold as psychoanalysis' and display a 'tendency to take psychological issues in isolation from other important perspectives' (Joyce 1995:73). This amounts to a lack of basic contextualisation.

Another example of retrospective diagnosis is Scurlock and Andersen's *Diagnoses in Assyrian and Babylonian Medicine* which argues that 'ancient Mesopotamian texts contain a great deal of useful information permitting us to be close to certain about the nature of the illnesses described' (Scurlock and Andersen 2005:xx). Similarly, despite urging caution about the legitimacy of comparing Akkadian texts with present-day disease categories, Adamson suggests that *rulibtu* 'clearly suggests that a weeping eczema of the lower limbs' (Adamson 1988:164).

Even Douglas comes rather close to retrospective diagnosis, when she describes 'disorders' in Leviticus,

> what modern medicine calls leprosy; but other disorders seem to be indicated by the diagnosis, perhaps skin cancer, which comes out in big red pimples, makes scabs, and dries out; perhaps psoriasis; probably tropical ulcers and yaws; the major infectious diseases, plague, smallpox, mumps, chickenpox, and measles (Douglas 1999:183–184).

38 Which Kahn and Solomon refer to as a 'therapeutic situation' and 'therapeutic process' (Kahn and Solomon 1975:90). Kahn is not alone in suggesting that the friends are offering medical therapy. For example, taking a psychoanalytic perspective, Merkur argues that 'Job's dialogue with his friends was therapeutic in facilitating the manifestation of Job's anger' (Merkur 2004). Similarly, Oeming and Schmidt argue that 'the complex structure of the Book of Job might also be understood as a counselling process' (Oeming and Schmid 2015:x). Therefore, instead of offering 'insensitive theological dogmatism', as commonly interpreted, Oeming suggests that the friends are 'are role models of kerygmatic pastoral theology who try to convince a suffering individual by means of the sufferer's own theological beliefs' (Oeming 2015:39; cf. Oeming and Drechsel 2007). Finally, Glasby also understands the dialogue between Job and his friends as a 'rudimentary form of psychotherapy [that] is instituted when the "friends" . . . seek to end Job's isolation on the ash-heap' (Glasby 2017:277). Finally, Dell uses a principle connected with psychotherapeutic intervention to depict Job's friends as unconnected, and thus threatening of the client (Dell 2017:99). It is sensible to acknowledge Newsom's argument here, however, regarding the cultural abyss between modern therapy and Job's composition. As she argues,

> What is expected in one culture may be deemed quite inappropriate in another . . . The gap is so great that most critics realize that they cannot simply rely on their own cultural norms to grasp and interpret what the friends are doing. . . . Very little information exists within biblical sources to show what the cultural expectations for consolation were in ancient Israel.
>
> (Newsom 2003:347)

(Houck-Loomis 2015:200; cf. Stein 2018; Job 7:14). Likewise, Dell suggests that Job's problem is one of mental torment or depression and that symptoms for this are his 'sleeplessness', his 'fear' and 'dread', 'restlessness', 'being unable to concentrate or settle to anything and feeling uncomfortable' (Dell 2016:68–69). Thus she argues,

> Job is clearly in pain and expresses this in a number of different ways. In ch. 3 he speaks of his 'sighing and groaning'. Groaning is something one does if one is hurting physically, but it is also a prime indicator of depression and despair.
>
> (Dell 2016:68)

Therefore, Dell's attempt to diagnose Job identifies his 'malady' as depression. At points in the argument, however, Dell loses sight of the physical symptoms (having listed these towards the beginning of the article), causing one to wonder if depression is an outcome of said symptoms or if depression emerged and the symptoms followed. Others refer to various conditions in passing, the most common being a 'skin disease' (de Joode 2014:562; Raphael 2004:401; Fohrer 1991:80).

The approaches earlier which attempt to diagnose Job are highly problematic, given the several centuries between the text and those scholars writing about it, which of course leads inevitably to anachronism. Moreover, we do not have access to a patient, only a literary figure from a text. As Seybold and Müller argue, any attempt 'to diagnose Job's sickness is, in reality, futile, since he is a fictional case, a pedagogical example, and a model both in the prose narrative (1–2; 42) and in the poetic dialogue' (Seybold and Müller 1981:78). Doctors don't usually diagnose without seeing a patient, making retrospective diagnosis from texts highly dubious (not to mention ethically problematic). Such a 'diagnosis' would only ever function as a label through which to interpret the literary figure and would fail to analyse the complex lifelong history of the 'disease' or the humanity of the 'patient'. Worse still, much of the literature which pseudo-diagnoses the character Job is not produced by medical practitioners in any case, but by non-experts with little more than a passing understanding of disease. Furthermore, we cannot assume that our modern concepts and categories of disease can simplistically be projected on to an ancient text such as Job: such an assumption supposes a privileged cultural position and fails to truly engage with the material. As Muramoto argues, 'these "hobbyist" historians are not following the methodological disciplines of historiography, literary criticism, and other relevant subject areas of the humanities and social sciences' (Muramoto 2014:1). Indeed, any attempt to 'diagnose' the character Job, completely fails to be sensitive to the book's historical and religious context, as well as its genres, by simplistically approaching it as if it were a scientific record. Moreover, the text itself wherein the character Job appears is likely to have been subject to editing over several centuries. How can we reconstruct this ailment or that when the text is not consistent, but exists in several versions and in various languages, with many of the terms used for ailments being *hapaxes*? Perhaps Rowley's observation 'it seems idle to try to give any precise identification of the disease' is apt here (Rowley 1976:35).

Alongside anachronism, perhaps one of the most distinctive difficulties connected with retrospective diagnosis is the level of cultural insensitivity it presupposes. Why, for instance, suppose Western medicine is the best point of comparison with Job? Problems relating to a lack of cultural competence became somewhat topical among medical anthropologists after Fadiman published *The Spirit Catches You and You Fall Down* (Fadiman 1997).[39] The book is an ethnographic narrative about a medical disaster which emerged on account of failed communication between Western biomedical doctors and a Hmong community in Merced, California. It resulted in a Hmong child being pronounced brain dead. Ironically, however, the book has been criticised on account of being 'racist' (Chiu 2004:1).[40] However, the point it attempts to make – however badly – about physicians requiring cultural competence is relatively helpful. Therefore, we can also acknowledge that cultural sensitivity, or better still 'cultural humility', is something which scholars examining the body in Job should also strive towards (Dasgupta 2008:981).

It should also be acknowledged, in light of the previous discussion, that suggesting the character Job suffers from some modern medical condition or another is both methodologically flawed and insensitive. Moreover, it flattens out potentially fascinating depictions of how the authors and early audiences thought about the body and pain. Surely it is more interesting to examine the social and cultural contexts surrounding the question of the body that are portrayed in Job? If this may be acknowledged, then a further question presents itself: How should we best refer to the body and pain in Job? What are the most appropriate categories? At this point, Lloyd's distinction between disease and illness[41] may prove helpful:

> We should distinguish between disease and illness. The first is what biomedicine will define as a pathological condition. The second relates to how you feel. The first is, in principle, objective and verifiable by certain tests that are generally agreed. The second is subjective. The distinction

39 Cultural competence is usually understood in medical settings to refer to 'the professional capacity to work within the context of the language, thoughts, communications, actions, customs, beliefs, values, and institutions of [patients'] racial, ethnic, religious, or social groups' (Jurecic 2012:117).

40 Anthropologists have critiqued the book for its 'simplified and romanticized explanations for Hmong beliefs and behaviour [*sic.*]' (Jurecic 2012:119). Likewise, the book is criticised for being insensitive about the ethics of storytelling. Chiu questions why the story should be told by a literary journalist who is neither a medical anthropologist nor an ethnographer since it 'raises puzzling questions about . . . her authorial method' and highlights how Hmong perspectives are filtered through Fadiman's own interpretations (Chiu 2004:4; cf. Taylor 2003).

41 The term 'sickness' is also sometimes used to refer both to 'illness' and 'disease'. As Pool and Geissler suggest, some scholars 'give "sickness" a more specialized meaning, using it to refer to the process in which illness and disease are socialized' (Pool and Geissler 2005:53).

> remains a useful one, even though it is less rigid than some of its early proponents suggested.
>
> (Lloyd 2003:1–2)[42]

Focusing on experience, meaning, and social or cultural interpretations of illness and pain, although more of a so-called 'subjective' approach, certainly reveals a lot about how illness was imagined and understood by early audiences and by the author/s of Job. Various compelling reasons for this focus exist, including the fact that concepts of 'health' and 'illness' 'embody value judgments that are rooted in metaphor' (Boyd 2000:9).[43] Therefore, exploring metaphors for pain, as well as various shades of meaning relating to the expression of bodily dysfunction and illness, can potentially be a means of gaining access to what types of values were associated with the body and with health in Job. For example, some present-day illnesses are particularly loaded with cultural meaning. By using the term 'illness' as a blanket term (and deliberately not providing details or diagnosis), perhaps we can ask which types of symptoms are related to different social meanings in Job? Moreover, given that all illnesses are 'socially constructed at the experiential level, based on how individuals come to understand and live with their illness', it is surely important to understand 'how the meaning and experiences of illness. . . [are] shaped by cultural and social systems' (Conrad and Barker 2010:67; cf. Kleinman 1988:417–148).[44] In essence, what we are attempting to uncover through a focus on the body, pain, and illness in Job is what type of social and cultural systems might have shaped the meaning and experiences of pain and bodily dysfunction. We are exploring

42 Some are critical of the limitations of definitions such as this (Timmermans and Haas 2008). Nevertheless, for our purposes in terms of examining Job, the distinction does begin to draw helpful nuances between terms and to distance us another step further from 'diagnosis'. Of course, many other definitions exist. For example, Carel suggests that 'illness (as opposed to disease) is a complete transformation of one's life' (Carel 2016:14).

43 Health is also difficult to define. The World Health Organization lists as its first principle of its constitution that health is a 'state of complete physical, mental, and social well-being and not merely the absence of disease and infirmity'. This is a rather optimistic way of thinking about 'health'. In general, it might be more sensible to suggest that what people mean by 'health' is 'a descriptive and . . . often culturally normative concept that plays a defining role in a given society' (Pilch 2000:24). As Lloyd states,

> [P]art of the human condition, and normal in the sense of frequent occurrence. But it conflicts with the norm when that is identified with the idea of well-being – as we too naturally think of the healthy state of the body as the natural one. In that way, or thanks to that ambivalence, the concept of disease enables one to normalize the paranormal, to treat as natural what nevertheless goes against the ideal. . .
>
> (Lloyd 2003:239)

This point is made in a sustained way in Canguilhem's evocative thesis on *The Normal and the Pathological* (Canguilhem 1989).

44 Conrad and Barker are referring here to chronic or long-term conditions rather than, for example, the passing cold in winter. Concerning social construction, which is the idea that meanings are constructed, rather than 'natural' depending on cultural and historical aspects of any particular

these themes in Job, not just in a narrow sense of what healers believed was happening to their patients but in a far broader perspective, asking questions about perceived causation and responsibility, about the self, identity, the body, about matters related to authority, purification and pollution,[45] and about reality and appearance. We are focusing on the way that illness and pain are described and in particular, the types of responses they elicit socially.[46] This is an important route into understanding how the authors of Job thought about illness and the body in their own culture because ideas about illness and what it affects are not cross-cultural, simplistic, or universal.

In doing so, it is important to acknowledge the huge influence of culture on the body and illness. Pilch argued that '[c]ulture dictates what to perceive, value, and express, and then how to live with illness (Pilch 2000:25; cf. Douglas 1970).[47] Nichter's research also illustrates this point: ethnophysiology studies

---

phenomena, refer to Berger and Luckmann 1966. As Freidson also points out, illnesses have social consequences, even in medicalised environments, regardless of biological factors,

> [W]hen a physician diagnoses a human's condition as illness, he [*sic.*] changes the man's [*sic.*] behaviour by diagnosis; a social state is added to a biophysiological state by assigning the meaning of illness to disease.
>
> (Freidson 1970:223)

Thus, the way that illnesses and illness labels are constructed can have palpable social consequences, and this in turn also has social consequences for how illnesses are depicted, experienced, and responded to. Therefore, when examining the body in Job, it will be especially important to consider the implications of the language and metaphors that are used to communicate.

45 Allusion to the possibility of framing illness in terms of divine interest also opens the possibility of exploring the matters of purity and pollution in Job, both in terms of religious ritualisation and purging but also in terms of social dynamics: Is the one who is ill a potential pollutant to the body politic? As Douglas argued in her seminal work, *Purity and Danger*, the human body is 'bounded, and this boundedness can represent any bounded system and become a symbol for other complex structures. Thus, it is difficult to interpret rituals concerning excreta, breast milk, saliva and the rest without understanding the body as a symbol of society. Likewise, social structures contain powers and dangers which can be reproduced in a small scale on the human body' (Douglas 1966). Similarly, de Joode emphasises the widespread nature of the 'conceptual metaphor the body is a container', which 'is not restricted to modern, Indo-European languages, but can be also be found in the Hebrew Bible' (de Joode 2014:557; cf. Southwood 2019; van Hecke 2005; Berquist 2002; Lakoff and Johnson 1980:58). There are some similarities here to the metaphor 'tent', as a bounded entity which Job uses to refer to the human body (Job 4:21; 5:24; 8:22; 11:14; 12:6; 15:34; 18:6, 14–15; 19:12; 20:26; 21:28; 22:23; 29:4; 31:1; Jones 2013:851). There are also connections to Scheper-Hughes and Lock's three perspectives here distinguishing between the 'individual body-self', a 'social body', and a 'body politic' (Scheper-Hughes and Lock 1987:8).

46 Even before the ground-breaking work of medical anthropologists such as Good and Kleinman, Douglas recognised that illness was intensely communal: it threatens behavioural norms, values, and conceptions of order. For Douglas, what is required is the restoration of order by placing the threat in its proper framework and making the entire event personally and socially meaningful (Good 1994; Kleinman 1988; Douglas 1970).

47 Pilch has made a decisive beginning in exploring how medical anthropology may be helpful as a tool for biblical studies in his exploration of the healing miracles in the New Testament (Pilch 2000). Pilch's work demonstrated that a major benefit of using a cross-cultural discipline such as medical anthropology is that it enables scholars to interpret texts in a more nuanced manner through

'how bodily processes are understood in different cultures and how such understanding influences perceptions of health, physical development, illness, medicines, and diet'; this in turn influences perceptions of 'what physical symptoms are deemed normal and abnormal at particular times' (Nichter 2008:25). We should, however, go a step further: In many cases culture defines what actually counts as illness. For instance, using the Greek example provided by Lloyd, we may question whether, at the time, love may have been perceived to be an illness, given that it was 'so often described in terms of a burning, of fire, indeed of fever' (Lloyd 2003:239). Similarly, homosexuality in America was, until 1973, 'defined by the American Psychiatric Association (APA) as an illness' (Gabe and Monaghan 2013:61). When viewed from this perspective, even healthcare, and what is deemed 'illness', might be considered 'a system of interacting ideologies, resources, personnel, and strategies' (Johnston 2004:160). For example, in the UK in 2019, youth and health are valued but 'other cultures and periods value old age and the wisdom and experience associated with it' (Carel 2016:74).[48] Part of the reason why values and ideology have such a large role to play is because, at a granular level, the expression of pain and illness involves categories, idioms, and modes of experience that are greatly diverse.

Even here, however, it is possible to go another step further and argue that culture also has a role in the way bodily sensations are interpreted. Insights from phenomenology suggest embodied modes of attention are elaborated culturally (Csordas 1994; cf. Baldwin 2007). As Csordas explains, attending to a body sensation is 'not to attend to the body as an isolated object, but to attend to the body's situation in the world'; therefore, even a bodily sensation can 'become a mode of attending to the intersubjective milieu that gives rise to that sensation' (Csordas 1994:138).[49] An extended example of this is Throop's analysis of pain in Yap, where virtue is considered to be all-important. As Throop describes, '[i]t is not that pain hurts less here. It does not, nor do wounds reopened by the strain of continued work heal more quickly. The pain simply matters less' (Throop 2010:159). Therefore, we can argue that no illness or pain is strictly biological. Instead, it must be considered as socially meaningful. The body does

---

highlighting areas of similarity and difference comparatively. A similar use of medical anthropology in biblical scholarship is Esler, who devoted a chapter to the 'madness' of Saul, using helpful models derived from cross-cultural healthcare to emphasise the commonality of spirit aggression (Esler 2012). A major contributor to the area is also Avalos, a trained anthropologist and biblical scholar, whose monograph on healthcare as the core of a new religious movement (Christianity) is particularly helpful (Avalos 1995). A further contribution to this area is Hong's study of the metaphor of illness and healing in Hosea, which suggests that illness metaphors in Hosea relate to an eighth-century oppressive socio-economic system (Hong 2006).

48 Leach takes this a step further, arguing that in modern settings 'subliminally the general public's idea of good health is all mixed up with ideas about sexual vigour' (Leach 1975:85).

49 Douglas took a similar line of argument, calling the body 'the field in which a feedback interaction takes place. It is itself available to be given as the proper tender for some of the exchanges which constitute the social situation. And further it mediates the social structure by itself becoming its image' (Douglas 1978:296).

not merely experience sensations with overlays of meaning; instead, 'we need to speak of pain as permeated with meaning – permeated with culture' (Jackson 1994:210). Given the evidence connecting culture and language with the body, it becomes even more vital and interesting to explore the expression of pain and illness in Job and how it is reacted to. The book lends itself very well to this type of investigation, given the sustained and in-depth focus on the body of the character Job. Indeed, as Jones argues, 'Job's view of the world is of a cosmos with his own body at the center [*sic.*]' (Jones 2013:846). Therefore, we can recognise that potential insights into the author's and early audiences' understandings of the body are facilitated through approaching Job using medical anthropology.

Having stated what we are *not* doing (retrospective diagnosis) and the reasons why, it is now important to examine a part of what we *are* doing. Specifically, the next sections will outline the research within medical anthropology concerning illness narratives and expressions of pain and explore some of the potential perils of using said research in a comparative way to interpret the book of Job.

Illness narratives and the quest for meaning: pain resists language?

Fuelled by concerns about blame, Sontag fiercely critiqued the idea of seeking meaning in illness, stating 'nothing is more punitive than to give a disease meaning' (Sontag 1978:58).[50] However, given the way that culture impacts upon embodied experience,[51] meaning is inescapable: Illness and pain cannot *not* have meaning. A common response to illness is 'Why me? (the question of bafflement), and What can be done? (the question of order and control)' (Kleinman 1988:29). This is because illness and pain can contribute to a breakdown of meaning.[52] As Carel argues '[o]ne's body, and the fundamental sense of embodied normalcy in which habits and values are rooted, is . . . disrupted'

50 Therefore, Sontag proposed:

> The age-old, seemingly inexorable process whereby diseases acquire meanings (by coming to stand for the deepest fears) and inflict stigma is always worth challenging, and it does seem to have more limited credibility in the modern world. . . . With this illness, one that elicits so much guilt and shame, the effort to detach it from these meanings, these metaphors, seems particularly liberating, even consoling. But the metaphors cannot be distanced just by abstaining from them. They have to be exposed, criticized, belaboured.
>
> (Sontag 1990:182)

Thus, according to Sontag, since metaphoric interpretations of illness distort stark biological facts and infuse disease with moral and ideological components, it would be best to simply not give them meaning (Sontag 1978:58).

51 Concerning the idea of how the body shapes experience refer to Bonan 2005; cf. Baldwin 2007; Marshall 2008; Romdenh-Romluc 2010.

52 Mattingly and Garro's observation about chronic illness particularly emphasises this point,

> Many anthropological and sociological studies have emphasized the disruption and despair – the lack of hope or struggle for hope – that can accompany chronic and serious medical conditions.
>
> (Mattingly and Garro 2000:5)

(Carel 2016:14).[53] Indeed, one's very sense of identity, friendships, and social status can be eroded by pain and illness. As Lupton argues,

> illness can redefine close relationships and become an occasion for questioning the direction of one's life. . . . Often the question 'Why me?' is answered through the construction of illness narratives. It is a means by which people seek to give meaning to their experiences, to make sense of them and to begin to formulate a revised identity and new context for living after the disruption of illness.
>
> (Lupton 1994:95)

Illness narratives can take myriad forms. For example, Frank suggests three key 'stories' (Frank 1995).[54] People draw selectively on cultural resources and dominant discourses when constructing narratives about pain and illness as a means of organising their experiences. One distinctive contribution that medical anthropology has recently made is the focus on patient experiences, particularly in the form of illness narratives. This approach was pioneered by Kleinman and Good, but it also became popular to examine illness narratives – or 'narrative medicine' – as part of medical education (Kleinman 1988; Good 1994; cf. Charon 2006; Bury 2001; Hurwitz 2000). Illness narratives are, '[s]tories that patients (but also friends, relatives, healers) tell about sickness' (Pool and Geissler 2005:52). These narratives are often told or written in order to provide coherence to events surrounding experiences of illness.[55] Patients and those around them construct narratives for various reasons. For example, Bury refers to 'biological reconstruction' through which 'moral narratives' occur; that is, narratives where individuals feel the need to present themselves as culturally competent. Moral narratives are, in some senses, social apologia wherein the ill person closes the chasm between their previous identity and their perception of

53 Carel describes lucidly her reaction to the onset of her life-altering condition:

> I fell into the beginner's trap of suffering and asked: why did this happen to me? . . . I suffered from what Joan Didion calls "magical thinking": the irrational, self-blaming, mystic thought that is apparently common in situations of distress. I blamed myself for writing a book on death. I blamed myself for going to the doctor so late. I blamed myself for being arrogant and not budgeting for something like this from the beginning. . . . I spent several months asking: why did this happen to me?
>
> (Carel and Cooper 2013:31–32)

This quotation highlights vividly the important role of blame and perceived justice which accompany the search for meanings associated with illness. It also highlights the assumption that health is a norm. Mattingly and Garro make a similar point, arguing that serious illness 'does not permit one to go on living in an undisputed, familiar world' (Mattingly and Garro 2000:88).

54 These include the restitution story, the chaos story, and the quest story (Frank 1995). Bury also suggests that there are 'core narratives' wherein the narrator emplots themselves in a more dramatic fashion, which may be comic, didactic, heroic, or tragic (Bury 2001:278).

55 An interesting example of this is Steffen's article on Alcoholics Anonymous where telling the story in a ritualised context 'brings thoughts and emotions into form in a process where listening and performing goes hand in hand' (Steffen 1997:106).

current failure as a consequence of the effects of an illness (Bury 2001:278). In contrast, Mattingly and Garro's analysis of Mexican cancer patients focuses on social and personal empowerment. Mattingly and Garro give the example of a cancer patient who had been suffering domestic violence and who 'cited his [her husband's] abuse as the cause of her brain cancer, and she thereby publicly challenged her husband' (Mattingly and Garro 2000:99). Entitlement to tell a story can serve as a marker for various types of relationships and power relations between individuals and groups (Ochs and Capps 1996). Essentially, therefore, narratives are a principal mechanism through which cultural understandings about illness are acquired, confirmed, refined, or modified. This is particularly useful for thinking about how illness, pain, and the body are represented in Job.

However, there is some significant critique of these so-called 'misery memoirs' and 'victim art'. This is because compositions about illness take on multiple genres and forms,[56] but there is no clear critical consensus about how they ought to be analysed. Moreover, the critical distance between those who create narratives and the scholarly community analysing them can be somewhat divisive. Jurecic sarcastically illustrates this: '[w]hen the smoke clears from the proclamation that testimonies are produced by agentless puppets of power, no one is left standing but the critic who sees what the rest of us, caught up in sentiment, do not' (Jurecic 2012:14). The result of this is a disembodied scholarly community who transforms the world 'into naïve believers, into fetishists, into hapless victims of domination' (Latour 2004:243).[57] Literature about illness and pain poses a specialised problem for critical engagement, especially in light of a hermeneutic of suspicion: Biblical scholars are trained not simply to take the text at face value, and this is entirely appropriate. This is especially the case for Job, where there is no clear patient writing about a specific condition, only a pedagogical example in a text. Nevertheless, it is still possible to engage with the material the authors place on the lips of the character in order to reconstruct some of the ideas about the body and pain that lie behind the text. Jurecic makes a compelling case for engaging with modern illness narratives:

> A blanket dismissal of testimony and emotional engagement can only be made from a position of distance and privilege. Such a critical stance imposes a falsely absolute divide between everyday experience and critical

56 As Vickers notes:

> Illness narrative is a capacious category. It is comparable to life-writing in that it is defined as much by what it doesn't exclude as by what it includes. Illness narratives can be fictional or non-fictional. They can be written by carers as well as patients. They can run to any length and can take the form of poetry and drama as well as prose.
>
> (Vickers 2016:388)

57 Jurecic's later analogy for this is powerful: '[i]f the non-participatory anesthetized patient is in many ways more convenient for the surgeon, the inarticulate sufferer is so for the theorist' (Jurecic 2012:55).

> engagement. It does not serve literary and cultural criticism well as a tool for understanding life's precariousness.
>
> (Jurecic 2012:14)

However, Jurecic's point here also provides an analogous argument for interpreting the speeches of Job as a character expressing the body in pain. Engaging with the dialogues concerning Job's body and pain does not mean that we cannot use our critical training. However, it does require us to acknowledge the text's emotional aspects and to imagine critically expressions cast on the lips of the main character about his body in pain and the reactions that they elicit socially.

If we do understand Job's speeches about the body in pain as socially constructed expressions of pain, then how should we navigate the argument that pain is inexpressible? Scarry, for example, argued that acute pain is world-destroying – it shatters and resists language but is instead expressed in cries and shrieks (Scarry 1985:5). This is on account of pain's 'unsharability' and its enduring nature in body memory.[58] Therefore, for Scarry, the disintegration of the body results in the world's disintegration from the perspective of the one who is in pain. This perspective might be applied to Job as signalling some sort of disintegration in the character's speeches. However, before doing so we ought to acknowledge that Scarry has been quite strongly criticised by medical anthropologists, although there are some modern publications whose arguments actually align somewhat with Scarry's arguments (Conway 2013).[59] While Scarry's argument here is sound with respect to torture, less extreme forms of pain are surely expressible, as is evident from the abundance and variety of autopathographies that exist (Aronson 2000). Indeed, for many, the problem is not how to find language for pain, 'but how to make readers receptive to stories of pain' (Jurecic 2012:44). Thus, the failure is not in the lack of language, but in the listener. Similarly, Jackson, who suggests that there is an 'anti-language' for pain, cites migraine sufferers who use vibrant metaphors and similes, such as it is like 'pliers on the optic nerve' or like wearing 'a football helmet seven sizes too small' (Jackson 2000:163; cf. Jurecic 2012:51).[60] Das and others also reject Scarry's

58 Scarry's point here is that 'it is not possible to compel a person to unlearn the riding of a bike, or to take out the knowledge of a song residing in the fingertips, or to undo the memory of antibodies or self-replication without directly entering, altering, injuring the body itself' (Scarry 1985:61).

59 And indeed, by biblical scholars such as Koch, who points out that one problem is that 'Scarry repeats the Christian *topos* of salvation on the level of her cultural theory' (Koch 2012:24).

60 Despite these examples, overall Jackson's position is more similar to Scarry's. This is illustrated well by an earlier article wherein Jackson concludes that

> pain, in a sense, *is* a language, and that it competes with everyday-world language. . . . Whatever form the language of chronic pain assumes, when sufferers attempt to translate it into everyday-world language – using gestures, cries, or metaphors – they say they feel a sense of failure, a sense of speaking a nonsense language, so poorly does the one map onto the other.
>
> (Jackson 1994:220)

central premise that pain resists language, arguing that pain is not 'inexpressible. . . . Instead, it makes a claim asking for acknowledgement, which may be given or denied' (Das 1996, cf. 2007; Jurecic 2012:62). Finally, Throop emphasises pain's temporal orientation, which 'often provides a means for suffering to be configured in terms of more coherent varieties of experience' while acknowledging that in Yap 'there. . . [were] a number of occasions in these narratives in which past experiences of pain continue to defy meaningful categorization for . . . sufferers' (Throop 2010:188–189).[61] A similar point is made by Jackson, who emphasises the paradox of language being at once urgently necessary in expressions of pain, yet at the same time insufficient, given the tension between the body as subject and object in encounters between the one in pain and the onlooker:

> They are exiles in the province of pain, and they find everyday-world language inadequate for communicating about their experiences there. And yet, because they are unwilling sojourners, they continue to turn periodically to that very same everyday-world language to avail themselves of its promised rationality, order, explanation, and control.
>
> (Jackson 1994:224)

While narratives and more general expressions of pain may be partial and incoherent, their very existence points towards the use of language to express pain. While language may resist full expression, given the unassumability of another's feelings, it is incumbent upon listeners to attempt to understand. Therefore, when analysing the expressions of pain in Job, it is important not to dismiss them on the basis of the fact that they are not simply cries, shrieks, and yells. What is almost more important, as the discussion has hopefully demonstrated, is how the expressions of pain are responded to and contextualised socially. For our analysis of Job's expressions of pain, therefore, it will be important to trace who talks and when, to pay close attention to expressions of pain, and to explore the nuances of the social reactions that these expressions elicit. However, doing so is not straightforward. As with any interdisciplinary work that attempts to take seriously the research of another discipline outside of biblical studies, analysis of Job using illness narratives and exploring expressions of pain in a heuristic way is a task requiring serious reflection about method.

Avoiding pitfalls: using illness and pain narratives to analyse Job's speeches

The different responses to illness and pain that exist both in ancient and present-day settings are striking. Through considering the topic of illness and pain in Job, we can potentially gain a wealth of detailed information about the culture and values of the society and the social architecture of ideas about pain

61 We should acknowledge here that chronic pain does not have the same past/present temporal orientation. Chronic illnesses 'tend to oscillate between periods of exacerbation, where symptoms worsen, to periods of quiescence, where disability is less disruptive' (Kleinman 1988:7; cf. Manderson and Smith-Morris 2010; Mattingly and Garro 2000; Garro 1994).

and illness at the time of its composition. Important questions begin to open up through this approach. Given that illness triggers ideas about self and identity, it has the potential to also shape social groups and class structures in society, provoking new, or even resurrecting old, boundaries between groups and constructing profound ideas about sameness and difference between human beings. This also directly relates to questions about power: Who has the power and authority in the dialogue? What kind of an authority is it? How does the idea of supposed wrongdoing, which is visibly inscribed on our main character's body, change the power dynamic of the relationships between Job and his friends? How do depictions of an attacking deity in Job contribute toward symbolic protest against Job's friends? How does interpreting Job as 'sin visualised' change the power dynamic between the protagonist and his friends?

In order to answer these questions, we must identify areas wherein bringing disparate material together for interpretation – in this case, medical anthropology and the biblical material – proves challenging. We have already covered some difficulties in our introductory discussion. Retrospective diagnosis, or as we have called it elsewhere 'exploring ancient texts through snake oil and exegetical quackery', will be avoided (Southwood 2019:232). One larger complication is the problem of language and texts: Job is 'notoriously difficult on a textual level' (Tollerton 2012:7). In terms of language itself, Aramaisms[62] and other idiosyncrasies[63] are relatively common, and there 'are more *hapax legomena* . . . and rare words in Job than in any other biblical book' (Pope 1965:XLII). Likewise, Job has 'a greater diversity of forms and a larger density of strange and foreign words than in any other book of the Bible' (Greenstein 2003:651). It is not clear why this is the case.[64] One thing that is for certain is

62 This is further complicated by the fact that there are sometimes Aramaic words and at other points also Aramaic forms (Greenstein 2003).

63 Such as the 'propensity to omit the definite article on the noun governing a construct genitive' and the 'suffixation of paragogic *nun* to prefixed verbs is also disproportionately high' (Greenstein 2007:82; cf. regarding the definite article Sarna 1996). Furthermore, Greenstein argues compellingly that features of Job's language are the precise selection of term, its multilingual character, polysemy and puns, its intricately metaphorical nature, and intertextuality (Greenstein 2007).

64 Perhaps it is an attempt at 'archaising' or 'exoticising, given that the book seems to display a decided and remarkable 'absence of any national feeling' (Treves 1995:269)? As Greenstein argues, 'the repeated use of non-Hebrew features lends the poetic dialogues an air of foreignness – which is particularly appropriate with regard to Job and his companions, who are all apparently Transjordanian figures' (Greenstein 2003:654). Hurvitz has suggested that the language of the prose tale is Late Biblical Hebrew, thus placing Job alongside Chronicles, Ezra-Nehemiah, Esther, Ecclesiastes, and Daniel (Hurvitz 1974; *pace* Young 2009). Joosten cautions, however, that 'our knowledge of ancient Hebrew being limited by the size of the corpus, we cannot ascertain beyond doubt that a unique word or usage is an invention of the Joban poet' but does also suggest, however, that given 'the amount of unique vocabulary and strange usages one finds in Job increases the likelihood that an unparalleled word or usage was coined by the author, especially when one cannot find a similar word or usage in Hebrew texts of the early postbiblical period' (Joosten 2014:334). Refer also to Greenstein concerning the invention of language in Job (Greenstein 2014). Joosten's crimes were not known about prior to this publication, which emerged in the UK in Summer 2020. Our lives as scholars cannot be separated from our work. The ethics of citation are important to me, hence this note, added retrospectively, and I will not be citing Joosten again.

that the book is 'a drama of words', and the author seems to manifest 'a poet's love of words' (Greenstein 2003). This is a problem because at many points it might actually not be at all clear how the text should be translated, and this is an acknowledged problem. Perhaps the most sensible route forward is to attempt to acknowledge varieties in translation throughout the analysis.[65] Indeed, doing so can only enrich our grasp of how Job was being understood and interpreted at an early point.

Another potential pitfall is genre (Johnson 2004; Cheney 1994; Schlobin 1992). Amongst other categorisations, Job could be understood as 'a dramatized lament . . . a paradigm of the answered lament . . . speeches of litigation . . . or a sapiental disputation' (Perdue 2008:127). The use of the legal metaphor as an organising principle in the work remains a theory which still has a following (Shveka and van Hecke 2014).[66] The book in its entirety represents a mixture

65 Although a 'few scholars have supposed that the shorter Greek version represents the earlier form of the text, the weight of the evidence is against them' (Pope 1965:xl, xlii). Therefore, as Seow states, '[t]he most important source of the text of Job is the Masoretic Text' (Seow 2013:3).

There are at least five extant versions of the Greek book of Job. The most important of these is 'the pre-Origen "Old Greek text" . . . also known as the "Job-Septuagint". . . . This version represents the putative Greek original' (Witte 2007:33). Furthermore, Witte also notes the Old Greek 'is succeeded by the translations of Aquila, Symmachus and Theodotion. . . [t]here are also fragments of a translation which some early fathers name τὸ ἑβραϊκόν' (Witte 2007:33). To complicate things further, the Old Greek is 'a sixth shorter than Masoretic Text', and the result is 'a version that in substance is at variance with the Hebrew' (Seow 2009:565). Furthermore, in the Old Greek the speeches of Job 'are less vitriolic than the Hebrew and Job comes across as a patient man' (Seow 2009:565; cf. Dhont 2017; Balentine 2015; Gard 1952).

Other versions worth noting are the Qumran Hebrew fragments, the most important of which is written in Paleo-Hebrew script (4QpalaeoJob[c]), and Qumran Aramaic texts (4QtgJob; 11QtgJob) which seem to 'corroborate the order of MT in the places where scholars are wont to rearrange' (Seow 2013:13). The Peshitta, or Syriac translation is mostly a 'literal translation of a consonantal Hebrew text that diverges from MT in many places' (Seow 2013:16).

66 This emerges from the term ריב in Job 31:13, 35. The metaphor has broader implications in terms of the book's anti-retribution theology. As Guillaume notes

> Job, nevertheless, takes up the juridical explanatory option, owed both to the sapiential and the deuteronomic-deuteronomistic traditions, to account for his situation marked by deep terror . . . and agonizing unrest. . . . Once brought into play, the thought that justice causes life; piety causes wellbeing; and religious, moral, and social integrity brings about blessings . . . can no longer be pushed aside. Whoever attempts to do that, as Job does . . . is stuck in a double trap: when he denies the connection between God's justice and human fate, he is seen as a wicked person who deserves a bad life. . . . If he follows the traditional interpretative path, however, he is caught – because of his awareness of his own innocence – in a swirl of self-justification. . . . This raises the question whether the failure of a theology of law for Job is ultimately also the demise of the theology of Deuteronomy.
>
> (Guillaume 2008:86; cf. Witte 2013)

This is certainly the case with regard to Job's body. As Raphael suggests, for Job, 'disease and disability are the beginnings of new insight, rather than the middle of a sin-and-repentance narrative, as the friends would have it' (Raphael 2008:103). However, Newsom cautions against pushing the interpretive implications of legal metaphor, suggesting that 'the reader often must make an active judgment whether to hear legal overtones or not' (Newsom 2009:150–151).

of genres known from Psalms, Wisdom, and Law, and 'even sometimes from the prophetic writings' (Witte 2013:81). It is 'a conscious literary combination . . . of predetermined genres' (Witte 2013:81; Dell 1991). Can we engage meaningfully with the themes of pain and illness within the material in Job without making a specific decision about categories? Indeed, as stated, we are imagining the book as something which was dramatised in the manner of a play and something which is a comedy of advice.[67] If we are imagining the book of Job in that way, does that affect how useful the anthropological research is for comparative interpretation? Perhaps, but only if we acknowledge existing scholarship on the question of genre and remain aware that delimitations between genres in the ancient world scarcely ever coincide with our own and to that extent any genre categories. We should further clarify here on a point related to genre: We do not have access to performative information, given that we cannot do participant observation or any other form of fieldwork. The work is imagined here as a play to be performed to an audience, but this is impossible to prove. However, modern autopathologies can be analysed without the narrator's presence, so this is not an insuperable hurdle (Aronson 2000). Obviously, this analysis is not claiming that Job is an autopathography or an illness narrative. Instead, what we are trying to achieve is an evaluation using heuristic comparisons with research in medical anthropology concerning illness narratives and pain which has, as demonstrated, the potential to inform us about the culture, values, and attitudes of its author/s and early audiences.

A related problem is that of categorisation. Our focus is mainly on chapters that are poetic, although it does not exclude the prologue and epilogue (Job 3–27; 29–37).[68] The poetic dialogues are particularly good for analysis through comparing illness narratives and behaviours because in them Job self-narrates at length about his body and pain. These sections of Job have been understood as making the prose prologue and epilogue seem like 'mere

67 Several scholars suggest the genre is comedy and the implication of the retelling of the text in the Testament of Job also points to comedy. Whedbee is particularly committed to the thesis that the genre is comedy, claiming:

> once the poem is set in its full and final literary context, replete with Prologue and Epilogue as well as the Elihu speeches, the most apt and compelling generic designation of the book of Job is comedy. In my judgment, the broad, overarching category of comedy is able to illuminate best the wealth of disparate genres, formulas, and motifs which are now interwoven in the total structure of the book.
>
> (Whedbee 1977:3–4; cf. Pelham 2010)

This argument is quite convincing because the comedy only really works by putting the entire book together. For example, as discussed, without informing the audience that Job is blameless and upright at the beginning, the advice of his three friends would perhaps seem quite correct for audiences who adopt a rather simplistic perspective of retribution. This is not to argue that a single author compiled Job. Rather, the argument is that in the text's final form, when the parts work together as a whole, comedy is the result.

68 Though the question of what Hebrew poetry actually *is* has been contentious. Refer to Alter 2011; Berlin and Knorina 2008; Kugel 1981; Watson 1984.

flourishes which are pale in comparison' to 'the sublime poetry of the book's core' (Steinmann 1996:87).[69] However, the material we are comparing this 'sublime poetry' with is largely narrative. This is not an insurmountable hurdle, given that, as Woods argues, narrative 'does not have a monopoly on expressivity' (Woods 2013:124).[70] Newsom's argument is relevant here, when she suggests that part of the power of Job's speeches is the extreme response to his friends, which goes beyond challenging the narratives of his friends and instead 'challenges the very narratability of human experience' (Newsom 2009:132). As Newsom explains,

> One could, of course, refer to the images and self-descriptions Job invokes as little narratives, but their configuration is vastly different from those of Eliphaz and Bildad. Much as the antinovels of Alain Robbe-Grillet contest the assumptions of the novelistic tradition by imitating aspects of its form but utterly refusing its structures of emplotment, so Job's little "narratives" undermine the integrative assumptions of the friends' attempt to narrativize human experience.
>
> (Newsom 2009:132)

Thus, for Newsom, the character Job is radically pushing back against a certain set of assumptions to which his friends subscribe about the 'configuration' or 'structure' and 'form' of narrative and about human experience being integrated and ordered. This argument aligns well with the method of comparing and contrasting the character Job's speeches on the body with modern illness narratives. Indeed, as Newsom's argument on narrative progresses, she suggests that it is the friends' conceptions of time which Job profoundly rejects. As Newsom argues, 'the "narrative" of his life extends no further than the end of each day' (Newsom 2009:133).[71] This is a somewhat persuasive argument,

69 Unfortunately, as van Hecke argues, some readers

> are inclined to pass over the long dialogues, in order to move quickly from the initial setting of the story to its dénouement. The dialogues at the heart of the story are often seen as contributing little to the development of thought in the book. They are merely the verbose repetition of essentially analogous or like ideas.
>
> (van Hecke 2013:69–70)

70 Poetry and other forms of expression also play an important role in modern research concerning illness experiences (Poindexter 2002; Glesne 1997). Indeed, as Kendall and Murray point out in their study of patients living with heart failure,

> All [these patients] acknowledge the special role and power of poetry: "poetry, as a special language, is particularly suited for those special, strange, even mysterious moments, when bits and pieces suddenly coalesce" as they do in the participants' illness narratives.
>
> (Kendall and Murray 2004)

71 In contrast, as Newsom points out,

> For Eliphaz narrative temporality is inscribed in the body's regenerative capacity. It is the time of a weakened body recovering its strength (4:3–4), the time configured by the healing of a wound

given that the character Job is presented as being in pain and, as argued earlier, the expression of pain is often less important than its acknowledgement by listeners (Das 1996; Jackson 2000:163; Jurecic 2012). The theme of time emerges a lot in illness narratives where illness is sometimes interpreted as a 'biographical disruption' in which individuals are forced to recast themselves in terms of new and unexpected plot developments and to reconstruct their identity through illness (Bury 1982; refer also to Bury 2001). Becker argues that illness narratives reflect the struggle to come to terms with moral ideologies concerning what is normal in the face of disruption. Narrative, for Becker, therefore 'ameliorates disruption: it enables the narrator to mend the disruption by weaving it into the fabric of life, to put experiences into perspective' (Becker 1997:166–167). What this monograph aims to do, therefore, is to both explore how Job's narratives are reconfigured to exclude the assumptions made by his friends and to uncover said assumptions on the part of the friends.

Anachronism is also potentially problematic. Although illness might be considered a 'universal' phenomenon – as Frank notes 'illness . . . cuts across worlds of race and gender' – expressions of pain and illness, as well as the ways meanings are constructed during, and in response to, illness, abound in variety (Frank 1995:170).[72] We acknowledge that comparing Job and modern research into patient narratives is anachronistic. However, this does not render the comparison pointless: The very fact that, as argued earlier, diverse meanings are constructed in light of pain and illness means there is the potential for some cross-cultural (and perhaps, therefore, cross-temporal?) continuity. The aim is not to dilute unique features or to force any of the text into some pre-existing pattern to make Job 'fit' with modern research: Such an exercise would simplistically homogenise both the medical anthropology and biblical evidence. Instead, the goal is to locate areas of potentially significant similarity and also,

---

> (5:18), or in Bildad's allegory, the time sketched by a damaged and uprooted plant sprouting again from the dust (8:19). Even "timely" death in old age is transcended by the body's capacity to generate offspring "like the grass of the earth" (5:25–26). These narrative metaphors of healing, sprouting, and seeding are powerful images by which the discordant is made concordant.
>
> (Newsom 2009:134)

However, Eliphaz's experience is presented as markedly different from Job's. Eliphaz can structure narrative from the perspective of health. Time is plentiful, and narrative can be tightly structured to fit his exact moral calculus where the wicked are 'like chaff that the wind blows away' but the righteous is 'like a tree planted by streams of water' (Ps. 1:3–4).

72 This is noted by Avalos, who draws attention to cross-cultural comparisons of how the senses are conceptualised, noting that

> differential privileging of senses can be detected by, among other methods: (1) contrasting expressions of valuation ("hearing is better than seeing"); (2) expressions of antipathy toward particular senses; and (3) narratives about the performance of valued tasks and functions in the absence or diminution of certain senses.
>
> (Avalos 2007:49)

This is, of course, relevant to the final chapters of Job wherein the character emphasises the privileged information that is gained through seeing rather than merely hearing (Job 19:26–27; 42:5).

importantly, differences. Moreover, the research we have selected from medical anthropology concerning illness and pain has not been 'cherry-picked' to 'match' Job. Every attempt has been made to grasp fully the complexity and abundance of modern research into illness narratives and pain in medical anthropology in order to maintain rigorous and sophisticated, rather than two-dimensional, analysis.

It is also necessary to emphasise that anachronism's counterpart, cultural projection, must be avoided. As discussed earlier, the aim is to maintain cultural humility and respect when engaging with Job. However, we must acknowledge here our lack of easy access to 'culture'. Since we cannot engage in fieldwork or participant observation, we must work within the limits of the available evidence in Job. This does not mean that the data in Job are invalidated. But it does mean that we have to acknowledge that what is meant by 'culture' when looking at Job will be filtered through the author's attitudes and values, some of which may have been shaped by setting and community at the time of composition. It is worth acknowledging, however, that medical anthropologists regularly do study texts and regularly do engage with historical matters, so lack of direct engagement through present-day fieldwork is not actually all that unusual.[73] Therefore using anthropology to ask these sorts of questions is not all that uncommon, even among anthropologists. Furthermore, whether we are studying texts or people, we should note the possibility of interpretive variation. As Pool and Geissler argue,

> Social researchers always influence the reality they study: recording conversations, or simply the presence of a researcher or a tape recorder, influences what people say, how they say it and how they act. . . . Social knowledge is always positional, shaped by the observer's point of view, and there is no independent vantage point from which to view, neutrally, a given society.
> (Pool and Geissler 2005:17)

However, just because social knowledge is 'positional' does not mean that there is no point in attempting to acquire it. This is partly a problem of hermeneutics: All interpretations depend on what evidence is selected, assumptions made about said evidence, how the evidence is analysed, and what sources are used to contextualise the analysis. All it is possible to do in response is to be clear about why Job is selected for this type of analysis and why and how we will utilise medical anthropology, specifically research into illness narratives and

73 For example, Hsu has published a monograph analysing medical case histories in early Chinese medicine. This involves translation from early Chinese, alongside anthropological analysis, a method which is perhaps analogous to the type of work a biblical scholar using anthropology might undergo (Hsu 2010). Furthermore, many of the publications in the Cambridge University Press monograph series 'Studies in Medical Anthropology' and in Oxford's 'Epistemologies of Healing' series include sections focusing on history and texts (e.g. 'history and ethnography of biomedicine', Brodwin 1996; cf. Pritzker 2014; Kreager and Schroeder-Butterfill 2004).

behaviours and pain, in the analysis. This entire subsection of discussion is an attempt to gain said analytical clarity.

A further important matter for clarification is what we mean by 'illness' and 'pain'. For our analysis, we will need to restrict the definition of pain to embodied symptoms and sensations, rather than exploring 'suffering' more generally (although the analysis does also have ethical and epistemological implications).[74] This means that in the analysis we will focus on the metaphors in Job's speeches wherein somatic and corporeal expressions are used. Since a high occurrence of these metaphors and expressions of pain exist in the shocking form of supernatural violence, we will especially focus on the melodramatic metaphors of 'deity attack' and violent 'deity surveillance' in Job. It should be noted here that since 'God' is referred to variously in Job and the tetragrammaton not usually used in the dialogues, we have chosen, in this monograph, to refer to the 'deity' rather than 'God'.[75] Given that we are not concerned with diagnosis, it is of little consequence whether or not an expression of bodily pain is 'just a metaphor' for suffering more generally. The way that language is configured to express pain still gives us clues about the way the body was thought about among early audiences and contextualised socially. 'Illness' in this analysis is used as a blanket term for bodily dysfunction. It is particularly important not to be specific about this given the perils associated with retrospective diagnosis, as argued formerly. Nevertheless, we can attempt to uncover, from the reactions of Job's friends and from the main descriptions that are placed on Job's lips, the author's social architecture surrounding the characterisation of Job and his expressions of pain. For example, we can examine whether Job's condition is thought to be stigmatised, how visible it is, and what difference it makes in terms of social structures.

An additional area for clarification is how aspects of language might be important for the analysis. Particularly notable here is the presence of metaphor

74 At times, when necessary, terms emerging outside of biblical studies will be used. This is not an attempt to submerge Job in generalities resulting in a loss of distinctiveness, but instead, an attempt to sharpen analytical clarity. Thus, we are not attempting to use what might be considered 'useless jargon' for its own sake; rather, this is an attempt to gain critical precision. We will endeavour to provide definitions where necessary.

75 Referred to variously in the poetic sections of Job, commonly as אֱלוֹהַּ 'eloah', and more familiarly, שדי 'the almighty', as well as אל 'god'. Interestingly, the tetragrammaton is hardly used in the dialogues, only in the mouth of the narrator (save for Job 12:9). Job 12:9, however, is sometimes understood to be an interpolation, perhaps as Job's ironic way of '"citing" the words of his friends, whom he envisages as deploying religious clichés' (Clines 1989:294). The term יהוה occurs in Job 1:6, 7, 8, 9, 12, 21; 2:1, 2, 3, 4, 6, 7, 9; 38:1; 40:1, 3, 6; 42:1, 7, 9, 10, 11, and 12. Concerning the various deity names in Job refer to Witte 2007:50–52; Szpek 1997; Cheney 1994:239–241; Strauss 1994. The near absence of the tetragrammaton in the dialogues helps to keep them as a hypothetical scenario at a distance from 'reality'. This is a useful device for the comedy because the divine violence is not directly attributed to Yahweh. Like the fact that Job is a foreigner from the mythical, timeless place called Uz, this acts as a veil hiding the serious points being made, which, as this monograph seeks to demonstrate, are directly about Yahwism at the time.

in the expression of illness and pain.[76] The tendency to use metaphor is marked both in modern illness experience and narrative research and also in Job. As Berlin argues, metaphor is 'just as important a constituent of poetry as parallelism' (Berlin and Knorina 2008:35). There has been a lot of work recently in medical anthropology focusing on the ways individuals use metaphor when communicating about illness. Metaphor is helpful for communicating about pain and illness because of its assistance to cognition through representing what is unfamiliar in familiar terms. It transforms conventional representation and as a consequence opens possibilities for new meanings. Through doing so, metaphor 'provides the intellectual and linguistic tools for communication . . . and yet also offers a plan for personal transformation' (Gibbs and Franks 2002:141). Metaphor represents an 'attempt to have a stronger relationship to disease by refusing to let it be only a medical condition' (Raffel 2013:48). Furthermore, metaphorisation of distress is a powerful critical tool for working with experience. As Kirmayer suggests,

> Because of their embodied nature, metaphors create meaning not only through representation but through enactment or presentation. The presentation of metaphor takes two forms: metaphors as cognitive tools that work on our concepts to fashion new meaning . . . and metaphors as communicative acts or gestures, constrained by social structure yet giving rise to new patterns of social interaction and modes of discourse.
>
> (Kirmayer 1992:337)

Therefore, metaphor is not just a rhetorical device, but an embodiment of expression.[77] Embodied metaphors and somatisation are particularly interesting

76 Sontag objected to the use of illness metaphors, arguing that they only 'contribute to the stigmatizing of certain illnesses and, by extension, of those who are ill' (Sontag 1990:99; *pace* Clow 2001; Raffel 2013). Sontag's point was specifically with regard to cancer and to AIDS. With regard to cancer, it is worth recognising the dominance of the military metaphor. As Clarke and Everest highlight:

> Dealing with cancer is likened to 'battling the deadly disease'. . . . Cancer is described as 'an implacable enemy'. . . . Scientific research into cancer treatments is described as rewriting 'the battle plan against cancer'. . . . Treatments are often portrayed with metaphors of war and aggression. Chemotherapy and radiation are likened to 'carpet bombing techniques'. . . . Drugs are said to be, 'ways to disarm the disease' . . . and used to 'destroy the renegade tissues'. . . . 'New medicines are like snipers firing on cancer cells alone and targeting their weakest links'. . . . Treatment is described as aggressive and 'war-like', as 'smart missiles' and, 'better targeted medication' . . . as a 'silver bullet' . . . an 'arsenal' offering service in the 'Boer war' . . . and 'ways to disarm the disease'.
>
> (Clarke and Everest 2006:2597)

For research concerning metaphor refer to Ricœur 2003; Lakoff and Turner 1989; Lakoff and Johnson 1980. Also refer to research on metaphor in Job (van Hecke 2005, 2013; Perdue 1991; cf. Southwood 2019). In addition, refer to Hong's work on the metaphor of illness and healing in Hosea (Hong 2006).

77 This notion of embodied expression is illustrated well in Mazanderani, Locock, and Powell's article on identity tension among patients whose experiences are 'differently the same' (Mazanderani *et al.* 2012).

in terms of their potential relevance for Job. Numerous medical anthropologists have followed, and critiqued, Nichter's work which focuses on embodied 'idioms of distress' (Nichter 1981, 2010; cf. Janes 1999; Parsons and Wakeley 1991).[78] Idioms of distress emerge when there are 'sociocultural constraints against and opportunities for expression' and function as 'alternative modes of expression' (Nichter 1981:402). In light of this insight, we might interpret a somatised idiom of distress as a symbolic protest which constitutes a language for suffering when other forms of communication are repressed. Therefore, we will need to analyse in detail the metaphors used by Job and his friends. In doing so, it needs to be established that this monograph is not primarily about conceptual metaphor theory, although it uses some of the excellent work from within this field (Hawley 2018:45–66; van Loon 2018:10–32; de Joode 2018:12–66). The somatic metaphors used by Job and his friends will often be analysed by identifying and reconstructing social dynamics and power structures between the characters. Through doing so we can uncover what is, and what is not, socially acceptable in the eyes of the author/s and in terms of illness metaphors.

A final reflection is in order here. Medical anthropology, if applied cautiously, we hope is helpful for gaining insight into the sections of Job wherein the protagonist describes his body in pain and for examining the nuances of the dialogue. However, it is recognised and fully acknowledged that social anthropology is, like concepts of illness themselves, socially constructed, just as biblical studies is socially constructed. No discipline is 'neutral' – this much ought to be obvious – just as no scholar can ever fully claim impartiality and detachment. Therefore, it would be naïve to suggest some kind of status imbalance between anthropology and biblical studies as if the one discipline can only ever inform the other without mutual benefit. However, it would also be rather simplistic – especially in an increasingly interdisciplinary, and even multidisciplinary, context in academia – to dismiss research engaging with material outside of what is traditionally thought to be biblical studies on the basis of some preconceived ideas about what is 'central' (with an implied 'peripheral') to biblical scholarship. There are examples of good interdisciplinary scholarship – and lesser examples – just as there are examples of successful and less successful arguments that emerge from biblical scholarship that is not interdisciplinary. A diverse range of approaches in the field is helpful, just as a more diverse range of people would be helpful too, for bringing new perspectives, energy, and richness to the discipline.

This chapter has surveyed some of the material relating to the body and illness in Job, arguing against the tendency to retrospectively diagnose. It has emphasised the importance of culture: Not only does culture dictate explanatory

78 Idioms of distress may be defined as 'socially and culturally resonant means of experiencing and expressing distress in local worlds. They are evocative and index past traumatic memories as well as present stressors, such as anger, powerlessness, social marginalization and insecurity, and possible future sources of anxiety, loss and angst' (Nichter 2010:405).

models and illness taxonomies, but also even body sensations are permeated with culture. We have argued that expressions of pain are possible, abundant, and important, and we have identified and addressed some potential methodological pitfalls associated with bringing biblical material together with research from medical anthropology. We now turn to analyse specifically corporeal and somatic expressions of pain in Job, which as noted, usually occur in the form of deity attack metaphors.

Outline

The following analysis will proceed in three chapters. Chapter 2, which is the heart of the monograph, focuses on Job's inflated expressions of pain through his use of the deity attack metaphor. It goes through each deity attack metaphor in Job, systematically discussing complications and significant details concerning the language, translation, and versions – the context within the dialogues. It then moves on to a broader discussion of how Job's speech relates to what his friends have said in addition to their reactions to his speech.[79] However, where the analysis develops depth and sophistication is, it is hoped, through using interdisciplinary techniques of analysis based on research concerning expressions of pain and illness narratives. This chapter is rather lengthy, partially on account of the many occurrences of the deity attack metaphor in Job's speeches which, it is argued, are the character Job's symbolic protest against his friends' constant moralising that uses retribution-centred language. Specific deity attack metaphors occur in Job 6:4, 9–10; 9:17–19; 16:7–9, 12–14; 19:7–12; and 30:16–19. This material will be examined both in light of its comic and tragic features but also, importantly, through using research from medical anthropology concerning illness narratives and expressions of pain.

79 It should be noted here that tracing the friends' responses is not always possible because the characters do not directly engage in argument. Instead, as Newsom points out,

> Although there are moments at which Job and his friends appear to reply specifically to each other's claims, their speeches largely ignore the substantive arguments made by the other party, as they dismiss one another's words as windy babbling.
>
> (Newsom 1999:239)

This lack of logical, structured argumentation adds to the comic, nonsensical nature of the play (or text), especially as Job and his friends' crescendo in their frustrations with one another towards the end of the dialogues.

An alternative perspective to the lack of structure is taken by Oeming and Schmid, who observe that 'interpreters of the book of Job have often complained that the dialogues in the middle section of the book show no continual train of thought, no progress of argument' and suggest 'from the perspective of counseling experience' that the reason for this is so that 'we can recognize how wisely the poet turned these recurring waves of dark meditation into a text' (Oeming and Schmid 2015:29). However, this argument comes very close to retrospective diagnosis through treating the text as though it were a scientific medical record (refer to the section: '"Illness", "Sickness", "Disease" and the Perils of Retrospective Diagnosis').

The next two chapters are significantly smaller and are essentially satellites to the main chapter, which focuses on deity attack. Both proceed in a similar systematic way as in Chapter 2, looking first at language and then supplementing this with broader interdisciplinary analysis. Chapter 3 focuses on implied divine violence through metaphors communicating intimidating and unwanted deity surveillance, again arguing that these are symbolic protests against Job's friends' moralising emphasis on the idea of retribution. Divine surveillance metaphors occur with implied (and sometimes explicit) attack in Job 7:17–20; 10:14–16; and 13:27–28; 14:3, 6, 16. Again, analysis will proceed by identifying comic and tragic features and through using interdisciplinary techniques, avoiding the aforementioned pitfalls.

Chapter 4 focuses in more detail on the social aspects of Job's experience of his body, looking specifically at Job 19:13–22 and 21:5–6. The same system of analysis outlined earlier will be followed. Finally, the conclusion (Chapter 5) will highlight the substantive ways in which the material in Job may be considered tragic and comic, depicting Job as a comedy of advice wherein bodily experience is pitted against traditional wisdom. The conclusion will address Job's response to Yahweh in Job 42:2–6, focusing especially on the crux in 42:6 and using Clines's and Greenstein's translations to suggest that that Job's response here is sarcastic and petulant (Clines 2011; Greenstein 2019). A key technique used to undermine the idea of retribution in the play is through providing Job with endless moralising advice that contests his seemingly ridiculous suggestions that he is blameless (which, ironically, the audience has been told from the start). Job's body is a particularly important device used to make this point. It is an ingenious site for the debate on account of the connection between pain or illness and wrongdoing. This connection is widespread, and it recurs in numerous present-day cultures, throughout history, and in particular in response to stigmatised illnesses. Indeed, even nowadays, in many wellness and healthy lifestyle campaigns, complex connections between illness, responsibility, and agency occur. The age-old problem of Job endures.

Bibliography

Aaron, D.H., 2001. *Biblical ambiguities: Metaphor, semantics and divine imagery*. Leiden: Brill.

Abusch, T., 2007. Witchcraft literature in Mesopotamia. In: G. Leick, ed, *The Babylonian world*. New York, NY; London: Routledge, pp. 373–385.

Adamiak, R., 1982. *Justice and history in the Old Testament: The evolution of divine retribution in the historiographies of the wilderness generation*. Cleveland: J.T. Zubal.

Adamson, P., 1988. Some infective and allergic conditions in ancient Mesopotamia. *Revue d'Assyriologie et d'Archéologie Orientale*, **82**(2).

Albertz, R., 1990. The Sage and pious wisdom in the book of Job: The friends' perspective. In: J.G. Gammie and L.G. Perdue, eds, *The Sage in Israel and the ancient Near East*. Winona Lake: Eisenbrauns, pp. 243–271.

Alter, R., 2011. *The art of biblical poetry*. New and Rev. edn. New York: Basic Books.

Anderson, B.A., 2011. *Brotherhood and inheritance: A canonical reading of the Esau and Edom traditions.* London: T&T Clark.

Annus, A. and Lenzi, A., 2010. *Ludlul bēl nēmeqi: The standard Babylonian poem of the righteous sufferer.* Helsinki: Neo-Assyrian Text Corpus Project.

Apte, M.L., 1985. *Humor and laughter: An anthropological approach.* Ithaca; London: Cornell University Press.

Aronson, J.K., 2000. Autopathography: The patient's tale. *British Medical Journal*, **321**, pp. 1599–1602.

Avalos, H., 1995. *Illness and health care in the ancient near East: The role of the Temple in Greece, Mesopotamia, and Israel.* Atlanta, GA: Scholars Press.

Avalos, H., 2007. Introducing sensory criticism in biblical studies: Audiocentricity and visiocentricity. In: H. Avalos, S.J. Melcher and J. Schipper, eds, *This abled body: Rethinking disabilities in biblical studies.* Atlanta, GA: Society of Biblical Literature, pp. 47–60.

Avalos, H., Melcher, S.J. and Schipper, J., 2007. *This abled body: Rethinking disabilities in biblical studies.* Atlanta, GA: Society of Biblical Literature.

Baldwin, T., 2007. *Reading Merleau-Ponty: On phenomenology of perception.* London; New York: Routledge.

Balentine, S.E., 2015. *Have you considered my servant Job? Understanding the biblical archetype of patience.* Columbia: University of South Carolina Press.

Barnwell, H.T., 1982. *Molière, Le malade imaginaire.* London: Grant & Cutler.

Bartlett, J.R., 1989. *Edom and the Edomites.* Sheffield: JSOT Press.

Becker, G., 1997. *Disrupted lives: How people create meaning in a chaotic world.* Berkeley; London: University of California Press.

Bengtsson, S., 2014. On the borderline – representations of disability in the Old Testament. *Scandinavian Journal of Disability Research*, pp. 1–13.

Berger, P.L., 1997. *Redeeming laughter: The comic dimension of human experience.* Berlin: Walter de Gruyter.

Berger, P.L. and Luckmann, T., 1966. *The social construction of reality: A treatise in the sociology of knowledge.* 1st edn. Garden City, NY: Doubleday.

Berlin, A. and Knorina, L.V., 2008. *The dynamics of biblical parallelism.* Rev. and expanded edn. Grand Rapids, MI; Cambridge; Dearborn, MI: William B. Eerdmans, Dove Booksellers.

Berquist, J.L., 2002. *Controlling corporeality: The body and the household in ancient Israel.* New Brunswick, NJ; London: Rutgers University Press.

Bonan, R., 2005. *Merleau-Ponty: de la perception à l'action.* Aix-en-Provence: Publications de l'Université de Provence.

Bosworth, D., 2015. Ancient prayers and the psychology of religion: Deities as parental figures. *Journal of Biblical Literature*, **134**(4), pp. 681–700.

Boyd, K.M., 2000. Disease, illness, sickness, health, healing and wholeness: Exploring some elusive concepts. *Journal of Medical Ethics*, **26**(1), pp. 9–17.

Brodwin, P., 1996. *Medicine and morality in Haiti: The contest for healing power.* Cambridge: Cambridge University Press.

Brown, M.L., 1995. *Israel's divine healer.* Carlisle: Paternoster Press.

Brown, W.P., 1999. Introducing Job – a journey of transformation. *Interpretation*, **53**(3), pp. 228–238.

Bury, M., 1982. Chronic illness as biographical disruption. *Sociology of Health and Illness*, **4**, pp. 167–182.

Bury, M., 2001. Illness narratives: Fact or fiction? *Sociology of Health & Illness*, **23**(3), pp. 263–285.

Canguilhem, G., 1989. *The normal and the pathological.* New York: Zone Books.

Carel, H., 2016. *Phenomenology of illness.* 1st edn. Oxford: Oxford University Press.

Carel, H. and Cooper, R.V., 2013. *Health, illness and disease: Philosophical essays.* Durham: Acumen.

Charon, R., 2006. *Narrative medicine: Honoring the stories of illness.* Oxford; New York: Oxford University Press.

Cheney, M., 1994. *Dust, wind and agony: Character, speech and genre in Job.* Stockholm, Sweden: Almqvist & Wiksell International.

Chiu, M., 2004. Medical, racist, and colonial constructions of power: Creating the Asian American patient and the cultural citizen in Anne Fadiman's the spirit catches you and you fall down. *Hmong Studies Journal*, **5**, pp. 1–36.

Claassens, L.J., 2013. Countering stereotypes: Job, disability, and human dignity. *Journal of Religion, Disability & Health*, **17**(2), pp. 169–183.

Clarke, J.N. and Everest, M.M., 2006. Cancer in the mass print media: Fear, uncertainty and the medical model. *Social Science & Medicine*, **62**(10), pp. 2591–2600.

Clines, D.J.A., 1989. *Job 1–20.* Dallas, TX: Word Books.

Clines, D.J.A., 1998. The arguments of Job's three friends. In: D.J.A. Clines, ed, *On the way to the postmodern: Old Testament essays, 1967–1998. Volume II.* Sheffield: Sheffield Academic Press, pp. 719–734.

Clines, D.J.A., 2011. *Job 38–42.* Nashville: Thomas Nelson.

Clow, B., 2001. Who's afraid of Susan Sontag? Or, the myths and metaphors of cancer reconsidered. *Social History of Medicine*, **14**(2), pp. 293–312.

Conrad, P. and Barker, K.K., 2010. The social construction of illness: Key insights and policy implications. *Journal of Health and Social Behavior*, **51**(1), pp. S67–S79.

Conway, K., 2013. *Beyond words: Illness and the limits of expression.* Albuquerque: University of New Mexico Press.

Crenshaw, J.L., 1992. Job. In: D.N. Freedman, ed, *Anchor Bible dictionary, volume 3.* London; New York: Doubleday, pp. 858–868.

Crouch, C.L., 2014. *Israel and the Assyrians: Deuteronomy, the succession treaty of Esarhaddon, and the nature of subversion.* Atlanta, GA: Society of Biblical Literature.

Csordas, T.J., 1994. *Embodiment and experience: The existential ground of culture and self.* Cambridge: Cambridge University Press.

Das, V., 1996. Language and body: Transactions in the construction of pain. *Dædalus: Journal of the American Academy of Arts and Sciences*, **125**(1), pp. 67–91.

Das, V., 2007. *Life and words: Violence and the descent into the ordinary.* Berkeley; London: University of California Press.

Dasgupta, S., 2008. Narrative humility. *The Lancet*, **371**(9617), pp. 980–981.

Day, J., 1994. How could Job be an Edomite? In: W. Beuken, ed, *The book of Job.* Leuven: Leuven University Press, pp. 392–399.

De Joode, J.D., 2014. The body and its boundaries: The coherence of conceptual metaphors for Job's distress and lack of control. *Zeitschrift fur die Alttestamentliche Wissenschaft*, **126**(4), pp. 554–569.

De Joode, J.D., 2018. *Metaphorical landscapes and the theology of the book of Job: An analysis of Job's spatial metaphors.* Leiden; Boston: Brill.

Dell, K.J., 1991. *The book of Job as sceptical literature.* Berlin: Walter de Gruyter.

Dell, K.J., 2000. *"Get wisdom, get insight": An introduction to Israel's wisdom literature.* London: Darton Longman & Todd.

Dell, K.J., 2007. Job: Sceptics, philosophers and tragedians. In: T. Krüger, M. Oeming, K. Schmid and C. Uehlinger, eds, *Das Buch Hiob und seine interpretationen: Beiträge zum Hiob-symposium auf dem Monte Verita vom 14.-19. August 2005.* Zürich: Theologischer Verlag Zürich, pp. 1–20.

Dell, K.J., 2016. What was Job's malady? *Journal for the Study of the Old Testament*, **41**(1), pp. 61–77.

Dell, K.J., 2017. *Job: An introduction and study guide: Where shall wisdom be found?* London: Bloomsbury, T&T Clark.

De Villiers, François T., 2004. Symptoms of depression in Job – a note on psychological exegesis. *Old Testament Essays*, **1**(17), pp. 9–14.

Dhont, M., 2017. *Style and context of old Greek Job.* Leiden; Boston: Brill.

Douglas, M., 1966. *Purity and danger: An analysis of concepts of pollution and taboo.* London: Routledge & Kegan Paul.

Douglas, M., 1968. The social control of cognition: Some factors in joke perception. *Man*, **3**(3), pp. 361–376.

Douglas, M., 1970. The healing rite. *Man*, **5**, pp. 302–308.

Douglas, M., 1978. Do dogs laugh? A cross cultural approach to body symbolism. In: T. Polhemus, ed, *Social aspects of the human body: A reader of key texts.* Harmondsworth; New York: Penguin Books, pp. 296–301.

Douglas, M., 1999. *Leviticus as literature.* Oxford: Oxford University Press.

Driver, S.R., 1902. *A critical and exegetical commentary on Deuteronomy.* 3rd edn. Edinburgh: T&T Clark.

Driver, S.R. and Gray, G.B., 1986. *A critical and exegetical commentary on the book of Job: Together with a new translation.* Edinburgh: T&T Clark.

Ducrot, O. and Todorov, T., 1972. *Dictionnaire encyclopédique des sciences du langage.* Paris: Éditions du Seuil.

Duhm, B., 1897. *Das Buch Hiob, erklärt.* Freiburg: I. B. & C.

Eagleton, T., 2019. *Humour.* New Haven: Yale University Press.

Engljähringer, K., 2003. *Theologie im Streitgespräch: Studien zur Dynamik der Dialoge des Buches I Job.* Stuttgart: Verlag Katholisches Bibelwerk.

Erbele-Küster, D., 2017. *Body, gender and purity in Leviticus 12 and 15.* New York: Bloomsbury, T&T Clark.

Eskenazi, T.C., Phillips, G.A. and Jobling, D., 2003. *Levinas and biblical studies.* Semeia Studies; No. 43. Atlanta, GA: Society of Biblical Literature.

Esler, P.F., 2012. *Sex, wives, and warriors: Reading Old Testament narrative with its ancient audience.* Cambridge: James Clarke & Co.

Fadiman, A., 1997. *The spirit catches you and you fall down: A Hmong child, her American doctors, and the collision of two cultures.* New York: Farrar, Straus and Giroux.

Fohrer, G., 1991. Man and disease according to the book of Job. In: *Studien zum Alten Testament (1966–1988) mitsamt Bibliographie Georg Fohrer (1991).* Berlin: Walter de Gruyter, pp. 80–84.

Foster, B.R., 1996. *Before the muses: An anthology of Akkadian literature.* 2nd edn. Potomac, MD: CDL Press.

Frank, A.W., 1995. *The wounded storyteller: Body, illness, and ethics.* Chicago; London: University of Chicago Press.

Freidson, E., 1970. *Profession of medicine: A study of the sociology of applied knowledge.* New York: Dodd, Mead.

Frye, N. and Bloom, H., 2000. *Anatomy of criticism: Four essays.* First Princeton Paperback edn. Princeton, NJ: Princeton University Press.

Gabe, J. and Monaghan, L.F., 2013. *Key concepts in medical sociology.* 2nd edn. Los Angeles; London: Sage.

Gard, D., 1952. *The exegetical method of the Greek translator of the book of Job.* Philadelphia: Society of Biblical Literature.

Garro, L.C., 1994. Narrative representations of chronic illness experience: Cultural models of illness, mind, and body in stories concerning the temporomandibular joint (TMJ). *Social Science & Medicine*, **38**(6), pp. 775–788.

Geller, M.J., 2015. *Ancient Babylonian medicine: Theory and practice.* Chichester, West Sussex: Wiley Blackwell.

Gibbs, R.W. and Franks, H., 2002. Embodied metaphor in women's narratives about their experiences with cancer. *Health Communication*, **14**(2), pp. 139–165.

Glasby, M., 2017. *Wholeness and holiness: Medicine, disease, purity and the Levitical priesthood.* London: Apostolos Publishing.

Glesne, C., 1997. That rare feeling: Representing research through poetic transcription. *Qualitative Inquiry*, **3**(2), pp. 202–221.

Good, B., 1994. *Medicine, rationality, and experience.* Cambridge: Cambridge University Press.

Gorman, S. and Kaplan, D.L., 1999. The affliction of Job: Poisoned! *Journal of the American Academy of Dermatology*, **40**(1), pp. 126–128.

Gotto, A., 2012. Suffering, medicine, and the book of Job. *Journal of Religion, Disability & Health*, **16**(4), pp. 420–431.

Greenstein, E.L., 2003. The language of Job and its poetic function. *Journal of Biblical Literature*, **122**(4), pp. 651–666.

Greenstein, E.L., 2007. Features of language in the poetry of Job. In: T. Krüger, M. Oeming, K. Schmid and C. Uehlinger, eds, *Das Buch Hiob und seine Interpretationen: Beiträge zum Hiob-Symposium auf dem Monte Verita vom 14–19 August 2005.* Zürich: Theologischer Verlag Zürich, pp. 81–96.

Greenstein, E.L., 2014. The invention of language in the poetry of job. In: J.K. Aitken, J.M.S. Clines and C.M. Maier, eds, *Interested readers: Essays on the Hebrew Bible in honor of David J. A. Clines.* Atlanta, GA: Society of Biblical Literature, pp. 331–346.

Greenstein, E.L., 2019. *Job: A new translation.* New Haven; London: Yale University Press.

Guillaume, P., 2008. Dismantling the deconstruction of Job. *Journal of Biblical Literature*, **127**(3), pp. 491–499.

Hallo, W.W. and Younger, K.L., 1997. *The context of scripture: Canonical compositions, monumental inscriptions, and archival documents from the biblical world.* Leiden: Brill.

Handelman, D. and Raskin, V., 1990. *Humor: International Journal of Humor Research*, **1**(1).

Hawley, L.R., 2018. *Metaphor competition in the book of Job.* Göttingen: Vandenhoeck & Ruprecht.

Heinlein, R.A., 1984. *Job: A comedy of justice.* Sevenoaks: New English Library.

Hillers, D.R., 1964. *Treaty-curses and the Old Testament prophets.* Rome: Pontifical Biblical Institute.

Hong, S., 2006. *The metaphor of illness and healing in Hosea and its significance in the socio-economic context of eighth-century Israel and Judah.* New York; Oxford: Lang.

Houck-Loomis, T., 2015. When fast-held God images fail to meet our needs: A psychoanalytic reading of Job chapters 6 and 7. *Pastoral Psychology*, **64**(2), pp. 195–203.

Hsu, E., 2010. *Pulse diagnosis in early Chinese medicine: The telling touch.* Cambridge: Cambridge University Press.

Hunter, R.L., 1985. *The new comedy of Greece and Rome.* Cambridge: Cambridge University Press.

Hunter, R.L., 2012. Attic comedy in the rhetorical and moralising traditions. In: M. Revermann, ed, *The Cambridge companion to Greek comedy.* Cambridge: Cambridge University Press, pp. 373–386.

Hurwitz, B., 2000. Narrative and the practice of medicine. *The Lancet*, **356**(9247), pp. 2086–2089.

Irwin, W.A., 1950. Job and prometheus. *The Journal of Religion*, **30**(2), pp. 90–108.

Jackson, J.E., 1994. Chronic pain and the tension between the body as subject and object. In: T.J. Csordas, ed, *Embodiment and experience: The existential ground of culture and self.* Cambridge: Cambridge University Press, pp. 201–228.

Jackson, J.E., 2000. *"Camp pain": Talking with chronic pain patients.* Philadelphia, PA: University of Pennsylvania Press.

Jackson, M.A., 2012. *Comedy and feminist interpretation of the Hebrew Bible: A subversive collaboration.* Oxford: Oxford University Press.

Janes, C.R., 1999. Imagined lives, suffering, and the work of culture: The embodied discourses of conflict in modern Tibet. *Medical Anthropology Quarterly*, **13**(4), pp. 391–412.

Johnson, T.J., 2004. *Job as proto-apocalypse: Proposing a unifying genre.* ProQuest Dissertations Publishing.

Johnston, S.I., 2004. *Religions of the ancient world: A guide.* Cambridge, MA; London: Belknap.

Jones, A., 2010. Justice and biblical interpretation beyond subjectivity and self-determination: A contrapuntal reading on the theme of suffering in the book of Job. *Political Theology*, **11**(3), pp. 431–452.

Jones, S.C., 2013. Corporeal discourse in the book of Job. *Journal of Biblical Literature*, **132**(4), pp. 845–863.

Joosten, J., 2014. Linguistic clues as to the date of the book of Job: A mediating position. In: J. Aitken, J.M.S. Clines and C.M. Maier, eds, *Interested readers: Essays on the Hebrew Bible in honor of David J. A. Clines.* Atlanta, GA: Society of Biblical Literature, pp. 347–357.

Joyce, P., 1995. Reading the Bible within the public domain. In: F.M. Young, ed, *Dare we speak of God in public? The Cadbury lectures for 1994.* London: Mowbray, pp. 67–79.

Jung, C.G., 1979. *Answer to Job.* London: Routledge & Kegan Paul.

Jurecic, A., 2012. *Illness as narrative.* University of Pittsburgh Press.

Kahn, J.H. and Solomon, H., 1975. *Job's illness: Loss, grief and integration: A psychological interpretation.* Oxford: Pergamon.

Kaminsky, J.S., 2015. Would you impugn my justice? A nuanced approach to the Hebrew Bible's theology of divine recompense. *Interpretation: A Journal of Bible and Theology*, **69**(3), pp. 299–310.

Kelber, W.H., 1997. *The oral and the written Gospel: The hermeneutics of speaking and writing in the synoptic tradition, Mark, Paul, and Q.* Bloomington: Indiana University Press.

Keller, C., 2003. *The face of the deep: A theology of becoming.* London: Routledge.

Kendall, M. and Murray, S., 2004. Poems from the heart: Living with heart failure. In: B. Hurwitz, T. Greenhalgh and V. Skultans, eds, *Narrative research in health and illness.* Malden, MA; Oxford: Blackwell Publishing, pp. 52–72.

Kiel, M.D., 2012. *The "whole truth": Rethinking retribution in the book of Tobit.* London; New York: T&T Clark.

Kirmayer, L., 1992. The body insistence on meaning: Metaphor as presentation and representation in illness experience. *Medical Anthropology Quarterly*, **6**(4), pp. 323–346.

Kitz, A.M., 2014. *Cursed are you! The phenomenology of cursing in cuneiform and Hebrew texts.* Winona Lake, IN: Eisenbrauns.

Kleinman, A., 1988. *The illness narratives: Suffering, healing and the human condition.* New York: Basic Books.

Koch, A., 2012. Reasons for the boom of body theories in humanities and social sciences. In: A. Berlejung, J. Dietrich and J.F. Quack, eds, *Menschenbilder und Körperkonzepte im Alten Israel, in Ägypten undim Alten Orient.* Tübingen: Mohr Siebeck, pp. 3–42.

Konstan, D., 2012. Defining the genre. In: M. Revermann, ed, *The Cambridge companion to Greek comedy.* Cambridge: Cambridge University Press, pp. 27–42.

Kreager, P. and Schroeder-Butterfill, E., 2004. *Ageing without children: European and Asian perspectives.* New York; Oxford: Berghahn Books.

Krüger, T., 2007. Did Job repent? In: T. Krüger, M. Oeming, K. Schmid and C. Uehlinger, eds, *Das Buch Hiob und seine Interpretationen: Beiträge zum Hiob-Symposium auf dem Monte Verita vom 14–19 August 2005*. Zürich: Theologischer Verlag Zürich, pp. 217–230.

Kugel, J.L., 1981. *The idea of biblical poetry: Parallelism and its history.* New Haven; London: Yale University Press.

Lakoff, G. and Johnson, M., 1980. *Metaphors we live by.* Chicago; London: University of Chicago Press.

Lakoff, G. and Turner, M., 1989. *More than cool reason: A field guide to poetic metaphor.* Chicago; London: University of Chicago Press.

Lambert, W.G., 1960. *Babylonian wisdom literature.* Oxford: Clarendon Press.

Lambert, W.G., 1987. A further attempt at the Babylonian "man and his God". In: F. Rochberg, ed, *Language, literature and history: Philological and historical studies presented to Erica Reiner.* New Haven: American Oriental Society, pp. 187–202.

Lambert, W.G., 2013. *Babylonian creation myths.* Winona Lake, IN: Eisenbrauns.

Latour, B., 2004. Why has critique run out of steam? From matters of fact to matters of concern. *Critical Inquiry*, **30**(2), pp. 225–248.

Lazarus, B.M., 2014. *Humanist comic elements in Aristophanes and the Old Testament.* Piscataway: Gorgias Press.

Leach, E., 1975. Society's expectations of health. *Journal of Medical Ethics*, **1**(2), p. 85.

Lenzi, A., 2010. Invoking the God: Interpreting invocations in mesopotamian prayers and biblical laments of the individual. *Journal of Biblical Literature*, **129**(2), pp. 303–315.

Lenzi, A., 2011. *Reading Akkadian prayers and hymns: An introduction.* Atlanta, GA: Society of Biblical Literature.

Lenzi, A., 2015. Scribal hermeneutics and the twelve gates of Ludlul bēl nēmeqi. *Journal of American Oriental Society*, **135**(4), pp. 733–749.

Lilly, I., 2016. Rûaḥ embodied: Job's internal disease from the perspective of Mesopotamian medicine. In: A. Weissenreider, ed, *Borders: Terms, ideologies, performances.* Tübingen: Mohr Siebeck, pp. 323–336.

Lloyd, G.E.R., 2003. *In the grip of disease: Studies in the Greek imagination.* Oxford: Oxford University Press.

Lundbom, J.R., 2013. *Deuteronomy: A commentary.* Grand Rapids, MI: William B. Eerdmans.

Lupton, D., 1994. *Medicine as culture: Illness, disease and the body in Western societies.* London: Sage.

Magdalene, R.J., 2007. The Ane legal origins of impairment as theological disability and the book of Job. *Perspectives in Religious Studies*, **34**, pp. 23–60.

Manderson, L. and Smith-Morris, C., 2010. *Chronic conditions, fluid states: Chronicity and the anthropology of illness.* New Brunswick: Rutgers University Press.

Marshall, G.J., 2008. *A guide to Merleau-Ponty's phenomenology of perception.* Milwaukee, WI: Marquette University Press.

Mattingly, C. and Garro, L.C., 2000. *Narrative and the cultural construction of illness and healing.* Berkeley; London: University of California Press.

Mattingly, G.L., 1990. The pious sufferer: Mesopotamia's traditional theodicy and Job's counselors. In: W.W. Hallo, B.W. Jones and G.L. Mattingly, eds, *The Bible in the light of cuneiform literature.* Lewiston, NY: Mellen, pp. 305–348.

Mayes, A.D.H., 1979. *Deuteronomy.* London: Oliphants, Marshall, Morgan & Scott.

Mazanderani, F., Locock, L. and Powell, J., 2012. Being differently the same: The mediation of identity tensions in the sharing of illness experiences. *Social Science & Medicine*, **74**(4), pp. 546–553.

McCracken, D., 1995. Narration and comedy in the book of Tobit. *Journal of Biblical Literature*, **114**(3), pp. 401–418.

Merkur, D., 2004. Psychotherapeutic change in the book of Job. In: J.H. Ellens and W.G. Rollins, eds, *Psychology and the Bible: A new way to read the scriptures, volume 2: From genesis to apocalyptic vision*. New York: Greenwood-Praeger, pp. 119–139.

Meshel, N., 2015. Whose Job is this? Dramatic irony and double entendre in the book of Job. In: L. Batnitzky, I. Pardes and R. Alter, eds, *The book of Job: Aesthetics, ethics, hermeneutics.* Berlin: Walter de Gruyter, pp. 47–76.

Milgrom, J., 1991. *Leviticus 1–16: A new translation with introduction and commentary.* New York; London: Doubleday.

Moss, C.R. and Schipper, J., 2011. *Disability studies and biblical literature.* Basingstoke: Palgrave Macmillan.

Müller, H., 1995. *Das Hiobproblem: Seine Stellung und Entstehung im alten Orient und im Alten Testament.* 3. um Nachträge erweiterte Auflage edn. Darmstadt: Wissenschaftliche Buchgesellschaft.

Muramoto, O., 2014. Retrospective diagnosis of a famous historical figure: Ontological, epistemic, and ethical considerations. *Philosophy, Ethics, and Humanities in Medicine: PEHM*, **9**, p. 10.

Nelson, R.D., 2002. *Deuteronomy: A commentary.* Louisville, KY: Westminster John Knox Press.

Newsom, C.A., 1993. Cultural politics and the reading of Job. *Biblical Interpretation*, **1**(2), pp. 119–138.

Newsom, C.A., 1999. Job and his friends – a conflict of moral imaginations (An examination of a scriptural model of divine moral answerability). *Interpretation-A Journal of Bible and Theology*, **53**(3), pp. 239–253.

Newsom, C.A., 2002. The book of Job as polyphonic text. *Journal for the Study of the Old Testament*, **26**(3), pp. 87–108.

Newsom, C.A., 2003. *The book of Job: A contest of moral imaginations.* New York; Oxford: Oxford University Press.

Newsom, C.A., 2009. *The book of Job.* Oxford: Oxford University Press.

Nichter, M., 1981. Idioms of distress: Alternatives in the expression of psychosocial distress: A case study from South India. *Culture, Medicine and Psychiatry*, **5**(4), pp. 379–408.

Nichter, M., 2008. *Global health: Why cultural perceptions, social representations, and biopolitics matter.* Tucson: University of Arizona Press.

Nichter, M., 2010. Idioms of distress revisited. *Culture, Medicine, and Psychiatry*, **34**(2), pp. 401–416.

Niditch, S., 1996. *Oral world and written word: Ancient Israelite literature.* Louisville, KY: Westminster John Knox Press.

Nougayrol, J., 1968. juste souffrant. In: C.F.A. Schaeffer, ed, *Ugaritica*. Paris: Imprimerie Nationale, pp. 265–273.

Ochs, E. and Capps, L., 1996. Narrating the self. *Annual Review of Anthropology*, **25**(1), pp. 19–43.

Oeming, M. and Drechsel, W., 2007. Das Buch Hiob – ein Lehrstück der Seelsorge? Das Hiobbuch in exegetischer und poimenischer Perspektive. In: T. Krüger, M. Oeming, K. Schmid and C. Uehlinger, eds, *Das Buch Hiob und seine Interpretationen, Beiträge zum Hiob-Symposium auf dem Monte Verità vom 14–19 August 2005, Abhandlungen zur Theologie des Alten und Neuen.* Zürich: TVZ, pp. 421–440.

Oeming, M. and Schmid, K., 2015. *Job's journey: Stations of suffering.* Winona Lake, IN: Eisenbrauns.

Olyan, S.M., 2008. *Disability in the Hebrew Bible: Interpreting mental and physical differences.* Cambridge: Cambridge University Press.

Ong, W.J., 1988. *Orality and literacy: The technologizing of the word*. London: Routledge.

Oring, E., 2008. Humor in anthropology and folklore. In: V. Raskin, ed, *The prime of humor research*. Berlin and New York: Walter de Gruyter, pp. 183–210.

Oshima, T., 2014. *Babylonian poems of pious sufferers: Ludlul Bēl Nēmeqi and the Babylonian Theodicy*. Tübingen: Mohr Siebeck.

Pachmuss, T., 1979. Prometheus and Job reincarnated: Melville and Dostoevskij. *The Slavic and East European Journal*, **23**(1), pp. 25–37.

Parker, R., 2007. *Polytheism and society at Athens*. Oxford: Oxford University Press.

Parsons, C. and Wakeley, P., 1991. Idioms of distress: Somatic responses to distress in everyday life. *Culture, Medicine and Psychiatry*, **15**(1), pp. 111–132.

Pelham, A., 2010. Job as comedy, revisited. *Journal for the Study of the Old Testament*, **35**(1), pp. 89–112.

Perdue, L.G., 1991. *Wisdom in revolt: Metaphorical theology in the book of Job*. Sheffield: Almond Press.

Perdue, L.G., 2008. *The sword and the stylus: An introduction to wisdom in the age of empires*. Grand Rapids, MI: William B. Eerdmans.

Piccin, M. and Worthington, M., 2015. Schizophrenia and the problem of suffering in the Ludlul hymn to Marduk. *Revue d'Assyriologie et d'Archeologie Orientale*, **109**(1), pp. 113–124.

Pilch, J.J., 2000. *Healing in the New Testament: Insights from medical and Mediterranean anthropology*. Minneapolis: Fortress Press.

Poindexter, C.C., 2002. Research as poetry: A couple experiences HIV. *Qualitative Inquiry*, **8**(6), pp. 707–714.

Pool, R. and Geissler, W., 2005. *Medical anthropology*. Maidenhead: Open University Press.

Pope, M.H., 1965. *Job*. Garden City, NY: Doubleday.

Portier-Young, A., 2001. Alleviation of suffering in the 'book of Tobit': Comedy, community, and happy endings. *Catholic Biblical Quarterly*, **63**(1), pp. 35–54.

Pritzker, S.E., 2014. *Living translation: Language and the search for resonance in U.S. Chinese medicine*. New York; Oxford: Berghahn Books.

Quick, L., 2017. *Deuteronomy 28 and the Aramaic curse tradition*. Oxford: Oxford University Press.

Radday, Y.T., 1990. On missing the humour in the Bible: An introduction. In: Y.T. Radday and A. Brenner, eds, *On humour and the comic in the Hebrew Bible*. Sheffield: Almond Press, pp. 21–38.

Raffel, S., 2013. *The method of metaphor*. Bristol; Chicago: Intellect.

Raphael, R., 2004. Things too wonderful: A disabled reading of Job. *Perspectives in Religious Studies*, **4**(31), pp. 399–424.

Raphael, R., 2008. *Biblical corpora: Representations of disability in Hebrew biblical literature*. London; New York: T&T Clark.

Revermann, M., 2012. Divinity and religious practice. In: M. Revermann, ed, *The Cambridge companion to Greek comedy*. Cambridge: Cambridge University Press, pp. 275–288.

Ricœur, P., 2003. *The rule of metaphor: The creation of meaning in language*. London: Routledge.

Romdenh-Romluc, K., 2010. *Routledge philosophy guidebook to Merleau-Ponty and Phenomenology of perception*. Milton Park; Abingdon, Oxon; New York: Routledge.

Rowley, H.H., 1976. *Job*. Rev. edn. London: Oliphants.

Ruch, W., 2008. The primer of humor research. In: V. Raskin, ed, *The primer of humor research*. Berlin; New York: Walter de Gruyter, pp. 17–100.

Sarna, N.M., 1996. Notes on the use of the definite article in the poetry of Job. In: M. Haran and M.V. Fox, eds, *Texts, Temples, and traditions: A tribute to Menahem Haran*. Winona Lake: Eisenbrauns, pp. 279–284.

Scarry, E., 1985. *The body in pain: The making and unmaking of the world*. New York; Oxford: Oxford University Press.

Scheper-Hughes, N. and Lock, M.M., 1987. The mindful body: A prolegomenon to future work in medical anthropology. *Medical Anthropology Quarterly*, **1**(1), pp. 6–41.

Scheyhing, H., 2011. Babylonisch-assyrische Krankheitstheorie: Korrelationen zwischen medizinischen Diagnosen und therapeutischen Konzepten. *Welt des Orients*, **41**(1), pp. 79–117.

Schipper, J., 2006. *Disability studies and the Hebrew Bible: Figuring Mephibosheth in the David story*. New York: T&T Clark.

Schlobin, R., 1992. Prototypic horror: The genre of the Book of Job. *Semeia*, **60**, pp. 23.

Schmid, K., 2008. The authors of Job and their historical and social setting. In: L.G. Perdue, ed, *Scribes, sages, and seers: The sage in the Eastern Mediterranean world*. Göttingen: Vandenhoeck & Ruprecht, pp. 145–153.

Sciama, L.D., 2016. *Humour, comedy and laughter: Obscenities, paradoxes, insights and the renewal of life*. New York: Berghahn Books.

Scurlock, J.A. and Andersen, B.R., 2005. *Diagnoses in Assyrian and Babylonian medicine: Ancient sources, translations, and modern medical analyses*. Urbana, IL: University of Illinois Press.

Seow, C.L., 2009. Reflections on the history of consequences: The case of Job. In: D.L. Petersen, J.M. Lemon and K.H. Richards, eds, *Method matters: Essays on the interpretation of the Hebrew Bible in honor of David L. Petersen*. Atlanta, GA: Society of Biblical Literature, pp. 581–586.

Seow, C.L., 2013. *Job 1–21: Interpretation and commentary*. Grand Rapids, MI: William B. Eerdmans.

Seybold, K. and Müller, U.B., 1981. *Sickness and healing*. Nashville: Abingdon Press.

Sharp, C.J., 2009. *Irony and meaning in the Hebrew Bible*. Bloomington: Indiana University Press.

Shveka, A. and Van Hecke, P., 2014. The metaphor of criminal charge as a paradigm for the conflict between Job and his friends. *Ephemerides Theologicae Lovanienses*, **90**(1), pp. 99–119.

Sontag, S., 1978. *Illness as metaphor*. New York: Farrar, Straus and Giroux.

Sontag, S., 1990. *Illness as metaphor and Aids and its metaphors*. New York: Picador.

Southwood, K.E., 2019. Metaphor, illness, and identity in Psalms 88 and 102. *Journal for the Study of the Old Testament*, **2**, pp. 228–246.

Southwood, K.E., Forthcoming. The "innards" in the Psalms and job as metaphors for illness. *Horizons in Biblical Literature*.

Sparks, G., 1903. The Hebrew prometheus or the book of Job. *The Sewanee Review*, **11**(1), p. 49.

Steffen, V., 1997. Life stories and shared experience. *Social Science & Medicine*, **45**(1), pp. 99–111.

Stein, G., 2018. *The hidden psychiatry of the Old Testament*. New York: Hamilton Books.

Steinert, U., 2018. *Assyrian and Babylonian scholarly text catalogues: Medicine, magic and divination*. Berlin: Walter de Gruyter.

Steinmann, A., 1996. The structure and message of the book of Job. *Vetus Testamentum*, **46**(1), pp. 85–100.

Strauss, H., 1994. Bemerkungen zu Gebrauch und Bedeutung von לא in der Hiobdichtung und Gesamtkomposition. In: P. Mommer and W. Thiel, eds, *Altes Testament: Forschung und Wirkung. Festschrift für Henning Graf Reventlow.* Frankfurt am Main: Peter Lang, pp. 95–101.

Szpek, H., 1997. An observation on the Peshiṭta's translation of Šdy in Job. *Vetus Testamentum*, **47**(4), pp. 550–553.

Taylor, J.S., 2003. The story catches you and you fall down: Tragedy, ethnography, and "cultural competence". *Medical Anthropology Quarterly*, **17**(2), pp. 159–181.

Throop, C.J., 2010. *Suffering and sentiment: Exploring the vicissitudes of experience and pain in Yap.* Berkeley, CA; London: University of California Press.

Timmermans, S. and Haas, S., 2008. Towards a sociology of disease. *Sociology of Health & Illness*, **30**(5), pp. 659–676.

Tollerton, D.C., 2012. *The book of Job in post-holocaust thought.* Sheffield: Sheffield Phoenix Press.

Treves, M., 1995. The book of Job. *Zeitschrift für die alttestamentliche Wissenschaft*, **107**(2), pp. 261–272.

Van Der Toorn, K., 1991. The ancient near Eastern literary dialogue as a vehicle of critical reflection. In: G.J. Reinink and H.L.J. Vanstiphout, eds, *Dispute poems and dialogues in the ancient and mediaeval near East: Forms and types of literary debates in semitic and related literature.* Louvain, Belgium: Department Oriëntalistiek, pp. 59–75.

Van Hecke, P., 2005. *Metaphor in the Hebrew Bible.* Leuven: University Press.

Van Hecke, P., 2013. "I melt away and will no longer live": The use of metaphor in Job's self-descriptions. In: A. Labahn, ed, *Conceptual metaphors in poetic texts: Proceedings of the metaphor research group of the European association of biblical studies in Lincoln 2009.* Piscataway: Gorgias Press, pp. 69–90.

Van Loon, H., 2018. *Metaphors in the discussion on suffering in Job 3–31: Visions of hope and consolation.* Leiden: Brill.

Vayntrub, J., 2019. *Beyond orality: Biblical poetry on its own terms.* 1st edn. London: Routledge.

Venter, P.P., 2015. Wealth, poverty and mutual care: Towards a reconstructive reading of the book of Job. *Verbum et Ecclesia*, **36**(3), pp. 1–7.

Vickers, N., 2016. Illness narratives. In: A. Smyth, ed, *A history of English autobiography.* New York: Cambridge University Press, pp. 388–401.

Watson, W.G.E., 1984. *Classical Hebrew poetry: A guide to its techniques.* Sheffield: JSOT Press.

Weinfeld, M., 1988. Job and its mesopotamian parallels – a typological analysis. In: W.T. Claassen, ed, *Text and context: Old Testament and semitic studies for F.C. Fensham, journal for the study of the Old Testament.* Sheffield: JSOT Press, pp. 217–226.

Whedbee, J., 1977. The comedy of Job. *Semeia*, **7**, pp. 1–39.

Witte, M., 2007. The Greek book of Job. In: T. Krüger, M. Oeming, K. Schmid and C. Uehlinger, eds, *Das Buch Hiob und seine Interpretationen: Beiträge zum Hiob-Symposium auf dem Monte Verita vom 14–19 August 2005.* Zürich: Theologischer Verlag Zürich, pp. 33–54.

Witte, M., 2013. Job in conversation with the Torah. In: B.U. Schipper and D.A. Teeter, eds, *Wisdom and Torah: The reception of "Torah" in the wisdom literature of the second Temple period.* Leiden: Brill, pp. 81–100.

Woods, A., 2013. Beyond the wounded storyteller: Rethinking narrativity, illness and embodied self-experience. In: H. Carel and R. Cooper, eds, *Health, illness and disease: Philosophical essays.* Durham: Acumen, pp. 113–128.

Young, I., 2009. Is the prose tale of Job in late biblical Hebrew? *Vetus Testamentum*, **59**(4), pp. 606–629.

2 Methinks the Job, he doth protest too much

Introduction

The amount of space given to the character Job in order to express his perceptions of bodily pain in the book is remarkable. Long sections of the material are devoted to this, with their length matched only by the intensity of expression. Indeed, the language placed on the character Job's lips is highly dramatic and often very shocking. Perhaps the most shocking aspect of it is the way the deity is continually blamed for Job's negative experiences of his own body. Of course – as we shall discuss – this is highly ironic, given that audiences have already been made aware that the responsibility lies ultimately with the deity who, cast as YHWH, in the prologue and epilogue allows the Satan to strike Job's body (Job 2:6–7). Nevertheless, the character's long and detailed descriptions of extremely violent attacks by the deity as an expression of pain are certainly worth analysis. As Whedbee argues, Job's 'language of attack against God is probably the most searing in the Hebrew Bible' so that 'God often emerges as a grotesque, demonic deity' (Whedbee 1977:15; cf. Heinen 1979). What could possibly drive an author to depict the character this way, and how might early audiences have engaged with the material? What is the significance of the deity attack metaphor for Job? Is this metaphor's prominence in the material and intensity haphazard, or does it have some function? The following chapter will try to answer these questions, bringing together scholarship on the biblical text with research into illness narratives and expressions of pain. The satirical nature of the material will be explored, and it will be suggested that throughout these depictions of Job's pain, tragedy tips over into comedy, often via the routes of exaggeration, absurdity, and incongruence.

'The arrows of Shaddai': Job's body and the deity attack metaphor in Job 6

At several points during the dialogue sections of Job, the main character describes what is happening to his body using language and metaphors which evoke attack. More shockingly, the one wielding the instruments of attack generally seems to be the deity. As Von Rad noted in his classic work *Weisheit in Israel*

> [H] ier ist ein neuer Ton. . .: Gott als der direkte Feind des Menschen, der ihn mit Lust quält, der . . . im Zerrbild eines Teufels über ihm erscheint,

DOI: 10.4324/9781003029489-2

> mit seinen Zähnen knirscht und seine Augen wetzt . . . und der Hiobs Eingeweide spaltet.
>
> (Von Rad 1970:280)

This chapter will explore the theme of the body in pain as the 'attacked' body. Of particular interest here are the following sections of material: Job 6:1–10; 9:17–19; 16:6–17, 19:7–12, and 30:16–20. We will then turn to material in Job which also focuses on Job's body, but interestingly combines the deity attack metaphor with the deity surveillance metaphor. Erickson highlights that in Job's speeches, 'corporeal imagery is both abundant and multivalent', meaning that 'Job's disintegrating, decaying, broken, and abused body lurks like a spectre in the dialogue between Job and his friends' so that 'all commentators take notice of Job's descriptions of physical suffering' (Erickson 2013:295). Perhaps one reason for this is, as Schipper suggests, 'Job often uses imagery of diseased skin to help him express and articulate his pain rather than his wrongdoing'; therefore, 'when he mentions his skin or flesh, he does so to express his circumstances and inspire those who hear of it, including God, to be with him' (Schipper 2010:19).[1] This argument aligns neatly with Das and Jurecic's points, discussed earlier, about the acknowledgement of pain (Das 1996; Jurecic 2012). Instead of his friends' problem-solving attitudes, the character seeks acknowledgement and empathy.

One peculiarity of the speeches which focus on Job's body is the vehemence of Job's rhetoric, especially when focused on the 'deity attack' metaphor. Eloah is characterised 'als der direkte Feind des Menschen, der ihn mit Lust quält' (Von Rad 1970:280). This is clear from the statement,

> For the arrows (חץ) of the Almighty (שדי)[2] are in me[3];
> my spirit drinks their poison (חמה);
> the terrors (בעותים)[4] of God (אֱלוֹהַּ "eloah") are arrayed against me.[5]
>
> (Job 6:4)

1 Greenstein also notes the emphasis on skin as the protective boundary to the body, arguing that 'Job's blistering skin reduces him to a fraction of his former self. He becomes so emaciated that his "bone sticks to [his] sin and [his flesh]" and protrudes' (Greenstein 2018:43; cf. Raz 2014:87). Concerning the motif of broken skin, which is usually connected with Job's emaciated figure, refer to Job 7:5; 10:11; 19:20; 19:26; and 30:30.

2 The Old Greek has κύριος 'the lord', at this point.

3 The Old Greek has ἐν τῷ σώματί μού 'in my body', which makes the image more strikingly somatic.

4 This term seems to come from the verb בעת, meaning 'to terrify'. The word occurs only here and in Psalm 88:16, where it is in parallelism with the term חרון meaning 'burning anger'.

5 This third line is a 'poetic triplet that stands out amid a sea of couplets' emphasising the severity of the personal and terrifying attack (Seow 2013:456).

The term יערכוני is derived from √ערך meaning 'to arrange' or 'put in order'. Thus 'they are arrayed against me'. This is not particularly problematic since the verb ערך is fairly common. Clines notes, 'יערכוני is a perfectly acceptable reading, the suffix being datival (GKC §117x)' (Clines 1989:158). Datival suffixes are common in Job (Blommerde 1969:87). This slightly undermines the suggestion in *Biblia Hebraica Stuttgartensia* that we understand the term to have a meaning similar to the Latin 'vexant me' on the basis of the Arabic term *araka*. Connecting this Arabic root without

Is it striking that, as Rowley comments, the 'author of his [Job's] distress' is Shaddai (Rowley 1976:58). Habel supposes that 'the designation of Shaddai as the archer is a veiled reference back to Rešef in 5:7' (Habel 1985:145).[6] This way of depicting Shaddai fits well with the theme of illness, given that Rešeph, the Canaanite god of pestilence, usually bears the epithet 'the archer' and his arrows produce disease.[7] This image of Rešeph also occurs in an Ugaritic incantation where the arrows 'are a reference to deadly diseases that this demon shoots into one's vital organs (CTU 1.14.I.16–20)' (Seow 2013:438). The suggestion seems to be that Shaddai is like Rešeph, a deity within whose arsenal is sicknesses.[8] This is in very sharp contrast to the perspective on the deity that Eliphaz provides as one who 'wounds, but he binds up; he strikes, but his hands heal' (Job 5:18; cf. Deut. 31:19).[9] Two parts of Eliphaz's argument in the previous chapters – this and the warning against the passions of food (Job 5:2 // Job 6:3) – are reformulated here. At various points in the book of Job the character is depicted as the target of an archer-like God (Job 7:20; 16:12–13). This is not an unfamiliar image in the Hebrew Bible more generally (Deut. 32:23, 42; Pss, 7:13; 38:2; 64:7; Lam. 2:3; 3:12). In this context, the arrows are poisonous, and this is emphasised by the syntax רוחי שתה חמתם literally 'it is *their poison* that my spirit drinks'. The term חמה is polysemous; it can mean 'poison' or 'anger' (as the Old Greek[10]

---

changing the consonantal text is based on Driver's suggestion and would produce a translation 'the terrors of Eloah frustrate me / wear me down' (Driver 1955:73).

6 Moore's article is particularly helpful for contextualising this metaphor (Moore 1993).

7 Most of the versions, including the Old Greek, Aquilla, Symmachus, the Vulgate, and the Pesharim, understand בני רשף in Job 5:7 as birds, leading Seow to suggest that 'the association of *rešep* with birds may have arisen in Egypt, where the Semitic deity Rešeph is identified with the gods Montu and Horus who are portrayed in the form of the falcon' (Seow 2013:437).

8 Some scholars take this metaphor quite far, suggesting that 'Job experienced his afflictions as a divine abuse and God as an abuser' (Verbin 2010:44; cf. Blumenthal 1993).

Perhaps more interesting is the way that the traditional language of prayer here is subverted. As Jones argues,

> The individual complaint psalms in the Hebrew Bible frequently employ the enemy motif, and on occasion they apply to God metaphors typically reserved for human enemies. So while God is commonly a shield (Pss. 3:4; 7:11; 18:3; 28:7; 33:20; cf. 35:2), a fortress (Pss. 9:10; 18:3; 28:8; 31:3–5), or a fortified city (Ps. 31:22) in which the psalmist takes refuge from enemy armies that besiege him with arrows (Pss. 11:2; 27:3; 37:14).
>
> (Jones 2013:849)

However, subverting traditional language through using arrows in the metaphor of a deity attack is not entirely without precedent, as Jones also notes in that 'Psalms 6 and 38 depict God as the one who strikes (6:2; 38:1–2) and shoots arrows (38:3) into the supplicant's body' (Jones 2013:849).

9 Job later ironically reworks this dialectical construction which here echoes *Ludlul Bēl Nēmequ* (as discussed earlier), stating 'if he tears down, no one can rebuild, if he shuts someone in, no one can open up' (Job 12:14). This is in stark contrast with Jeremiah, who has enough hope to venture in parallelism: 'heal me, O Lord, and we shall be healed, save me, and we shall be saved' (Jer. 17:14). Job has no such option.

10 ὧν ὁ θυμὸς αὐτῶν ἐκπίνει μου τὸ αἷμα: (Old Greek). There is a resumptive pronoun here: 'the arrows . . . whose wrath drinks my blood'. Perhaps this is a theological toning down or

and Vulgate[11] translate). Arrows are sometimes associated with destructive diseases (Deut. 32:23–24; Ps. 91:5–6).

The way that the character Job describes his body at this point is tragic and distressing. Like Prometheus on the rock, Job miserably suggests the arrows of Shaddai are within him. Newsom calls such depictions the 'disturbingly intimate violence of torture' (Newsom 2009:144[12]; cf. Clifton 2011:151; Hyun 2013:101). The metaphor casting Shaddai as Rešeph who throws down personified diseased arrows that Job's very spirit is forced to ingest is interesting.[13] Rather than saying 'I' drink, the author wrote 'my spirit' drinks. There is an absence of the later Cartesian dualistic division between 'mind' and 'body' here. Instead, we have an expression which aligns more closely with Merleau-Ponty's perspective of the body as the seat of personhood (Carel and Cooper 2013:20). Job's being is not separable from his body. Traditional responses to pain in the Hebrew Bible are here challenged in an accusatory manner. The result is a fissure, in the form of Job's body and his words, which re-imagines causality through subverting and distorting traditional language.

Within only a few verses, the metaphor of a malignant, attacking deity returns:

> . . . that it would please God [Eloah] to crush (דכא) me,[14]
> That he would let loose his hand and cut me off (בצע)![15]
> This would be my consolation;
> I would even exult[16] in unrelenting pain (חילה)[17]
> For I have not denied the words of the Holy One.[18]
>
> (Job 6:9–10)

---

anti-anthropomorphism (Gard 1952)? However, it could simply be the more natural Greek style of a translator 'who is comfortable with Greek usage' and 'less bound by the textual-linguistic make-up of the source text' (Dhont 2017:140).

11 sunt quarum indignatio ebibit spiritum meum: 'the range of which drinks up my sprit'.

12 Newsom's reference is to Job 9 at this point, but the comment could apply here too.

13 Raz suggests a rather compelling alternative way of thinking about the verse by emphasising the significance of the deity name 'Shaddai' here, arguing that 'the archaic divine epitaph also suggests breasts; this would render the scene a reversal of primal nurturing, as here the maternal God force feeds Job venom' (Raz 2014:85).

14 Other possible synonyms which occur in parallelism with דכא might include טחן 'grind' (Isa. 3:15) and ענה 'afflict' (Ps. 94:5). The Old Greek has the terms τρωσάτω 'wound' and for בצע, ἀνελέτω 'abolish/kill'.

15 Cf. Isa. 38:12 which uses a striking simile referring to life being cut off like the thread from a weaver's loom (Clines 1989:159).

16 Grabbe notes the various translations here: LXX has 'I would not draw back' (οὐ μὴ φείσωμαι); the Vulgate and Targum use the 'spare' (*parcat* יחוס). The Syriac, however, has 'I will become perfected (ואשתמלא) in strength'. Grabbe suggests that the translations 'could be the result of guessing' (Grabbe 1977:48).

17 The *hapax* is usually masculine, חיל. Seow observes that this could be a 'pseudo-Qedemism, a form that is meant to evoke a feeling of foreignness' (Seow 2013:474). The term is often used of a woman during childbirth (Ps. 48:7; Isa. 13:8; Jer. 6:24; 22:23; 50:43; Mic. 4:9).

18 Some commentators suggest that the final line is a pious gloss. As Rowley states, 'Siegfried, Duhm, Peake, and many other editors delete this line as inappropriate here' (Rowley 1976:60).

With pressing sarcasm, Job declares his hope. Job begins with an imitation of piety, asking 'may it please god. . . ' in a way which sardonically mirrors traditional language where the expectation is of the deity's blessing and choice.[19] However, the author/s quickly turn him to his more familiar ironic style of perverting Eliphaz's advice in the former speech. Instead of hoping for a better future based on his innocence, Job mirrors Eliphaz's term (דכא) suggesting he hopes to be 'crushed'[20] by Eloah (Job 4:6, 19). As Habel argues, to 'be eliminated by God would not be punishment, as Eliphaz implied (4:8–9), but freedom' (Habel 1985:147). The irony of this suggestion is heightened further by the image of Eloah unfastening his hand, rather than stretching out his 'strong hand' in rescue (Exod. 6:1; Neh. 1:10; cf. Job 30:16). Thus, the author/s paint a picture where the prime mover of Job's pain is Eloah. This is a pointed and satirical reversal of the retribution model that his friends emphasise. The incongruity of Job's dysfunctional body moves from the ironic to the ludicrous to the comical and ridiculous, where the character paradoxically and bizarrely froths 'I would even exalt in unrelenting pain!' Far from being the stereotypical 'patient Job' or 'exemplary sufferer', this is a character depicted as angry and challenging: certainly *not* the 'patient' patient.[21] Instead, we see an irate (if exaggerated to the point of being nonsensical) plea to be seen and recognised as human. Job, the 'theological whistle-blower', as Seow calls him, refuses to be quarantined to the sinners' ward by his friends (Seow 2013:460). Rather than adhering to Eliphaz's moralising advice, therefore, Job insists on pointing out the 'Eliphaz in the room', so to speak, by uncovering his friends' argument's shortcomings.

Ironically however, through drawing attention to Eliphaz's problematic position, Job's own inadequacies also become increasingly apparent. The hyperbole associated with 'exulting' in pain depicts Job as a self-righteous would-be 'hero' who relentlessly struggles to maintain honour. As Pelham argues, 'he protests a bit too much to be taken seriously' (Pelham 2010:96). The character's body, when matched with his words about having not denied the words of the Holy One, make it seem to his friends that he is behaving falsely. This is because of the incongruity of Job's body and his claim to innocence. For his friends, Job's body is evidence which clearly signals retribution for some wrongdoing. As such, in the eyes of his friends, Job seems to be putting on airs and graces

19 Judg. 19:6; 1 Sam. 12:22; 2 Sam. 7:29; 2 Kgs 6:3; 1 Chr.17:27; Isa. 38:20; 1QH[a] 16:8.

20 The verb דכא in *piel* form can also refer to the deity 'trampling' on people (Lam. 3:34).

21 This is in contrast with the view of Job taken in the New Testament book of Job as a model of patience τὴν ὑπομονὴν Ἰὼβ ('the patient Job'; Jam. 5:11). The Qu'ran also reduces the story of Job to a model of endurance, wherein Job's response to calamity is 'Behold, affliction has visited me / And Thou art the most merciful of the merciful' (Surah 21:83). By the end of the tale, God praises Job as an excellent and penitent servant (Kermani 2011:129). This tradition of interpreting Job as a model of piety and patience has been maintained into modern times. For example, Kierkegaard suggests that the book of Job is a 'study of spiritual repetition, to be carried out in each instance, for the person in absolute relation to the absolute: life is invested, lost and yet gained back in each moment' (Dahl 2016:45).

that are in no way matched by the evidence that is his body in pain. Ironically, however, the audience has been told that he is blameless and upright. This conspiracy between the storyteller and the audience 'in which the teller makes the audience privy to information of which one or more characters are ignorant' and wherein 'the characters proceed unaware that their actions, speech, expectations, and so on will be upturned at some point' functions to make the scene rather amusing (Jackson 2012:19). The whole convoluted affair makes the audience feel superior: In the eyes of Job's friends he is some sort of rambling buffoon who can't accept the reality. However, in the eyes of the audience he might be likened to the Shakespearean fool: His words contain some truth, but he is not a character that is taken seriously. To use another analogy, Job is like Cassandra doomed not to be listened to by his friends, while all the time the audience knows that his puffed-up protestations of innocence are at least partly true. Job's confrontational body is matched by his confrontational words, which challenge the audience to rethink the connection between transgression and pain. However, this challenge is cast in such an overstated and satirical way that one wonders if audiences who agree with the retribution model are perhaps being teased. After all, nothing makes a dangerous and risky point more safely than comedy, given that it can elicit both emotional engagement from the audience and also critical detachment.

A profitable way to frame the social responses that are betrayed in the attitudes of Job's friends is to describe them as 'moralising language'. Several scholars have used this term to describe the friends' reactions.[22] This is certainly

22 For example, Sanders argues that the 'so-called friends engaged, actually, in blatant moralizing, which is what . . . static thinkers, are wont to do' (Sanders 2009:67). Similarly, Raphael argues that 'the friends insist on a moral meaning to Job's suffering, and Job says that there is none. His suffering has no moral cause, and no moral conclusion' (Raphael 2004:421). Likewise, Ferngren notes the 'tendency to moralize sickness by rendering its victims sinners in need of repentance' was popular, and he connects this with the attitude of Job's friends (Ferngren 2014:28).

Nevertheless, it should be noted that there are several more positive appraisals of Job's friends. For example, Pelham claims that they,

> . . . are rolled into the conglomerate of his identity. Adopting the signs of his suffering and grief, they make clear that it is his experience that is of central importance. Silencing themselves like the members of his community in chapter 29, they make clear that his words are valued above their own. Lowering themselves to the ground in his presence, they demonstrate their deference to him. They do not behave this way because he is suffering and they want to show how sorry they feel for what has befallen him. Rather, they behave this way because it is indicative of the relationship that exists between them – Job is the central figure in their world, because he is the most righteous and, by extension, the biggest – in spite of Job's suffering, which has stripped his greatness from him.
>
> (Pelham 2012a:59; cf Habel 1977)

It should be noted here, however, that Pelham's argument is restricted to the prologue. The dialogues take on a very different characteristic, wherein the 'defence of the traditional doctrine of retribution fails utterly to convince Job' (Burnight 2014a:369). Said dialogues proceed in a cantankerous crescendo until the comic character Elihu interrupts and brings to play to a disappointing anti-climax

a marked trait of Eliphaz's response,[23] and it emerges in Bildad's reactions to Job.[24] Indeed, 'moralising language' aligns well with the general trend of the friends who misapply 'the principle of retributive justice' (Aimers 2012:61).[25] Resistance to moralising language also emerges in Job's responses: His friends, who withhold kindness, 'are treacherous as a wadi' (Job 6:14–16, 21). As we shall see, several times throughout the book, Job makes similar protests. The mismatch of epistemologies is partly the problem here: As Greenstein argues, the friends' 'world view is theoretical and abstract, while his is felt in the bone' (Greenstein 2007a:76). As a consequence, there is a contest of authority embedded within the dialogue and an attempt on Job's part to 'reinvest his words with a power he perceives they have lost' (Pelham 2012a:334). This is perhaps achieved through the recourse to graphic[26] metaphors of the pain which is inflicted by the deity.

One helpful way of framing this is through the logic of criminalisation which is implicit within the retribution model that the friends adopt. Lloyd's observation is helpful at this point:

> The boundary between the criminal and the sick is also deeply contentious. . . . Not only are there powerful preconceptions of what is normal at work in the construction of the kind, but the type of abnormality in question may be deeply controversial, as between criminality on the one hand, disease on the other.
>
> (Lloyd 2003:244)

This logic then runs this risk of being understood as 'the basis for representations of what is good ethically and in the political domain' (Lloyd 2003:240). As Worsley argued, at a high level of abstraction, misfortune, including illness, is commonly attributed to some kind of offense against

(prior to the whirlwind speeches) by re-stating the arguments already raised by Eliphaz, Bildad, and Zophar.

23 E.g., the implied responsibility in the question 'who that was innocent ever perished?' and the advice to 'do not despise the discipline of the Almighty' (Job 4:7; 5:17). Refer to note 24 in Chapter 1.

24 E.g., as noted, the advice 'make supplication to the Almighty if you are pure (זך) and upright (ישר)' (Job 8:5–6). The prologue's depiction of Job as 'blameless' (תם) and 'upright' (ישר) adds an at once infuriating but also almost comical irony to the advice (Job 1:1). Refer to note 24 in Chapter 1.

25 Aimers argues that the friends' assumption that Job is undergoing retributive justice is 'the type of self-conceit [that] is thus called the Just World Delusion by social psychologists' (Aimers 2012:62). This connects well with Pelham's principle of contested creations: Eliphaz's belief in the stable 'world-as-it-ought-to-be' is 'troubled by Job's suffering' (Pelham 2012a:114).

26 While van Hecke suggests it 'should come as no surprise that Job speaks of his pain mainly in metaphorical terms', it is the violent nature of the somatised metaphors, casting the deity as an 'zorniger Tyrann', as Luther described it, which is as surprising as it is provocative (van Hecke 2013:70; Luther and Bornkamm 1989:60).

cultural values and social norms (Worsley 1982).[27] Job's refusal to adhere to the system of thought, as expressed through excessive metaphors of divine assault, emphasises the flaws in the explanatory model. Job's publicly and obviously different body reveals a lot about norms and expectations. Of course, it should be acknowledged at this point that norms can form in arbitrary ways.[28] Nevertheless, in protesting innocence despite his body, Job represents a broken norm to his friends. Ironically, however, the audience has been informed from the outset that Job is 'blameless' and 'upright', and this only serves to highlight the flawed approach of his friends (Job 1:1). Because of this paradox, in the eyes of his friends, Job is tantamount to matter out of order (Douglas 1966:35).[29] This is also potentially confronting, creating a dramatically high level of tension for early audiences if they adhere to the traditional retribution model's logic.

It is also helpful to compare the arguments of Job's friends with modern research about illness narratives. Moralising language is a regular feature which is common in this research. Good argues that a 'great many anthropological studies of illness have shown that sickness is universally experienced as a moral event, as a rupture of the moral order that invokes such "moralizing judgements"' (Good 1994:134). In Good's research, illness is a moral event raising soteriological issues and resorting to theodicy. Another example

27 This point is made by Gabe and Monaghan, who point out that,

> Medicalization is often associated with the control of deviance and the ways in which deviant behaviours that were once defined as immoral, sinful or criminal have been given medical meanings (Gabe and Monaghan 2013:59).

Similarly, with regard to obesity, Tomlinson suggests that two are categories available: 'the careless, or *immoral* lacking in self-respect "fatties" who, despite their better knowledge, continue to criminally abuse their "freedom" . . . and the *irrational* fatties, . . . guilty of "fatlogic"' (Tomlinson 2017:160). These are interesting statements given how closely they echo the retributive model of explaining illness present in much of the Old Testament and especially of Job's friends. Examples of this are plentiful, but one particularly insensitive remark emerges on the lips of Eliphaz, who suggests that Job is like somebody who 'drinks iniquity like water' and 'all the days of the wicked he writes [in pain]' (Job 15:20).

28 Goffman's comments about norms are relevant here:

> It can be assumed that a necessary condition for social life is the sharing of a single set of normative expectations by all participants, the norms being sustained in part because of being incorporated. (Goffman 1968:152)

Solomon makes a similar point, using the analogy '[i]f most people could flap their arms and fly, the inability to do so would be a disability' (Solomon 2013:29).

29 It should be noted here that in the experiences of those for whom illness is public information, the paradox of attempting to conform to expected norms of health can be deeply humiliating. Waskuil and Vannini allude to a study of rheumatoid arthritis wherein an informant described attending a cabaret (where one expected norm is likely to be health) on holiday. When the informant started to get up they reported: 'I had to stand there for a bit until we could get going and I know other people were looking at me and thinking that I was drunk' (Waskul and Vannini 2006:50).

of this is Lupton's research, examining numerous accounts of illness, which argues '[d]iscourses on the moral nature of illness seem pervasive in people's accounts' (Lupton 1994:111). Lupton's examples include the pattern of 'a confessional mode' being adopted when talking about illness and when 'relating supposedly unhealthy practices; "conscience" and "guilt" were regularly mentioned' (Lupton 1994:111).[30] Similarly, interviews in elderly populations in Aberdeen identified 'the common belief that constitutional strength was viewed as a moral matter. . . [depending on] will and a sense of responsibility' (Lupton 1994:111). This leads Lupton later to argue, in the case of obesity, that '[w]hen an illness is viewed as resulting from carelessness, lack of self-discipline or licentious or illegal behaviour, the ill person becomes treated with moral opprobrium' (Lupton 2012:50). In contemporary Western societies obesity is described in language inflected with moralising categories, coupled with socially constructed assumptions about behaviour. This may cause observers to judge obese people as morally inferior, based on a single physical trait. Through constructing meanings about the body using moralising sociocultural categories, an intrinsic ethical value is connected, with the body creating an additional burden of deviance for people who are visibly ill. However, the same may apply in non-Western contexts. Ferrari, for example, examining health and religious rituals in South Asia, problematises the question of responsibility in spirit possession. When 'a human being is possessed by a deity or by a spirit, the human being loses their agency' and this sets them outside of the normal rules of social interaction where 'health and well-being mostly depend on order' (Ferrari 2011:21, xvii). Similarly, Throop found that concerning pain in Yap 'a large majority of individuals' spoke about their 'experiences of pain within moral frameworks shaped according to a constellation of virtues' (Throop 2010:159). Likewise, addressing a North American religio-therapeutic community, Reynolds observes that '[e]xcessive consumption of such goods became pathologized when a moral distinction was made between "natural" (e.g. food) and "unnatural" (e.g. drugs) desires' (Reynolds 2016:124). Indeed, '[m]oralizing' can be found in many recent debates about 'individual responsibility for health . . . and the promotion of "heath behaviours" to support a "healthy lifestyle"' (Littlewood and Lynch 2016:161). Similarly, in relation to the body and shame, Dolezal argues that there is a 'contemporary tendency to moralise about "lifestyle" illnesses' (Dolezal 2015:567). This is because '[s]ickness makes the patient's stewardship of the body suspect' (Kirmayer 1988:62). In these examples, human agency and control over the body is exaggerated and, as a consequence, so, too, is responsibility. The cultural meanings ascribed to pain and illness therefore

30 Strangely, moralising about food has emerged in many places, though obviously it is not the case in many countries given the global variation in access to food, and was not the case historically. In a newspaper article in *The Guardian* in 2016, Baggini cites 'clean eating', 'dirty burgers', 'naughty' foods, 'sinful' foods, and foods which lead people 'astray'.

map to ideas about innocence and guilt. Two consequences of this internal logic are that alongside being criminalised as immoral, those who are ill or in pain might also be considered irrational. Using this material as a comparative lens through which to analyse Job's speech and his friends' reactions is helpful. Given the widespread and persistent nature of this response to the body in pain and illness in modern and present-day settings, it is not surprising to see the same response placed in the mouth of Job's friends. However, given that audiences are made aware from the book's beginning that Job is innocent, the moralising nature of the advice given is exposed and undermined. Therefore, we can observe that the book of Job presents to us an extremely progressive way of thinking about the body and pain at an early period.[31] If people are able to moralise illness even in a modern biomedical context where lots of information about the causation of pain is available, then the advanced nature of the book of Job is particularly emphasised. This level of nuanced sophistication is matched by a satirical and comic depiction of the interaction between the character and his friends.

A final observation here is in order with regard to power. Through allowing the character Job to narrativise illness in this manner, he is cast as authoritative and powerful. As Mattingly and Garro illustrate, '[n]arrative practices, including who is entitled to tell a story and when it can be told, "reflect and establish power relations in a wide range of domestic and community institutions"' (Mattingly and Garro 2000:18; citing Ochs and Capps 1996:35). Similarly, Good illustrates the case reporting an interview situation in Turkey where family members dominated the explaining of the illness of a daughter in law who, although present, was not allowed to tell her own story (Good 1994:160). Although in a position of disempowerment as a character who is cast at the triple intersectionality of being in pain, a foreigner, and fallen from status, the author/s nevertheless give Job a voice. Not only does the character have a voice, his words are provokingly shocking and disturbing. Job is given authority to speak about his own condition, and his words totally dominate the discordant conversation. Pelham's contribution is valuable here, pointing out the irony of Job's 'power': 'increasingly

31 It is also interesting to note that a range of receptions of Job among communities experiencing illness interpret the book, despite all the windy moralising, as comfort. For example, Carter uses the example of reading Job through the eye of people living with HIV/AIDS and leprosy amongst the Fang in Africa wherein 'suffering . . . is immersed in, if not wholly identifiable with, vehement accusations of moral blame, typically couched in the rhetoric of witchcraft' (Carter 2017:166). However, Carter also notes that from the perspectives of 'stigmatized sufferers, the sting of retribution clearly mirrored their own painful experiences of social exclusion' (Carter 2017:166). Similarly, Schroder, reading Job with communities living with HIV/AIDS in Brazil, notes that a relationship between the text of Job and individuals exists wherein a more positive reading of Job is possible. This is because of the dominance of the idea in Brazil of retribution and AIDS as a punishment from God for the sins committed by the individual exists (Schroder 2015). Likewise, Jones suggests that 'Siyaphila participants have the biblical text of Job as a comfort; Job's story begins to break God's silence for them' (Jones 2010:445).

aware that his previously powerful words have been sapped of their former force. . . [Job] speaks in powerful words . . . his aim is to invest them with the power they lack by convincing his hearers that they are in fact powerful' (Pelham 2012a:333). This power is certainly achieved: The friends listen and respond to Job on his terms and in the end, to some extent, so, too, does the deity. The deity, the cause of Job's pain, is supposedly the powerful one. Ironically, however, Yahweh is never allowed by the author/s to defend himself until the very end of the dialogues, where he is not actually given that much space in the text relative to that of Job and his friends. The device of giving only a few lines to the supposedly all-powerful creator deity for defence is also highly comical: The deity's voice emerges at the upturned U-point of the comedy, just before the happy ending. These speeches are highly incongruent and do not fit well with the preceding dialogue. In the whirlwind speeches, where God's 'ontological stammer' – as Sontag phrases it – is finally broken, Job's questions are not meaningfully engaged with, and it takes rather a lot of exegetical acrobatics to decipher how, if at all, the questions relate to the dialogues (Sontag 1969:27). As Clines suggests, by not addressing Job or any of the matters he raises, the deity 'implicitly refuses his discourse and its terms' (Clines 1998a:256). Guillaume makes a similar point arguing 'Job did not hear God's still small voice because there was far too much racket. . . . This is no glorious restoration' (Guillaume 2008:496, 499). One also wonders if the character Job finds the speeches satisfactory. The usual translation of Job's final response is 'I despise myself', but it is possible to translate the verb מאס as 'refuse' or 'reject', possibly indicating Job's dissatisfaction.[32] If so, this would add a further irony to the ending: Far from experiencing 'post-traumatic' growth or there being any sense of pain and illness having some positive meaning, such as Throop's distinction between 'mere-suffering' and 'suffering-for', Job simply quits (Throop 2010:212; cf. Hefferon *et al.* 2009). In this case, even the 'happy ending' at the U-point in the comedy turns out to be an anti-climax.

'He multiplies my wounds rashly': Job 9:17–19 and the metaphor of deity attack

Bildad's short plea, described by Seow as 'the same Pollyanna theology', to accept the sovereignty of a God who is upright in chapter 8 is answered by Job's lengthy response in chapters 9 and 10 wherein Job begins to imagine the possibility of a legal dispute between himself and God (Seow 2013:549). Protesting his innocence and appealing for mercy (but assuming he will not be listened to), Job turns to his somewhat regular style of expressing his frustration through emphasising the body under attack from a violent deity. The deity attack metaphor is not particularly lengthy here in comparison with its appearances in

32 However, it must be acknowledged that the translation here is much debated (Krüger 2007). Refer to Chapter 5.

Job 16 and 30, for example. It does, however, warrant our attention, given its appearance, if we are to be thorough about examining the metaphor's function within Job. Job claims here that,

> He bruises (שׁוף)[33] me in a storm (שׂערה)[34]
> and multiplies my wounds (פצע) rashly
> He will not allow me to take breath (רוח)[35]
> but satiates (שׂבע)[36] me with poison
> If it is about power,[37] he is firm
> if it is about judgement, who will summon[38] for me?
>
> (Job 9:17–19)

Here Job directly contradicts Bildad's ironic claim that God, who according to Bildad, 'will not cast away the blameless (תם) man' and who will also fill the mouths of the pious with laughter (Job 8:21). Far from merely being 'filled' (מלא) with laughter and rejoicing, the character Job reports that he is 'satiated' (שׂבע) with 'poison' (Job 9:18).[39] Thus Job picks up on Bildad's moralising advice and parodies his example to the extreme in order to undermine it. Likewise, Bildad's use of the term 'blameless' (תם) is repeated three times after the deity attack metaphor in 9:17–17, wherein Job pointedly remarks that God destroys 'the blameless (תם) and the wicked' (Job 9:22, cf. 9:20, 21). Here, too, the usual simplistic binary distinction between the 'righteous and the wicked', which emerges regularly in the Psalms and Proverbs, is reworked and therefore caricatured by Job (Pss. 7:9; 11:5; 34:21; 37:21, 32; Prov. 11:8, 10, 31; 12:7; 13:5; 14:19; 21:18; 25:26). Rather than a God who wounds but he binds up,

33 The term שׁוף can also be translated 'falls upon' or 'attack'. Seow suggests this is possibly a 'wordplay' given that שׁוף 'may also mean to blow' (Seow 2013:563). This translation would align well with the emphasis on wind and storms in Job generally.

34 The term "storm", spelled here with a שׂ rather than a ס, occurs only here and in Nahum. The latter reference has the term 'storm' (שׂערה) alongside the term 'whirlwind' (סופה), with the latter perhaps being a gloss (Nah. 1:3). Clines, however, prefers the reading he bruises me 'for a hair', repointing thus בְּשַׂעֲרָה a reading which emerges also in the Syriac and Targums (Clines 1989:235).

35 Literally 'to cause my wind [רוח] to return' *hiphil* שׁוב. This idiom may also be used of venting anger, and that is a possibility for the translation here too (Job 15:13).

36 The term 'satiates', which is usually positive, also occurs in the deity attack and surveillance metaphor discussed later in Job 10. Refer to Chapter 3.

37 Pope notes that 'power' and 'judgement' here imply 'litigation' and 'legal authority' (Pope 1965:71).

38 The MT has the *hiphil* of the term יעד meaning 'summon' presumably to an imagined courtroom. The Old Greek has a very free translation here κρίματι αὐτοῦ ἀντιστήσεται ('will oppose his judgement'). Likewise, the Vulgate has *nemo pro me audit testimonium dicere* ('for no one dares bear me witness'). Gordis notes that 'most commentators emend יוֹעִידֵנִי מִי, "who will summon me," to יוֹעִידֶנּוּ מִי "who will summon him"' and notes that this may be a *tiqqun soferim* while cautiously pointing out that 'varying numbers of *Tiqqunei Sopherim* given in rabbinic sources are obviously incomplete' (Gordis 1978:107; cf. Clines 1989:218; McCarthy 1981).

39 On the prevalence of metaphors in Job and the Psalms focusing on eating and digestion in a moralising manner, refer to Southwood 'The "Innards" in the Psalms and Job as Metaphors for Illness' in *Horizons in Biblical Literature* (forthcoming).

as Eliphaz had envisaged, Job here depicts a set of circumstances where even the blameless has the same fate as the wicked and where the deity can attack a human rashly or without reason. If Job is righteous, or blameless, he is no more able to lift his head than if he were wicked (Job 10:15; cf. Ecc. 9:2). The caricature, which asserts that even if Job is blameless, he will not get a fair hearing, continues throughout the chapter.

Unlike the psalmist who wishes to be made clean (טהר) and 'whiter than snow', Job assumes that even if he were clean (זכך)[40] and washed with snow, the deity would plunge him in a ditch (Ps. 51:7; Job 9:30–31). Also particularly notable is the prominence of the motif of 'wind' in this deity attack metaphor.[41] As Habel notes,

> [t]he irony in Job's language is . . . evident in his allusion to Eliphaz's vision (4:15), where a "wind" [רוח] . . . glided . . . over Eliphaz's face and a whirlwind made his flesh shiver. Job here anticipates a scene where El, if he appeared in court, would overwhelm Job with a "whirlwind" and prevent him from catching his own "wind/breath" [רוח]. Job had already experienced the terror of a "mighty wind" wrecking his abode (1:9).
>
> (Habel 1985:193)

Wind is a prominent theme in Job, and, as Hawley recognises, 'WORDS ARE WIND' is one of the 'most perceptible cases of coherence and competition between multiple metaphorical expressions' as either destruction or ephemerality, and this is perhaps part of the comedy (Hawley 2018:90). A great wind רוח is part of the initial calamity in the prologue (Job 1:19), and both the friends and the character Job accuse each other of producing explanations that are windy and, by implication, thus lacking in substance. For example, Job compares Eliphaz's advice to 'wind' (Job 6:26). Bildad then asks Job how long the words of his mouth will be 'like a large wind' (Job 8:2). Eliphaz asks Job why he 'utters windy (רוח) knowledge' and fills his belly with the east wind (קדים Job 15:2). Job accuses his friends of attempting to comfort him with 'puff' and later of being 'ephemeral' (הבל Job 21:34; 27:12). Elihu is perhaps the most insulting here, accusing Job of opening his mouth 'in vain (הבל) and multiplying words without knowledge' (Job 35:16), an insult reworked by Yahweh in the whirlwind and then mimicked sarcastically by Job (Job 35:16; 42:3). To some extent the entire discussion is as pointless as 'chasing after the wind', given that none

40 Note the hyperbole: Job is not just clean (טהר) but instead the term he uses for clean is זכך, a term which is used in Lamentations of the Nazarites who were cleaner than snow and whiter than milk (Lam. 4:7).

41 The prominence of the theme of 'wind' in Job is highlighted by the numerous occurrences of the terms רוח ('wind', Job 1:19; 4:9, 15; 6:4, 26; 7:7, 11; 8:2; 9:18; 10:12; 12:10; 15:2, 13, 30; 16:3; 17:1; 19:17; 20:3; 21:4, 18; 26:13; 27:3; 28:25; 30:15, 22; 32:8, 18; 33:4; 34:14; 37:21; 41:16); the strategic significance of the 'whirlwind' (סער) at the end on the lips of YHWH (Job 38:1; 40:6); and the mention of windy 'storms' (שערה) Job 9:17; (שער) Job 27:21; (סופה) Job 21:18; 37:9.

of the characters will budge from their entrenched positions with the result that 'vexation of spirit' is multiplied as all the windbags repeatedly rehearse their views.[42] Instead, we begin the metaphor with the association between the deity Eloah and the 'storm' but quickly progress to Job's body with reference to 'wind': the breath he is unable to catch. It is a contest of unmatched parties with disproportionate weakness on Job's side. Rather than 'burning for burning' or 'wound for wound (פצע)' here Job's picture is of divine injustice and wounds wherein there is no responsibility on Job's part (Exod. 21:25). Furthermore, rather than experiencing the 'faithful wounds (פצע) of a friend' which improve the character, Job experiences his friends' words as windy 'puff' (הבל Prov. 23:29). However, the incongruous (if not peculiar) movement from the great storm to the trivial Job highlights the main character's self-importance. His body inflates to fill all the imagined space, as if the character were, in fact, the storm. Unlike Yahweh who speaks from the whirlwind (סופה), Job's windy words are likened merely to a storm (שערה).

The term 'satiated' (שבע) is also interesting here. Clines notes the link here with the deity attack image in chapter 6, arguing 'the imagery of attack with poisoned arrows (cf. 6:4) may also appear here in God's compelling him to "drink bitterness" . . . or poison' (Clines 1989:235). It is a term which is regularly positive.[43] In many of the Psalms, the metaphor of being satiated is applied to pious satiation through, for example, being sated with goodness or mercy (Ps. 65:4; 91:16 104:16).[44] However, in Job the term is used negatively: Job, who is full of tossing to and fro from sleeplessness, sarcastically echoes his friends' moralising, suggesting that the offspring of the wicked are not satiated. Moreover, for Job, his friends are not satisfied with his flesh, but instead feel the need to keep moralising to him (Job 7:4; 19:22; 27:14; 31:31). Only in whirlwind is the term שבע positive, wherein the dry ground is satiated by rain (Job 38:27). For Job's friends there is not even the appearance of the likeness of a shadow of a doubt that their moralising advice is not correct. Yet for the character Job, his own body tells a different story.

In examining the concept of Job being wounded, many scholars cite Scarry's thesis on pain resisting language and torture (as discussed earlier).[45] In her

42 Cf. Eccl. 1:14; 2:11, 17, 26; 4:4, 6; 6:9.

43 For example, it emerges in a positive sense with regard to having lived a full life (refer to note 30 in Chapter 3). Likewise, one may be satiated with food (Exod. 16:8, 12; Lev. 26:26; Deut. 6:11; 8:10, 12; 11:15; 14:29; 26:12; 31:20; Ruth 2:14; 2 Chr. 31:10; Neh. 9:25; Pss. 78:12; 81:16; 105:40; Prov. 1:31; 12:11, 20:14; 25:16; 28:19; 30:22; Hos. 4:10; Joel 2:19; Mic. 6:14).

44 Note, however, Psalm 88 wherein there is a focus on the body in pain: The psalmist claims he is sated with troubles (Ps. 88:1; cf. Southwood 2019). Being sated also emerges in a negative sense in Lamentations, where the complaint of being sated with 'poison' also occurs (Lam. 3:15; cf. Lam. 3:30).

45 Refer to Chapter 1. Raz, for example, argues that Job 'challenges and problematizes Scarry's reading of biblical text, especially her portrayal of the "Old Testament God" as wounder and a torturer' (Raz 2014:82). However, Raz's argument also sometimes sounds somewhat similar to Scarry's. For example, she suggests that 'in Job's speeches, God is nakedly exposed as wounder and original tyrant.

chapter on the Hebrew Bible, Scarry uses the metaphor of the 'weapon' as a way to describe the relationship of God to humanity.46 Newsom also focuses on the language of wounding in Job, taking a rather different position than Scarry. Newsom argues that,

> For Job the basic truth about the body is found in the image of the wound and in the pain of the wound. A significant number of Job's representations of the body are invasive images. . . . Only by exploring such images can one grasp the violation of reality Job hears in the friends' attempt to narrativize his experience as a story of expectation, a story both literally and metaphorically represented as healing. For Job the wounded body is a fundamental image of the limits of narrative time as adequate to human experience. Narrative time is a time of delay, for it tells of an end that can come only after the playing out of an indeterminate number of necessary events. But the time of a body in pain is a time of urgency. Whereas Eliphaz and Bildad privilege the future as the locus of meaning, for Job the present in all its immediacy is the hermeneutically privileged time. The combination of pain and relentless scrutiny, one of the common features of torture, makes the aggressive other always present and so deprives a person of the time and space of privacy essential to subjectivity.
>
> (Newsom 2009:134–135)

Newsom's emphasis here on what we have labelled the deity attack and deity surveillance metaphors is helpful. In particular, her interpretation of Job's friends – who she understands as attempting to 'narrativize his experience' through the lens of healing at some point in the near or distant future – aligns well with the evidence we have analysed in the dialogues. However, the connection Newsom draws between pain, scrutiny, and torture (with the

---

The divine warrior who fought mythological forces, thereby bringing order to the world, also pits his strength against vulnerable human bodies' (Raz 2014:93).

46 The following is a suitable example of this metaphor:

> Yet the positioning of God and humanity at the two vertical ends of the weapon itself recurs so regularly that it seems to become a central and fixed locus toward which and away from which the narrative continually moves. At times, this image seems to define the structure of belief itself. . . . . Man can only be created once, but once created, he can easily be modified; wounding re-enacts the creation because it re-enacts the power of alteration that has its first profound occurrence in creation.
>
> (Scarry 1985:183)

Scarry's assessment of the Hebrew Bible, which she describes as 'a monumental artefact' and a 'product of the human imagination' in this chapter, rather homogenises the depiction of God in the material in order to argue for the significance of the fact that God does not have a body. The connection between creation and wounding, which for Scarry 're-enacts the creation', is rather difficult to maintain, especially given the demythologised and undramatic nature of the creation narrative in Genesis 1 by comparison with *Enûma Eliš*.

implication that it is the deity who is torturing Job) is less convincing, partly because it aligns so closely with Scarry's now widely critiqued arguments.[47] The character Job certainly uses exaggerated language in employing the deity attack and surveillance metaphors, but his pain does not resist language. If anything, the character is cast as one only too pleased to describe his body in pain, often in inflated, sarcastic, and hyperbolic language. Indeed, the urgency of Job's situation is more than slightly undermined by his tendency to speak at length. Nor does Job's pain resist narrativising completely: The character himself forms a type of narrative through continually returning to the metaphors of deity attack and deity surveillance. What is being resisted, to slightly modify Newsom's position, is not his friends' 'narratives' about his experience per se, but their failure to accept his narrative.

The importance of compassion within the listener when faced with a character in pain is brought into sharp focus in the play (or book) of Job by the moralising advice of the main character's friends. Perhaps this is part of the reason for the exaggerated metaphors of deity attack being placed on Job's lips. In much of the research concerning social responses to pain, there is an emphasis on accepting and valuing patients' experiences. For example, Kleinman argues that 'legitimating the patient's illness experience – authorizing that experience, auditing it emphatically – is a key task' (Kleinman 1988:17). Similarly, Throop argues that 'the ethical problem posed by pain . . . is that it commands a turn toward, and recognition of the other' (Throop 2010:219). Throop develops this argument, claiming that

> In confronting the suffering of another, we may be compelled to reorient our attention to the other as a subject and not an object of experience, as a complex self-interpreting being and not a simple determinable thing. The other's unassumability as a suffering subject may bring forth a shift away from interpreting the other as a mere token of a type.
>
> (Throop 2010:223)

This ethical aspect of the interaction between those who are experiencing pain or illness and others is particularly important. However, this type of interaction is totally absent in the dialogue between Job and his friends. In this respect, the friends are characterised as rather two-dimensional. Rather than showing humanity, compassion, or genuine concern, they simply offer advice, and not just merely advice but instead moralising advice, betraying their lack of depth. For Job's friends, the character remains, to borrow Throop's language, a 'mere token of a type', an 'object' and a 'simple determinable thing' (Throop 2010:223).

The role narrative plays in the research concerning pain, in connection with empathy, is a particularly prevalent topic. For example, Nussbaum highlights

47 Refer to Chapter 1.

the role that narrative has in connection with respect and compassion, arguing that 'narrative imagination is an essential preparation for moral interaction' (Nussbaum 1998:90). Likewise Rorty argues that narrative 'increases our sensitivity to the particular details of the pain and humiliation of other, unfamiliar sorts of people' (Rorty 1989:xvi).[48] Similarly, Hurwitz and Bates argue that 'at its core, narrative makes no commitment to truth or falsity, to a real or merely imaginary subject matter . . . but it does bear a commitment to connectedness and to structure' (Hurwitz and Bates 2016:561). The interaction between Job and his friends couldn't be further from these observations and arguments. The main character is allowed by the author/s to express and narrativise his experience, but the reactions are not sensitive or concerned with deepening understanding of the Other.[49] Instead of using narrative and speech as a vehicle through which to emphasise connectedness, the friends focus on meaning in the sense of what is true and false. The effect that this has is to attempt to make Job into a passive victim of pain who needs care and advice. However, Job's resistance to his friends' advice, alongside his insistence on speech, puts him in a position of authority in the dialogue. As Mattingly and Garro argue, during illness, 'narrative performance is capable of enacting a new, more empowered position' (Mattingly and Garro 2000:101). The audience is forced to listen as Job continues to offend his friends by rejecting their versions of how the world works. Job may claim that 'if it is about power' then the deity would win, but that fact that it is Job who is assigned most of the speech means that for audiences, his is the dominant and most represented voice.

'He seized me by the scruff and shattered me': Job's body and the deity attack metaphor in Job 16

Job 16 is perhaps the most detailed and extended metaphor of the deity attack in the entire book (Job 16:7–9, 12–14). Here, 'divine violence develops in a graphic crescendo' (Newsom 2009:137). Dell describes this as Job launching 'into a tirade against God' (Dell 2002:123). This is certainly one way of interpreting the material. However, through using research concerning illness and pain narratives, we can also observe something more complex is being

48 So important is narrative in connection with pain and illness that there has been a movement in clinical medicine towards narrative. For example, Charon coined the term narrative medicine to refer to narrative skills (such as recognising, absorbing, interpreting, and being moved by the stories of illness) which she deemed to be necessary to honour the meaning of the patients' own interpretations of their conditions (Charon 2006). Charon deemed narrative skills to be so important that she set up a programme in narrative medicine at Columbia University to teach clinical practitioners active textual and cultural knowledge of narrative skills. Likewise, Hordern argues that in primary and community healthcare, compassion is important. This is because 'compassion alleviates suffering by participating in it. As an essentially alleviative affection, it reaches out in understanding and embodied service to engage with persons in need' (Hordern 2017:26).

49 Of course, we are not falling into the pitfall of attempting to argue that Job is a narrative, but instead use the term 'narrativise' in a very loose sense. In Job's speeches, the prevalence of the deity attack and deity surveillance metaphors does not form a coherent narrative, but it is a strikingly consistent *topos*. Refer to Chapter 1.

brought to audiences' attentions. Job here imagines God 'as a warrior who brutalizes him with an outstretched arm, a powerful hand, and a sharp eye' (Jones 2013:845).[50] The first description states that,

> Surely now God[51] has worn me out;
> he has made desolate all my company.
> And he has shrivelled me up,
> which is a witness against me;
> my leanness has risen up against me,
> and it testifies to my face.
> He has torn me in his wrath, and hated[52] me;
> he has gnashed his teeth[53] at me;
> my adversary sharpens his eyes against me.
>
> (Job 16:7–9)

Job's body is described at this point using three terms: 'worn out' (לאה), 'shrivelled up' (קמט), and 'lean' (כחש).[54] The first verb (לאה)[55] suggests exhaustion and lack of energy and ability (Jer. 12:5).[56] The second verb is not particularly regular, occurring twice in Job (Job 16:8; 22:16).[57] Seow comments, the 'image is

50 Or, as Perdue describes it, God is 'the divine sadist who has engaged in combat' (Perdue 1991:148).

51 NRSV assumes the subject is God; it is 'God' who has worn Job out and isolated him. However, none of the terms which Job uses for 'God' appear in Hebrew in this verse. Perhaps this is why the Vulgate assumes that the suffering mentioned in verse 6 is the subject (*Nunc autem oppressit me dolor meus* 'now my suffering has oppressed me'). However, as Seow notes, in the previous line 'Job's suffering comes from God . . . and the parallel line immediately makes it clear that God is involved' (Seow 2013:743).

52 Driver and Gray suggest the translation '*hate actively* for the form וישטמני, noting that the verb combines the ideas of *hatred* and *persecution*' (Driver and Gray 1921:105, italics original). Melcher, Parsons, and Young also note this and add that 'the sense of the imperfect' here represents 'continuous action' (Melcher *et al.* 2017:176).

53 Noegel suggests that this may be an example of Janus parallelism, which can be defined as:

> a type of word-play known as polysemous parallelism . . . in which a middle stich of poetry parallels in a polysemous manner both the line that precedes it and the line which follows it.
>
> (Noegel 1996:12)

This can be demonstrated here wherein the term 'teeth' שנן in the form of 'gnashing teeth' parallels both ילטוש 'stab', and טרף, 'tear' (Noegel 1996:102).

54 This is similar to the depiction of the Babylonian sufferer in *Ludlul bēl nēmeqi* who claims that *Šīri ištaḫḫa damī izzuba / Eṣettum ussuqat arimat maškī* '[My] flesh has wasted away, my blood drained / [my] bones have become visible, covering my skin' (Annus and Lenzi 2010; cf. Piccin and Worthington 2015; Oshima 2014). As Jones suggests, '[l]ike the Babylonian sufferer, Job believes that God's hand is too near' (Jones 2013:851).

55 This verb appears in the *hiphil* form, making it clear that Job's body has been made to feel this way (and clearly implicating the deity as the creator of this problem).

56 As noted, the Vulgate translates 'oppressed' here, which is slightly different. Seow has a helpful list of cognates (Seow 2013:392).

57 Seow notes the unfamiliar Hebrew term 'is attested in Aramaic and Arabic [*qamaṭa*] where it means in the basic stem "to grasp, crush (by the curling of fingers)"' (Seow 2013:744). This aligns well with Theodotion's version, which has καὶ ἐπελάβου μου 'and you grasped me'.

that of a hand crushing something fragile and leaving the object all crumpled" (Seow 2013:734).[58] The noun 'lean' (כחש) usually refers to fraud or deception,[59] but here and in Psalm 109:24 context suggests being thin or frail. Both terms suggest that Job's body is made smaller by illness. As Erickson argues, 'Job's description here in 16:8 also recalls 7:5, in which Job describes his body as losing definition and breaching its boundaries (Erickson 2013:303).[60] This is no surprise because, as Raz argues, 'the language of wounds and wounding is basic to the notion of God in the text' (Raz 2014:78). However, a case can also be made for Job's body having a symbolic value as a means of communicating with his friends too. As Eriksen argues, 'Job's broken and deteriorating body functions as a metaphor for the destruction of self – physical, spiritual, emotional, existential – he has experienced' (Erickson 2013:313). It is possible to add nuance to Eriksen's argument here through contextualising the character's continuous use of the deity attack metaphor in terms of an 'idiom of distress', as discussed earlier. The deity attack is a powerful metaphor in the text, but it might also be framed as the character's embodied symbolic protest against his situation, the loss of his children, wealth, and social status. The focus is ostensibly on Job's bodily appearance and his suffering; however, it is also possible to interpret it here as a somatic reflection of the character's changed identity.

There is a strong emphasis on Job's social status as communicated through the deity attack metaphor at this point. The way pain is communicated is significantly shaped by repeated statements about divine agency, as is obvious through the second-person subject. God has isolated Job from his companions,[61]

58 This image is more aligned with Aquila ἐρρωτίδωσάς με 'you have wrinkled me'.

59 This is the meaning understood by Symmachus (καταψευδόμενος) and the Vulgate (*falsiloquus*). The Peshitta, the Targum, Theodotion, and Aquila all read 'my lie'. This is, perhaps, a slightly ironic and amusing example of polysemy, but the translation 'lean' (כחש) which is also attested in Psalm 109:24, seems to fit the context better, in parallelism with 'shrivelled up' (קמט). Picking up on the forensic language in this verse, Eriksen suggests that this is a wordplay where 'Job's physical leanness acts as a personification of the lie his body communicates and deceives those gathered in the imagined courtroom' (Erickson 2013:303).

60 Concerning the body and its boundaries, refer to note 45 in Chapter 1. Greenstein makes a similar point, suggesting that:

> [I]n Job's mind, as it is reflected in his metaphorical conception, the various acts of destroying him . . . are for all intents and purposes the same. Wellness is wholeness, and illness is disintegration.
>
> (Greenstein 2018:47)

61 Clines and Pope note that the term עדה (congregation, assembly, family) is sometimes emended, substituting ר for ע (thus רעתי 'my calamity'). However, both prefer the Masoretic text (Clines 1989:381; Pope 1965:116). The Greek does not help at this point, providing a double translation of 'weary', νῦν δὲ κατάκοπόν με πεποίηκεν μωρόν σεσηπότα ('But now he has made me weary and a worn-out fool and you had laid hold of me').

Given the use of the term עדה here, the suggestion is, as Bastiaens states, 'Job is isolated by members of his own people, not by strangers, not by people who are in some way remote to him' (Bastiaens 1997:422).

and they are forced to recoil (*hiphil* √שמם)[62] in disgust when confronted with his body. As Bastiaens, comparing the language in Job 16–17 with that of the suffering servant passages in Deutero-Isaiah, argues, Job's friends 'are horrified by the one who suffers, whom they hold in contempt' (Bastiaens 1997:427). This reaction to Job's body is also vividly depicted in Job 19:14–19 where, as we shall discuss, even Job's wife is disgusted by the sight and smell of his body.[63] Another clue that the authentic focus is on social standing in light of the appearance of Job's body is the forensic metaphor of a courtroom.[64] As Habel comments,

> God has shrivelled up Job into a pathetic wrinkled wretch who has no credibility with his community. . . . With rhetorical flair Job depicts his gaunt form, like a ghostly shadow of his true self, "raising up" *(qwm)* in court. . . . His innocent inner self cannot be heard because the court sees only his gaunt outer self.
>
> (Habel 1985:271)

62 It is interesting that the verb שמם is used. The loaded term can refer to desolation in the sense of a city, nation, or people desolate and annihilated after an attack (Lev. 26:31; Ezek. 30:12, 14). However, it can also refer to a sense of being appalled or dismayed (Ezra 9:3–4; Ezek. 3:15) and, interestingly, to striking with illness which causes people to be desolate (1 Sam. 5:6).

63 Pelham's analysis, which cites Nemo is helpful here,

> Nemo makes the link between outsider status and the breakdown of the body explicit, writing that the members of Job's household, might have tried to overcome their moral repulsion . . . had Job's physical existence remained intact and healthy. However, confronted with his 'putrid' body odour and 'unbearable' bad breath, even his wife recoils. . . . The dissolution of the body automatically dissolves the convention of communication. That is, the affliction of the body can only ever signal moral failure requiring expulsion from the community, because the community cannot bear the presence of the one whose body is in a state of disintegration. The breakdown of the body cannot stand simply for itself, with no larger meaning.
>
> (Pelham 2012a; Nemo 1998, italics not in original)

Here the connection between moralising and Job's body is lucidly described. Job is 'metaphorically, physically secluded, so too socially he is no longer part of his friends and family' (de Joode 2014:564).

64 Concerning the legal metaphor refer to note 109, and note 66 in Chapter 1. There are several similarities between Job and the Australian comedy film entitled *The Man Who Sued God* which is surely derivative of Job. Areas of commonality include a relatively powerless man opposing the religious institutions, the emphasis on a lawsuit between the man in question and God, and the windstorm at the end of the lawsuit. Similarly, in the film, as the main character prepares for court verses from Proverbs are read out and deemed to be unsuitable, e.g. 'The one who digs a pit falls into it' (a strong statement of simplistic retribution, Prov. 26:27). Likewise, verses from Ecclesiastes appear, such as 'there is nothing new under the sun' on signs and in conversation. It is quite interesting to note that lawsuits against God appear also in non-fictional sources. These include the cases of Betty Penrose, Ernie Chambers, Pavel M, and Chandan Humar Singh. The case of Betty Penrose, wherein God was sued for 'negligence', was won in 1970 by default because God failed to turn up in court.

The idea of the body undermining acceptability, which also occurs earlier in Job,[65] indicates the possibility of a widespread understanding that interpreted the meaning of illness in terms of retribution.[66] By casting Job as innocent and then paradoxically having him made the victim of a metaphoric deity attack, the logic behind this perhaps normative assumption is undermined. However, the style used for this probing is highly satirical, over-stated, and paradoxical: In a pompous imagined courtroom, an ostentatious Job 'rises up' to speak and to be listened to. However, the character is forcibly humbled, admitting that his body acts like an unfamiliar alter ego that produces a counter-narrative to his protestations of innocence. The scene is delicately balanced on a sharp borderline.[67] It is so utterly ridiculous that it is humorous and comic, yet at the same time, it also tragically communicates to audiences a serious and profound message questioning the meanings assigned to the body and pain. This is not merely a character's 'effort to understand the meaning of his present terrifying and agonizing condition' (Bastiaens 1997:424). Rather, as Erickson states, 'images of disembodiment function not only to articulate Job's pain but also as a means to reinterpret and re-present his testimony. With no little irony, Job's rhetoric transcends the limitations and vulnerability of his body with metaphors of the body' (Erickson 2013:313). Therefore, while communicating and enacting the experience of suffering, these images also compel audiences and readers to question normative and traditional assumptions about the body and pain.

The theme of divine assault in Job 6 recurs here, where the deity is cast as a devouring animal hunting for prey. Ironically, at this point the stereotypical lament of the psalm, where enemies may be depicted with theriomorphic metaphors as predators from which Yahweh can save the psalmist, is inverted here to make the deity the very one who is the predator (Pss. 7:1; 17:12; 22:12).[68]

65 Refer to Job 9:20–21, where, like here, the character grieves his own body's betrayal of his claim to innocence.

66 For the popularity of this association refer to note 21 in Chapter 1.

67 Pelham expresses this well, arguing that,

> Although Job may insist that he retains his moral integrity despite the affliction of his body, his friends do not believe him, viewing his loss of bodily integrity as proof of his loss of moral integrity, assuming that the two go hand in hand.
>
> (Pelham 2012a:157)

68 Using the concept of sensory mimicry, Tilford argues that one reason for this violent language in Job is to heighten the form of expression and engage readers. As she suggests,

> No one physically cuts the individual in half or crushes him under the foot. Rather, the individual experiences a loss, sickness, or death that has no identifiable cause. A superhuman agent is blamed, and the book uses tactile expressions to describe the experience in such a way that the reader can identify with it.
>
> (Tilford 2016:52)

It is also worth emphasising here the alignment of Job's metaphor with the deity attack metaphor in Lamentations. As Newsom notes, '[h]owever horrific these images, they closely echo . . .

The deity is depicted as a ferocious and angry wild animal that 'tears' (טרף),[69] 'gnashes' (חרק),[70] and places Job under 'surveillance' (לטש + עין).[71] The deity is also described as a hateful 'enemy' (צר) which Habel likens to 'Anath in the Baal myths of Canaan' (Habel 1985:272).[72] The way that Job's body is described has shifted focus from symptoms such as weariness and leanness or frailty, to the body as reacted to socially, and finally to the metaphor of a deity attack where God is depicted as a hunting animal. The final image is particularly striking. It has more intensity than the description of Eloah in Job 6, as explored previously, where Job merely wishes to be crushed and let loose. Ironically, Job's pompous and inflated wish for unrelenting pain back in Job 6:10 is all but exactly realised in the language the author/s place on his lips here.

Because of the pattern emerging in this analysis concerning the connection between Job's body and the way it is contextualised socially, it is important to also analyse the responses this elicits from his friends. Bildad's response displays a high level of resistance to Job's use of the deity attack metaphor. His initial remarks are particularly loaded: 'why are we reckoned as beasts, dense[73] in your eyes? Oh you who tear yourself apart in rage' (Job 18:3–4). The initial statement in verse 3 picks up on the metaphor of the deity as a wild animal and reapplies it

---

Lamentations 3, which uses as its central motif the figure of graphic divine violence. In Lamentations the extensively described violence (Lam. 3:1–20) serves as prelude to a word of hope (3:21), grounded in a conviction of the mercies of God (3:22–24)'. Therefore, '[s]ubmission to such suffering is appropriate (3:25–30), because God only reluctantly administers it as punishment for sin (3:31–39)' (Newsom 2003a:137). This perspective obviously aligns more closely with the retribution model than with Job, wherein pain and illness do not represent a punishment and forgiveness cycle.

69 The verb טרף ('tear') is associated with wild hunting animals such as wolves and lions (Gen. 37:33; 44:28; 49:27; Deut. 33:20; Ps. 7:2; 17:12; 22:13; Ezek. 19:3, 6; 22:25, 27; Hos. 5:14; Mic. 5:8; Nah. 2:12; 1QH^{a} 5:14; 4QpNah 3:1^{4}).

70 The onomatopoetic term חרק does not occur regularly, but in each of the occurrences teeth are associated with gnashing. The idiom occurs 'only in laments (Pss. 35:16; 37:12; 112:10; Lam. 2:16) where the subject is always the complainant's enemy/enemies' (Seow 2013:745). Refer also to 4QpPS^{a} 1:2^{12}; 1QH^{a} 1:39; 2:11. Given this and the other animal imagery, perhaps the metaphor of a lion is envisaged (Strawn 2005).

71 The last term, very loosely translated as 'surveillance', reads literally 'sharpen the eye' and conveys a sense of focused and scrupulous attention which is needed prior to pouncing on prey. A somewhat similar popular English idiom is to 'look daggers'. Clines describes this as 'the sharp look of a murderous intent' (Clines 1989:382).

72 The Greek does not go this far, but instead replaces the term enemy with the phrase 'the weapons of his robbers have fallen upon me' (βέλη πειρατῶν αὐτοῦ ἐπ' ἐμοὶ ἔπεσεν). As Gordis notes, 'some commentators have referred then [the epithets in stiches b and c of this verse] to human enemies revocalizing צָרִי to צָרַי' (Gordis 1978:176). This revocalisation might be supported by the Syriac and by Symmachus which also have the plural. The context, where throughout verses 3–9 God is subject and Job object, suggests that the attack is from the deity rather than other human enemies, but a certain level of ambiguity must be noted since human enemies feature in the next two verses (Job 16:10–11).

73 The word נִטְמִינוּ is not easy to translate. It may be a *niphal* from טמא ('unclean'). BHS suggests repointing נִטְמֹנוּ this assumes a *niphal* of the form טמם 'be stopped up', and therefore 'dense, thick'. Perhaps, as Grabbe suggests, both senses, stupid and unclean, are possible (Grabbe 1977:73–74). It would not be out of character entirely, given that polysemy is a feature of Job.

to the friends. This metaphor is then applied to Job himself in verse 4 wherein Bildad directly undermines the metaphor that Job uses in Job 16:9 where the deity is cast as a wild animal with the idiom טרף אף (cf. Amos 1:11). This idiom is deconstructed and reconstructed 'in literal terms . . . Job has "torn himself apart in his rage"' (טרף נפשו באפו Job 18:4, Greenstein 2014:335).[74] Essentially,

> Job's enemy is not someone else. Rather, it is Job himself who has acted so bestially. Job as the predator preys on none other than himself. This is an image not just of a wild animal, a stupid creature, but a demented, self-destructive beast!
>
> (Seow 2013:773)

Through this undermining reconfiguration of Job's own language the puffed-up and intense manner in which Job uses the deity attack metaphor is deflated. The satirical anti-climax totally undercuts the original force from Job's tragic case about his body in pain and portrays it as ridiculous and comic. Bildad's case is developed using the by now rather mundane characteristic of retribution in verses 5–21 where the 'wicked' person is terrified by 'terrors', is consumed by hunger and has his skin eaten away by illness, and he is given the unflattering title, the 'Firstborn of Death' (Job 18:11–13). It is interesting that Job's own pain metaphors are met also with illness metaphors by Bildad. Bildad's metaphors, however, are designed to destabilise Job's by emphasising Job's self-inflicted pain. Zophar also uses the metaphor of hunger and of eating but not being satiated, suggesting somewhat graphically that the food eaten by the wicked is vomited up again, having turned to poison in their stomachs, to emphasise the connection between the dysfunction of the body and wickedness (Job 20:14–16, 20–25).

Hyun suggests that Job's friends 'fail to reconnect with Job's language' and 'turn Job's speech into isolated, senseless moans' (Hyun 2013:120). However, this argument could be developed further: Not only do the friends fail to listen to and acknowledge Job's pain, they also actively engage with his words and arguments and reconstruct them to suit their own worldviews. The lack of acknowledgement of pain is a large part of the problem.[75] As Tham argues, Job 'wants to be heard and understood by his friends, not judged categorically with a mere theoretical link between sin and punishment. . . . Job wants friendship and empathy rather than a pronouncement of God's just retribution' (Tham 2013:86).[76] This aligns rather well with Kant's argument in response

74 Eliphaz has a similar response to Job, repeating the term 'shrivelled up' (קמט) by pointing out that 'shrivelling . . . leads to death' (Greenstein 2018:47). Indeed, Eliphaz suggests in chapter 15 that Job's 'own lips testify against you [him]' (Job 15:6).

75 This is also the case in modern illness narratives, as demonstrated formerly (see Chapter 1).

76 Kutz makes a similar point, arguing that the friends 'wish to reduce his suffering by espousing an age-old moral-theological theory of illness containing both aetiology and cure' (Kutz 2000:1613).

to the book of Job about the need for *authentic* theodicy.[77] However, what is so powerful about Job's speeches is partly that they are personalised accounts of pain. Given the 'unshareability'[78] and, more important, the 'unproveability' of pain, the speeches are, in a way, indisputable by any theorem, no matter how entertaining and impressive the friends' performances of linguistic acrobatics and attempts to undermine them are. As a consequence, irreducible personal experience is pitted against generalised theological theory. This is powerful because it makes Job a character that audiences can identify with and turns the friends into two-dimensional philosophers. As Raphael remarks 'Job starts with observation of his own life, not with a theological premise' (Raphael 2004:412). As a consequence of the friends' moralising, instead of acknowledgement of Job's pain, a breakdown in the social order occurs: The paradox of innocent suffering undermines the two-dimensional perspectives of Job's friends and highlights the complexity of experience and meaning to audiences.[79] This can be observed in Job's response to Bildad, which is an extended emphasis on the social consequences and implications of the moralising responses he receives, particularly emphasising the character's own isolation and ending again with the recurring motif of 'skin' (Job 19:13–20; cf. 18:13).

Research concerning illness narratives and behaviour is helpful here for drawing out the social implications of the dialogue. An initial point that is worthy of consideration is the value of experience in terms of what we know about the world. As we noted, Job's friends understand the world through a theoretical and traditional lens, but for Job it is bodily experience that informs his epistemology. This aligns well with the discussion in the previous chapter[80] concerning pain and meaning. Merleau-Ponty's classic research into the phenomenology of perception is helpful here. Carel provides a helpful definition of phenomenology as an approach that

> focuses on phenomena (what we perceive and experience) rather than on the reality of things (what there is). It focuses on the experiences of

77 Kant suggests that Job speaks as he thinks, and 'with the courage with which he, as well as every human being in his position can well afford; the friends, on the contrary, speak as if they were being secretly listened to by the mighty one' (Kant 1791; cited in Williams 2012:63). Kant's call for integrity and authenticity through his argument about the importance of 'sincerity of heart' over 'distinction of insight' may also apply in response to Job's friends.

78 This term is coined by Scarry 1985.

79 In many ways the moralising itself may be considered an instrument of comedy. As Whedbee argues, quoting Cox,

> moralizing leads toward incongruity for several reasons, not least of which is the fact that it usually takes the form of universal statements. Obviously universal statements gather so many things under a single heading that there is almost bound to be incongruity among the things brought together under that heading'. Cox ends his discussion with an observation that strikingly bears on the Joban poet's parody of the wise comforter: 'The pedant with his general maxims is simply a caricature of the basic comic character, who strives constantly . . . to justify and preserve his invented self against the onslaughts of the realities he encounters.
>
> (Whedbee 1977:12)

80 See Chapter 1.

> thinking, perceiving, and coming into contact with the world: how phenomena appear to consciousness. Phenomenology examines the encounter between consciousness and the world, and views the latter as inherently human-dependent; as can be seen from its name, it is the science (*logos*) of relating consciousness to *phenomena* (appearances), rather than to *pragmata* (things as they are).
>
> (Carel 2016:19–20)

The distinction between *pragmata* and *phenomena* here is helpful for framing and understanding some of the nuances in the discussion between Job and his friends. For Merleau-Ponty, the body is the ultimate medium of experience and thus of our understanding of the world (Merleau-Ponty and Smith 2002). Given that the body is inseparable from experience (and indeed the condition for experience), it is particularly effective that Job's body is featured in a discussion about suffering. Job's language concerning pain undermines the knowledge of the world that his friends rely on because his source of knowledge is bodily experience. In this way, bodily experience becomes a privileged source of knowledge because it challenges what Carel describes as 'the reality of things'. However, as discussed, bodily experience is not unconnected from the social world, and it overlays pain with meaning. This is because 'the ways in which we conceive of and describe illness . . . shape how we experience and respond to it' so that 'both the conception and narration of illness is interpersonally negotiated, rather than done by the ill person in abstraction' (Carel 2016:127). Thus, pain is permeated with culture. The meanings that the character Job is extrapolating from his experience operate within the limits of his known world: The character looks to Yahwism for meaning. However, they also go beyond the limits of his social and cultural context by powerfully challenging traditional ideas that lie at the heart of Yahwism.

Earlier in the argument, we touched on the topic of acknowledging pain, rather than finding words to describe it in contrast to Scarry (Jurecic 2012; Das 1996; Jackson 2000; *pace* Scarry 1985). The importance of this is emphasised in Carel's narrative about living with a life-limiting lung disease, where she argues,

> If I had to pick the human emotion in greatest shortage, it would be empathy. And this is nowhere more evident than in illness. The pain, disability and fear are exacerbated by the apathy and disgust with which you are sometimes confronted when you are ill. There are many terrible things about illness; the lack of empathy hurts the most.
>
> (Carel and Cooper 2013:37)

The theoretical and moralising emphasis in the responses of Job's friends limits his suffering to explanatory models instead of witnessing, affirming, and acknowledging his humanity. As a consequence, what is lacking is indeed empathy but also compassion, imagination, and sensitivity.[81] Instead of recognising Job's irreducibility and uniqueness – which *includes* in all its complexity his mortality, his inadequacies, and his capacity for suffering – the friends assume their own authority and simplistically offer him the 'comfort' of the retribution model. Therefore, the key failure of the friends is their lack of acknowledgement of Job. Acknowledgement is defined here as 'recognizing the complexity of living among others . . . in contrast to knowing or judging', and furthermore, 'acknowledging also entails recognizing one's own ignorance and vulnerability, as well as the unpredictability of social encounters and relationships' (Jurecic 2012:63). Through failing to acknowledge Job's pain, as it is described by the character, the friends prevent themselves from expanding their own horizons of experience. As Throop explains, 'in the face of the other's suffering, [the] very unassumability of the other's self-experience is revealed to us and in its self-presenting is evocative of a call to responsibility'; therefore, in such moments it is not possible 'to flatten out the other's self-experience by subjecting it to our own categories of understanding and expectation' (Throop 2010:219, 223). As a consequence of the failure to acknowledge Job in this way, by restricting his pain to their own planes of 'logical' understanding, the friends demonstrate a second failure: Their affective understanding of the situation seems to be absent. This is ironically dramatised throughout the dialogues with a crescendo on the part of all the characters of a failure to see any perspective other than their own. The friends' entrenched and unchanging positions, lack of sensitivity and emotional responsiveness, and repetitive moralising advice are somewhat exaggerated at points, not to mention protracted. It is almost difficult to decide, in response, whether the dialogues offer deeply profound insights into the human experience of suffering or whether they are so utterly absurd and ridiculous that they tip over into over-blown comedy.

Another interesting social consequence of Job's body emerges in the character's suggestion that his leanness witnesses and testifies against him. What is particularly striking about this statement is the way the character represents to his friends sin visualised through the emphasis on the explicit and obvious nature of his body's dysfunction. This aligns well with illness research concerning stigmatised conditions. In particular, Lupton's work on obesity is helpful as a comparative lens. Lupton argues that,

> Grotesque bodies deviate from the norm, mainly by exceeding it. They defy clear definitions and borders and occupy the liminal middle ground between life and death. They are permeable and uncontained, transgressive

81 Of course, Job's friends are not the only ones guilty of this. One interesting example is a response published in the *Guardian* newspaper in 2010 concerning moralising advice given to a cancer patient when she failed to conform to expectations. The patient's rejection of the 'must fight and be positive' attitude led to 'a chorus of rebukes' for a 'bad attitude' and for living the little life she had left 'in anger and bitterness'.

> of their own limits. They are the embodiment of ambiguity, which in itself creates apprehension in a cultural context in which ambiguity challenges privileged notions of certainty.
>
> (Lupton 2012:56)[82]

It is interesting that deviating from the supposed 'norm' and, as such, embodying ambiguity are key features singled out by Lupton here.[83] Embodying ambiguity and the tension it creates in terms of certainty is a useful way of thinking about the character Job.[84] For his friends he is the visualisation of sin: His body represents retribution for some crime whether known or unknown. Yet paradoxically, the visible symbol of sin that is represented in Job is, in fact, innocent. This creates a challenge and heightens tension for audiences, especially if they are accustomed to using the retribution model when confronted with misfortune.

Perhaps it will be helpful to explore how this tension is reconciled in modern illness narratives research. Lambek and Antze's research into illness narratives argues that one way of mediating paradoxes or embodied ambiguity associated with illnesses is through irony. Irony, they suggest, 'contextualizes and compromises naïve notions of agency' in social responses to illness (Lambek and Antze 2004:10). Therefore, for those who are ill, irony functions not to displace or conceal suffering but to recognise the reality of the body during illness, when

> there is often a fine line between tragic and comic interpretations of the recognition of the limits of moral agency. Irony can serve as a transfer point between tragedy and comedy. . . . what turns irony in one direction or the other? When does the despair of Job give way to what Laura Bohannan . . . memorably called a "return to laughter"? With respect to illness, one can abhor or appreciate the Rabelaisian effects of bodily or mental breakdown and the collapse of personal agency. Why not celebrate the carnivalesque or grasp the comic dimension of suffering? When is the situation seen as one of tragic linear inevitability and when of comic indeterminacy?
>
> (Lambek and Antze 2004:13)

82 The permeable and 'borderless' nature of incongruous bodies also aligns well with much of the secondary research concerning the body and its boundaries in the Hebrew Bible. Refer to note 45 in Chapter 1.

83 The matter of broken norms has already been discussed. See the earlier section: 'The arrows of Shaddai'. Refer also to note 28.

84 This aligns well with Merton's theory of social ambivalence which is created by illness. As Merton suggests,

> Suffering people are disposed to want a nostrum, in the realm of health as in the realms of politics and, sometimes, of religion. It requires cultural training in self-discipline to accept the fact, when it is a fact, that a prompt solution to one's troubles is not possible.
>
> (Merton 1976:71–72)

Lambek and Antze's research is helpful for contextualising the deity attack metaphors in Job. These also operate at a point where tragedy and comedy are divided. They are comical, at least partly, because they are so exaggerated and on account of their reuse, as sarcastic parodies, of traditional lament (Kynes 2011). Yet at the same time, their overstated nature only serves to highlight the poignant nature of the character Job's suffering. Claassens suggests this forms a type of 'tragic laughter' (Claassens 2015).[85] It is possible to push this theory a little further, however, by understanding the deity attack metaphors in Job as being at once deeply tragic yet also the polar opposite: outrageous, peculiar, and comical. Indeed, at many points the comic seems to outweigh the tragic.[86] As Fox notes, 'how seriously are we to take the tale of Job?. . . . Not very' (Fox 2011:145). Irony is also helpful in Job in relation to the question of the limits of moral agency. As noted Irony 'contextualizes and compromises naïve notions of agency' (Lambek and Antze 2004:10). Given the entrenched positions of Job's friends and their tendency to moralise about his body, Job's satirical parodies may be interpreted as attempts to undermine and resist their position, especially with regard to the idea that Job might have any agency in terms of his condition.

Finally, the concepts of stigma and shame are relevant in relation to the question of broken norms. Stigma may be identified as 'a negatively defined condition, attribute, trait or behaviour conferring "deviant" status, which is socially, culturally and historically variable' (Gabe and Monaghan 2013:68).[87] In Goffman's classic work on stigma he examined the complex process of attempting to maintain the integrity of the self in order to manage impressions when faced with a discredited or discreditable self. Where stigma is known about, it is a matter of managing tensions, where unknown, one must manage information (Goffman 1968).[88] When stigma is part of illness, it is sometimes referred to as a 'second illness' (Schulze and Angermeyer 2003). Kleinman argues that

85 Pelham also notes that there are characters in the book of Job who do directly laugh at him: 'The group of outcasts which Job calls "a senseless, disreputable brood" (30.8a) finds Job laughable. "They make sport of me" (30.1a), Job says. "They mock me in song; I am a byword to them"' (30.9) (Pelham 2010:95).

86 For example, Aitken points out that the 'comfort that the friends intend to offer is foiled since they only expected a brief period of mourning' (i.e. mourning rituals and sitting in silence Job for a week, Job 2:13). 'After this liminal period of mourning, instead of returning to reintegrate with society, Job launches off into cursing and lamentation (Job 3), followed by a lengthy dispute with his friends about the meaning of what happened' (Aitken 2013:214). For Newsom, this launch into self-pitying lament is a 'culturally inappropriate outburst' (Newsom 2003b:351). Regarding mourning refer to Olyan 2004.

87 The term stigma comes from the Greek στίζω meaning 'to mark or brand' and was originally used to refer to 'marks that publicly disgraced the person'; however, more recently it 'has come to refer more to the disgrace than to the actual bodily mark' (Kleinman 1988:158).

88 Goffman elaborates here, drawing out the paradoxical and socially ambivalent nature of stigma for identity:

> given that the stigmatized individual in our society acquires identity standards which he applies to himself in spite of failing to conform to them, it is inevitable that he will feel some ambivalence about his own self (Goffman 1968:130).

stigma in the case of bodily dysfunction has serious social consequences. This is because 'cultural meanings mark the sick person, stamping him or her with significance often unwanted and neither easily warded off nor coped with'; this significance, or mark, 'may be either stigma or social death' (Kleinman 1988:26).[89] This can be deeply discrediting, rendering the person somehow dishonourable and inferior. Such stigma, if sustained and internalised, can lead to a 'spoiled identity' or a 'feeling of being inferior, degraded, deviant, and shamefully different' (Kleinman 1988:159). Indeed, when stigma and shame go hand in hand, the shift in identity can completely transform a person's reactions. As Kleinman observes,

> In stigmatized disorders, the stigma can begin with the societal reaction to the condition: that is to say, a person so labelled is shunned, derided, disconfirmed, and degraded by those around him, though usually not by the immediate family. Eventually, the stigmatized person comes to expect such reactions, to anticipate them before they occur or even when they don't occur. By that stage, he [*sic.*] has thoroughly internalized the stigma in a deep sense of shame and a spoiled identity. His [*sic.*] behaviour, then, becomes shaped by his [*sic.*] negative self-perception.
>
> (Kleinman 1988:160)

This shift in identity aligns well with many present-day public health campaigns which are fanned by moral panic and what Lupton calls the 'pedagogy of disgust' (Lupton 2014).[90] Lupton argues that disgust is an 'unreasonable emo-

89 Dolezal makes a similar point about the specific type of shame that body shame elicits:

> Body shame is a particularly powerful and potent form of shame. Not only is the body the part of ourselves that is immediately observable to others, the body is also the seat of personhood and that which makes meaningful subjective experience possible.
>
> (Dolezal 2015:569)

90 Kleinman makes a similar point with regard to the role that religion and morals play when stigma and illness coincide, arguing that stigma

> carries a religious significance – the afflicted person is viewed as sinful or evil – or a moral connotation of weakness and dishonour. Thus, the stigmatized person is defined as an alien other, upon whose persona are projected the attributes the group regards as opposite to the ones it values. In this sense, stigma helps to define the social identity of the group. In certain societies, so powerful is the stigma brought to the patient by the culturally marked illness label that it affects all his [*sic.*] relationships and may lead to ostracism.
>
> (Kleinman 1988:159)

Therefore, the type of retributive logic used in Deuteronomy, as explored earlier, persists in response to illness, especially obvious or particularly stigmatised illnesses. Sontag strongly objected to assigning meaning to illness on the basis of the role of moralising during illness. She makes a similar point to Kleinman's, arguing

> The persistence of the belief that illness reveals, and is a punishment for, moral laxity or turpitude can be seen in another way, by noting the persistence of descriptions of disorder or corruption as a

tion because it projects our fear and anxiety about physical decay and death onto the certain individuals' and as a consequence 'instead of attempting to reduce their social disadvantage, our disgust positions them as inferior' (Lupton 2014:9). A major theme in research concerning illness narratives, and particularly in stigmatised illnesses and visible illnesses, is stigma and social reactions.

To some extent, this research aligns well with the depiction of Job. He is 'held in contempt by the contemptible' and publicly humiliated (Newsom 2009:189). He has 'no real place in the social world' and is treated as an outsider, or 'Other' (Newsom 2009:189). Furthermore, as Basson points out, to friends and family, 'Job has become the centre of infection. . . . In Job's case defilement leads to estrangement from the rest of the community. . . . Job is forced to reside at the boundaries of the prevailing social structure . . . he carries with him the danger of pollution' (Basson 2008:296).[91] Therefore, the picture which is painted of reactions to Job's body in the book aligns well with the thinking in other parts of the Old Testament, where the ill are socially outcast, shameful, and stigmatised.

However, in contrast to this research, the character Job seems to relish the opportunity to talk about his body in pain and to draw attention to it. Rather than 'managing information' through trying to conceal his body or 'managing tensions' by capitalising on the fact that the friends are there for him *at all* (no matter how dim-witted their advice), Job seems determined to provoke and annoy his friends. Likewise, rather than suffering from a spoiled identity and feeling inferior or ashamed, Job claims he is 'not inferior' to his friends and calls them 'useless quacks' for whom it would be better if they 'shut up' (Job 12:3; 13:2, 4–5).[92] Likewise, Job suggests they are 'comforters of misery' who

---

> disease. . . .[referring to the plague metaphor] A theodicy as well as a demonology, it not only stipulates something emblematic of evil but makes this the bearer of a rough, terrible justice.
>
> (Sontag 1990:145; *pace* Raffel 2013; Clow 2001)

In both the quotations, religious language and concepts underpin the connection between illness and responsibility. This is founded on social responses because of cultural meanings ascribed to illness, but said beliefs are also reinforced through being enacted socially.

91 Here, Basson quotes Douglas's comment: 'The polluting person has developed some wrong condition or simply crossed some line which should not have been crossed and this displaced unleashes danger for someone' (Douglas 1966:113; Basson 2008:296). Clines makes a similar point, arguing that '[t]he state of his [Job's] body identifies him as one who is undeserving of the protection afforded by inclusion within the human community' (Clines 1989:159). This is a helpful way to contextualise the social dynamics related to illness which the author/s convey through the book of Job.

92 'You are all quacks; if only you would shut up' is my own loose translation, attempting to capture the cantankerous nature of the dialogues (Southwood 2018). Refer also to Greenstein's nuanced argument about the phrase שקר טפל (forgers of lies) here. Greenstein asks 'should the medical metaphor that is manifest in the second colon be presupposed in the first colon as well? In that case the first colon would be presenting quack doctors who smear medicinal ointment that is false' (Greenstein 2007:89). Perhaps, we could take this idea further by suggesting that if advice is what is being undermined here, then this may an example of Janus parallelism hinging on the motif of 'worthless physicians' (Noegel 1996)?

'crush me [him] with words' and 'console me [him] with puff (הבל)' (Job 16:2; 19:2; 21:34 cf. 13:12). Job's body certainly evoked 'moral panic' among his friends, but his response is not humiliation: shame in the dialogues on the part of Job is simply a mechanism for spilling over into an inflated, sanctimonious outburst which regularly spills over into the deity attack metaphor. The idea of being consoled with wind taps into an important mechanism through which comedy emerges. The recurrent motif, expressed with several synonyms, of 'windy words', functions as a way of each party accusing the other of verbose arguments which lack substance: Bildad (Job 8:2), Eliphaz (Job 15:2), and Job (Job 16:3; 21:34). This makes the ending with a strangely incongruous interrogation from a 'whirlwind' highly ironic (Job 38:1). Both the friends and Job are caricatures of the 'wise'; the friends with their moralising advice and Job with his claim to knowledge and insight. Indeed, this motif of wind makes the beginning of Elihu's speech particularly comical.[93] He starts out, after no fewer than 30 chapters of speeches, with the message 'I am full of words' (Job 32:18). Even his words betray a sense of comedy, with a sound-play between the terms מלא and מלה 'מלתי מלים', a sound-play which may have sounded even more comical in the high-pitched voice of a youth, (Job 32:6). Just like the 'puffs' of advice from Eliphaz, Bildad, and Zophar, here Elihu suggests his intention to no longer be distressed by the 'wind in my [his] belly' (Job 32:18). Read one way, the statement is yet another example of advice on the lips of a pompous, pretentious counsellor; read another, the character himself inadvertently compares his own forthcoming advice with flatulence.

A further deity attack metaphor in Job 16

After a brief respite we return in Job 16 to further vivid, violent images of Job's body being attacked by the deity, El.

> I was at ease, and he broke me in two;
> he seized me by the neck and dashed me to pieces;
> he set me up as his target;
> his archers surround me.
> He slashes open my kidneys, and shows no mercy;
> he pours out my gall on the ground.
> He bursts upon me again and again;
> he rushes at me like a warrior.
>
> (Job 16:12–14)

93 Perhaps there is some similarity to the Athenian theatre here. Compare, for example, 'The Clouds' and 'The Knights' by Aristophanes in terms of the motif of 'wind' and 'flatulence'. Refer to Henderson for the various connotations to breaking wind in Attic comedy (Henderson 1991:187–203). For a full overview of comic elements in the Old Testament and in Aristophanes, refer to Lazarus (Lazarus 2014). Jarick also traces connections between Aristophanes and Menander, as well as Ecclesiastes (Jarick 2014).

At this point audiences are confronted with graphic images of the height of divine cruelty, but these images may also provide insights into perceptions of pain among early writers. What is being described here sounds rather like a cruelly calculated military attack, where El is depicted as a warrior and Job the target for the arrows. There are striking similarities with Job 6:4 where Eloah is scathingly cast as the Rešeph who fires infected needles at Job, as previously discussed (cf. 1 Sam. 20:20; Lam. 3:12).[94] However, here the pain appears to be both directly inflicted by El but also exacted by El's archers.[95] The military metaphor can only go so far here since, as Clines notes, this is 'more like a firing squad than a military engagement of matched forces' (Clines 1989:384). This is an image far worse than that depicted in chapter 6; as Habel comments the 'arrows of Rešeph bring pestilence; the arrows of El leave their victim impotent and close to death' (Habel 1985:273). However, this is depicted as a tightly organised attack, and responsibility still clearly lies with El, as the myriad third-person singular verbs confirm. Here, El is 'a brutal enemy who attacks hapless victims without restraint' (Balentine 2015:120). This is an unsettling and uncomfortable way of depicting the deity. Indeed, Balentine argues that such is the level of anxiety caused by these images that even the Greek translator/s felt the need to 'censor the defiant Job' (Balentine 2015:121).[96] Given the translators' possible uneasiness, one wonders how early audiences would have experienced listening to this explicit description of pain and loaded, sceptical accusation of responsibility? Perhaps early audiences would also have been made to feel uncomfortable?

In these verses, pain is expressed in personal and distressingly private somatic terms, yet it is also made public by the presence of the audience who is forced to look on in horror. The verbs associated with divine actions in these verses

94 Similarly, both here and in chapter 6, God is without 'compassion' (חמל; Job 6:10; 16:13).

95 The Hebrew here is slightly ambiguous: רב is quite a common term simply meaning 'many', 'great', or 'chief' both in Hebrew and Aramaic (cf. 2 Kgs 25:8; Ezr. 4:10; Ps. 31:20; Lam. 1:1; Dan. 2:14). This could be understood in the sense of bands of soldiers or in the sense of many arrows. The Old Greek has λόγχαις 'spears', as does the Vulgate, whereas the Targum and Peshitta have 'arrows'. However, the same word occurs in Jeremiah 50:20 explicitly referring to רבים bending the bow. This argument is bolstered by the related term רבב meaning to 'shoot', which also occurs in the context of archers (Gen. 49:23; Ps. 18:15).

96 The Hebrew and Greek are noticeably different here:

יָסֹבּוּ עָלַי רַבָּיו יְפַלַּח כִּלְיוֹתַי וְלֹא יַחְמוֹל יִשְׁפֹּךְ לָאָרֶץ מְרֵרָתִי
יִפְרְצֵנִי פֶרֶץ עַל־פְּנֵי־פָרֶץ יָרֻץ עָלַי כְּגִבּוֹר׃

ἐκύκλωσάν με λόγχαις βάλλοντες εἰς νεφρούς μου οὐ φειδόμενοι ἐξέχεαν εἰς τὴν γῆν τὴν χολήν μου κατέβαλόν με πτῶμα ἐπὶ πτώματι ἔδραμον πρός με δυνάμενοι

Balentine's comparison between the Hebrew and Greek version's third singular versus third plural at this point highlights the differences effectively:

Hebrew: *His* archers surround me. *He* slashes open my kidneys, and shows no mercy; *he* pours out my gall on the ground. *He* bursts upon me again and again; *he* rushes at me like a warrior.

Greek: *They* surrounded me with spears, hurling them into my kidneys, without sparing; *they* poured out my gall on the ground. *They* threw me down, fall upon fall; they rushed at me powerfully (as quoted in Balentine 2015:120, italics not in original).

By changing the number of verbs from the singular to the plural indefinite, God is removed from the passage. This may seem like a 'theological toning down' (Gard 1952:63). However, it is as well to note that the Greek translation 'is a literary ("free") rather than a literal translation' (Witte 2007:35).

are vicious, sadistic, and terrifying. El 'breaks' (פרר)[97] 'grabs by the neck' (אחז) 'slashes' (פוץ)[98] 'pours out' (שפך) 'bursts upon' repeatedly (פרץ),[99] and 'rushes at' (רוץ)[100] the character Job like a military leader. Image is heaped upon image of lethal aggression. Rowley notes Driver's suggestion that the picture intended here is of a beast preying on an animal (Rowley 1976:119). This certainly seems appropriate for verse 12 when the 'prey' is vigorously shaken and then grabbed by the neck. Job's answer to Eliphaz's speech on the fate of the wicked directly mirrors the language which Eliphaz uses of the wicked: they 'writhe in pain. . . [because they were] playing the warrior . . . running stubbornly against him [Shaddai]' (Job 15:20, 26). Here the ironic reversal of Eliphaz's advice is stronger than the first retorts to Eliphaz. The responses are, as the conversation progresses, 'increasingly acrimonious, with each side insisting that the others' words are useless' (Pelham 2012b:336). Furthermore, to add irony to injury, however challenging these images of the deity are, they 'do closely echo a traditional type of prayer, that found in Lamentations 3, which uses as a central motif the figure of divine violence' (Newsom 1999:247).[101] However one attempts to contextualise, aggression and brutality dominate this expression of pain.

Finally, the description focuses heavily on the effect that divine assault has on Job's body. Job's kidneys (כליה) have been slashed open and his gall (מררה) is on the ground. Similar body parts are referred to in traditional laments where bile or entrails are poured to the ground (Lam. 2:11; 3:13; cf. 2 Sam. 20:10). The kidneys are usually used metaphorically as the seat of desires and affections in Hebrew. Likewise, in Hebrew, the 'gall' has symbolic significance as something bitter. As Clines suggests if the 'affections and sympathies are assaulted, it is bitterness that spills out' (Clines 1989:385). Thus, coupling desires and affections

97 The verb פרר usually means to break into pieces or make void (2 Sam. 15:34). Here we have the only occurrence in the Hebrew Bible of the verb in the *pilpel* form, perhaps meaning something like 'shake' (the verb occurs at Isa. 24:19 in a description of apocalyptic violence as a *hithpoel* infinitive absolute in parallel with a *hithpael* infinitive absolute of מוט (totter, shake, move).

98 Like the verb פרר the term פוץ which is also in the *pilpel* form, means to break or dash in pieces (cf. Jer. 23:29; Lam. 3:12).

99 The Hebrew here reads יפרצני פרץ על פני פרץ 'he breached me, breach upon breach'. The term פרץ usually means to break down or scatter, but here it is to break forth upon, as in Exod. 19:22, 24; 2 Sam. 6:8; 1 Chr. 15:13. The terms פרר, פוץ, and פרץ are synonymous; therefore, this is semantic parallelism (Kugel 1981:49). Moreover, we can trace here what Berlin calls 'phonological parallelism', that is, 'lexical associations . . . which . . . seem to have a phonological dimension to their association. . . . These are word pairs which can also be considered sound pairs' (Berlin and Knorina 2008:106). Seow also notes that the attack is 'graphically (and phonologically)' represented with the repetition of the term 'breach' (פרץ) and the deity's 'charging' at Job (ירץ) (Seow 2011:80).

100 The verb רוץ + על means to 'rush at' something in a hostile manner.

101 For Newsom the reason for this 'linguistic sabotage' is Job's opposition to 'different moral imaginations – one grounded in the discourse of prayer, the other in the discourse of legal dispute' (Newsom 1999:248).

with bitterness and lack of mercy on the side of the attacker (El) illustrates the physical and brutal attack against the character Job.

Although this echoes the language of traditional lament, it pushes the metaphor of the deity attack to an extreme. As Newsom suggests, 'nothing in the psalms, nothing even in Lamentations 3, matches Job's disturbing account of divine violence. . . . Something else besides the mere heightening of a lament motif generates this language' (Newsom 2009:138). For Newsom, it is the perception on the part of Job that 'human and divine alterity' causes this language to emerge (Newsom 2009:139).[102] Tilford also comments on the deity attack metaphor at this point, suggesting that 'presumably Job experiences misfortune inside his body, the tactile descriptions focus the reader's attention on the external nature of Job's suffering' (Tilford 2016:53). Some scholars go beyond interpreting the metaphoric somatic language here as a reflection of suffering by emphasising the agency of the deity in this language. Verbin, for example, makes a case for Job being an example of divine abuse (Verbin 2010). Similarly, Blumenthal suggests that the deity in Job 'is an abuser' (Blumenthal 1993:255).[103] These arguments are helpful to an extent. The latter emphasises the question of the deity's responsibility in response to the moralising of Job's friends. The former examples focus on the connection between language and the body. Both of these aspects may be analysed using illness experience and pain research.

However, concerning the matter of language and the body in Job 16, perhaps one effective way of contextualising the violence of the deity attack metaphor at this point is through the notion of 'idioms of distress', as mentioned

102 This is a perspective which is in some ways similar to Scarry's argument about the relation between God and humans in the Old Testament which is 'often mediated by the sign of the weapon'. Scarry develops this point, arguing,

> The invented god and its human inventor (or, in the language of the scriptures, the creator and his creature) are differentiated by the immunity of the one and the woundability [*sic.*] of the other; as if the creature is not merely *woundable* but already deeply and permanently *wounded,* handicapped or physically marred in some way . . . then that individual is asserted to exist at an even greater moral distance from God than does the "normal" person.
>
> (Scarry 1985:183)

The connection between the human body being woundable but also once wounded, then at a 'greater moral distance from God' than the "normal" person, in the Old Testament is interesting. Scarry's statement about one who is wounded being at an 'even greater moral distance from God' certainly seems to correlate well with the depictions of Job's body and the way it is reacted to. However, we have noted previously problems with Scarry's overall argument.

103 Blumenthal notes the responses to Job by Weisel (*The Trial of God*) and Jung (*Answer to Job*), who emphasise the need for Yahweh to go on trial. Jung argues,

> it is Yahweh himself who darkens counsel. . . . He turns the tables on Job and blames him for what he himself does: man is not permitted to have an opinion about him. . . . For seventy-one verses he proclaims his world-creating power to his miserable victim, who sits in ashes and scratches his sores with potsherds, and who by now has had enough of superhuman violence.
>
> (Jung, cited in Blumenthal 1993:255; cf. Hyun 2013:116)

earlier.[104] Idioms of distress are not merely psychological somatised responses: they can also be considered in socio-political contexts. For example, Nichter points out that

> At the level of symbolic protest, they [idioms of distress] constitute a language for social suffering that cannot overtly be articulated in socio-political contexts where doing so causes a threat to both those who suffer from structural violence and those in positions of power.
>
> (Nichter 2010:412)

Nichter provides several examples of this 'symbolic protest' which is articulated through a focus on the body in pain. These include 'young barren women in Guinea Bissau' who used distress in a social movement to communicate post-war traumatic stress and suffering (Nichter 2010:412). Similarly, Havik women in Nichter's study expressed distress about sanctions against remarriage and divorce through '(a) Commensality, Weight Loss, Fasting, and Poisoning; (b) Purity: Obsession and Ambivalence; (c) Illness' (Nichter 1981:380). Interpreting the violent deity attack metaphor in Job 16:12–14 as a type of 'idiom of distress' reveals several, perhaps overlooked, points of significance about the force of the language. Initially, Job's body, interpreted by his friends as 'sin visualised', is the source of the problem. Through emphasising Job's high levels of pain using the metaphor of a violent deity attack, the source of the problem, Job's body, becomes the source of resistance to this interpretation. It is a symbolic protest against the retribution model and an attempt, placed on the lips of the character Job, to draw attention to his humanity and his suffering instead of moralising. It is also an attempt to regain power through questioning the existing power structures created by the retribution model of Job's friends. The hyperbolic level of violence in the language captures the attention of various audiences and of Job's friends effectively and communicates in a symbolic way the character's level of objection to his friends' explanatory models.

Even here, however, we find a type of double-edged poignant and tragic yet also ironic and comical dramatisation of pain. Job's overstated idiom of distress at this point ends up being a type of passive-aggressive defence. It is aggressive because of the level of violence being attributed to the deity, which has the capacity to shock and create tension. It is passive because it is addressed to nobody specifically from verse 6 through to the end of the chapter. Indeed, Job's strange soliloquy ends with a generalised call 'Oh Earth, do not cover my blood' wherein the character pretentiously compares himself with innocent Abel, wrongfully attacked by Cain whose unresolved innocent 'bloods cry out' from the ground (Job 16:18; Gen. 4:10).[105] The speech is, in some ways, com-

104 See Chapter 1.

105 The implication here at the end of the deity attack metaphor is that the attack is an attempt at murder (Deut. 19:10–13; 21:8–9; Isa. 26:21; Ezek. 24:7–8).

parable to Lear's ramblings about heaven's fury: 'blow winds, and crack your cheeks! Rage! Blow' (Lear III:1)![106] In both cases, a character fallen from power addresses no one in particular with overly inflated and dramatic language; Lear as if he could control the weather, Job as if his body is all-important to every listener. Both madly froth as a symbolic expression of their levels of suffering.

Concerning the deity's responsibility, as alluded to in the scholarship cited on divine 'abuse', audiences cannot help but notice the striking language wherein El is cast as the attacker. Thus, one major aspect of the problem is the matter of perceived lack of justice. As Newsom comments at 'the heart of Job's imagination lies the enigma of bodies broken for no reason. By insisting on speaking of and for such bodies, Job is drawn to the language of justice and accountability as it can be imagined in a court of law' (Newsom 1999:252).[107] Therefore, by juxtaposing the metaphor of a court of law with images of dismemberment and assault, the friends' own moralising advice is met with questions associated with blame, shame, and morality which, through the language of divine violence, come more sharply into focus. Furthermore, pain is strategically constructed through the metaphor so that it is transformed 'into a social asset, and role destruction into a chance for personal empowerment' because through narrative 'people find the power to resist and restructure ideas of normalcy that do not fit with their experiences and they reconfigure their disrupted identity' (Mattingly and Garro 2000:88–89; cf. Garro 1994). This is a good way of contextualising the severity of the language used in the deity attack metaphor here. Job uses the description of pain as currency to challenge and reconfigure ideas about norms. The problem is not the 'me' of the main character, it is the deity. This metaphor opens up and inverts traditional questions about justice, agency, and punishment.

It is important to recognise the role of certainty with respect to agency which is created by Job's vivid descriptions of perceived pain. The idea of a violent deity who inflicts illness indiscriminately removes the tensions around disease created by illnesses leitmotif 'why me/you?' For example, exploring witchcraft among the Azande of central Africa, Evans-Pritchard argues that the explanation that there are witches helps account for things going wrong and thus relieves anxiety. Similarly, in their *Oedipus and Job in West African Religion*

106 For a sustained comparison between Job and King Lear which focuses on reception, refer to Fisch 1999:116–150, cf. Lipshitz 2015.

107 Similarly, Newsom suggests

> The ravaged body serves not as the basis for compassionate appeal, as in Lam 3:43–48, but as the basis for accusation. Rather than engaging in self-examination and repentance, as the lament urges, Job envisions a witness who would testify against God concerning the wrong done to Job (Job 16:19–21).
>
> (Newsom 2009:137–138)

Thus, the character uses his body not as a symbol of divine punishment, but as a warning about divine injustice.

Forte and Horton expose 'how the Tallensi of northern Ghana address the uncertainties of existence and, most compellingly, how they understand the reality of "spoiled lives" by providing an ethic and psychological account of agency linked to troublesome spirits in order to explain the death of offspring' (Lambek and Antze 2004:7–8; Fortes and Horton 1983). Nevertheless, it also replaces such question with larger questions such as 'Who are the witches among us? Why, really, do they act as they do? What, actually, are we capable of doing?' (Lambek and Antze 2004:7; Evans-Pritchard 1937). Through deflecting agency, causation, and blame for illness on to demons, troublesome spirits, or even a deity who arbitrarily attacks, new questions emerge which also, importantly, deflect blame and agency away from Job, the one who is portrayed as being in pain. There is a certain level of irony even here, however, in the manner in which the retribution model is undermined. What has been achieved, ultimately, in this proliferated drama of finger-pointing, is not the reassurance of the deity's fairness in a just world. Instead, anxieties are likely to be raised through the troubling possibility that life, far from being reducible to some neat moral calculus of retribution, is in fact complex and chaotic. Indeed sometimes, as Job's random demise illustrates, it is brutally unfair.

Who can but moralise?: Job's body and the supernatural attack in Job 19

Job 19 is an interesting example of the deity attack metaphor at work. As Clines points out, 'there is a veritable kaleidoscope of images here, all images of assault' (Clines 1989:442). Here the character explicitly points to 'violence' on the part of the deity as the key reason for his somatised distress.

> If I cry out[108] "Violence!"[109]
> then I am not answered
> I shout out for help! But there is not justice.
> He has fenced up[110] my path so that I cannot cross over
> Over my footpaths he has set darkness.

108 The term צעק 'cry out' (sometimes spelt זעק) is usually a call to the deity for deliverance (Exod. 5:8, 15; 8:12; 14:10, 15; 17:4, 22:23, 27).

109 The word חמס 'violence' has a wide semantic range and can also mean 'injustice', 'cruelty', or simply 'wrong'. It is possible to translate 'injustice' here (Seow 2013:791). This is on account of the legal ריב metaphor (Job 13:6; 29:16; 31:13, 35; cf. Jer. 20:8; Hab. 1:2). It is also perhaps because we are told at the outset that it is the deity who has allowed Job to suffer, a translation perhaps strengthened by the term 'justice / judgement' (משפט) which occurs in parallelism. However, given the regularity of the deity attack metaphor in Job, 'violence' is the preferred translation here, and indeed a translation which many commentators also use (Habel 1985:290; Gordis 1978:196; Rowley 1976:134; Pope 1965:128; Clines 1989:426). Seow's suggestion that 'the shout of "Injustice!" may be the ancient Hebrew for "Help!"' is compelling in context given the parallelism with the verb שוע 'help'.

110 The verb גדר refers to the repair of a wall. However, the Old Greek and Vulgate translations suggest the idea is building a wall or fence around (κύκλῳ περιῳκοδόμημαι). There is a similar expression, though using a synonym 'hedged in' (סכך) in Job 3:23.

He has stripped my glory from me
And removed the crown from my head.
He has torn me down all around and I have gone
  He has pulled up my hope like a tree.
His anger is kindled against me
  He imagines me as one of his enemies
Together his troops come and they and their ways rise up against me[111] and encamp around[112] my tent.

(Job 19:7–12)

The term 'violence' is usually used by the innocent when crying out to the deity for deliverance (Hab. 1:2). Ironically, here it is on the lips of the character Job who cries out for vindication against the deity who violently attacks. This characteristic repurposing of traditional language perhaps makes the audience feel uncomfortable, a technique which has the silver lining of the fact that they are engaged and listening. Indeed, the accusation of divine violence may have increased the tension for audiences listening to Job. The accusation develops the metaphor of the stripped royal. Job's 'crown' and his 'glory' are stripped off. This metaphor within the deity attack scene has the effect of emphasising Job's own opinion of himself if the figurative idiom of 'crown' for head is understood literally. This is a thoroughly ironic twist on the psalmist's mawkish claim that man is 'a little lower than the angels' and 'crowned with glory and honour' (Ps. 8:6). Seated at the epicentre of the calamity of traditions being overthrown is the character Job whose very presence represents a tragic form of social inversion: the rich and honourable Job has been brought to nothing. He is an uprooted tree, perhaps a euphemism for death.

The tension continues to mount as another powerful metaphor – that of encircling the city wall in siege – is employed. As Jones comments 'God piles up siege ramps against him [Job] as if he were a fortified city with high walls' (Jones 2013:851).[113] As in Job 16, so, too, here the deity's assault on Job's body is expressed through the hyperbole of a city's destruction (cf. Job 16:14). However, the way that the deity is described here moves quickly from the menacing to the extremely peculiar. In another puffed-up overestimation of his own self-importance, Job's description suggests that the character imagines the deity as threatened by him, as if an entire celestial army of troops were needed for Job's defeat. If the character Job were any more puffed up at this point, he would need to borrow the hot-air balloon in which Aristophanes placed Socrates in *The Clouds*. As Moss argues, Socrates 'who is presented . . . as conceited, arrogant, pedantic, and full of sophistry, spends the duration of the play in a hot air balloon, literally puffed up with air' (Moss 2012:323). However, having ramped up the tension and confusion to this

111 BHS notes that the Hebrew here is close to Job 30:12 at this point, although the latter has a synonym for 'ways' דרך (ארח).

112 For לאהלי the preposition ל is rather awkward, perhaps accounting for the rare term 'spies / lying in wait' used by the Greek translator (ἐγκάθετος).

113 Greenstein makes a similar comment, 'Job imagines that God has brought an army to surround and lay siege to his home' (Greenstein 2018:47).

point, we now realise that these exaggerated metaphors were misdirection: instead of the drama of a large celestial battle between King Job and the deity, we are presented with the weedy anti-climax of Job's 'tent'.[114] This anti-climax is an example of classic relief theory: nervous energy has been allowed to build in the audience as tensions increased on account of Job's tragic language. Habel expresses this well: 'the mighty fortress against which God has marshalled his entire siege works and militia is, in fact, a mere "tent"' (Habel 1985:301). The sudden incongruence of the tent versus the celestial army flips the tragic over into the comical and absurd. Yet again, we have gone from the catastrophic to the ludicrous.

The theme of justice is interesting here: Once more the connection between sickness and criminality, as previously discussed, is challenged by Job.[115] The injustice of his situation is a theme which dominates the dialogues. Here the term picks up on Job's former mention of משפט in 13:18 and 14:3. This theme is taken up by Eliphaz in response to Job's speech, who asks:

> Will he [*El*] not reprove (יכח) you for your fear?
> Will he enter with you into judgement (משפט)?
> Is your wickedness not great?[116]
> And your iniquities infinite?
>
> (Job 22:4–5)

Eliphaz's moralising has moved in this speech about justice from his former judgemental style of advice to full-blown accusation (Job 5:17; 15:2–6). The advice undermines Job by asking several rhetorical questions, including the suggestion that El might make his judgement based on Job's piety or fear (ירא). Loaded notions of the seriousness of 'fearing' God which emerge regularly in the Psalms are echoed here (Gen. 22:12; 42:18; Ps. 22:23, 25).[117] Indeed, audiences may be reminded of the Satan's opening gambit 'does Job fear God for nothing?' (Job 1:9).[118] From Eliphaz's perspective, if Job would only be uncompromisingly obedient, as Abraham before him who was also 'tested', then things would go better for him (Gen. 22:1). This aligns neatly with Eliphaz's less irate moralising advice for Job at the beginning of the dialogues wherein he asks, if

114 Clines notes the added layer of metacritical irony here, observing that 'So unexpected is the last word of the line, "my tent" . . . that some commentators have felt there must be some mistake. . . . There is the grimmest of humour here' (Clines 1989:445).

115 Refer to the section 'The arrows of Shaddai'.

116 Note the morphologic similarity, and perhaps sound-play, here between רע and רב.

117 Refer also to Pss. 15:4; 25:12, 14; 31:19; 33:18; 34:7; 60:4; 61:5; 66:16; 85:9; 103:11, 13, 17; 111:5; 115:11, 13; 118:4; 119:74, 79; 128:1, 4; 135:20; 145:19; 147:11.

Habel goes as far as to suggest that there is a double-entendre here, suggesting that God's fear of Job might be what is meant. This translation, adopted by the AV ('Will he reprove thee for fear of thee?'), renders Eliphaz's speech 'fraught with bold sarcasm' (Habel 1985:338). If this translation is adopted, an ironic reversal has taken place between the character Job and the deity El. This perhaps foreshadows the character Job's playing the God in chapter 29, as discussed in section 'By night he chews at my bones within me'.

118 This connection may be strengthened by the recurrence of the term 'for nothing' (חנם) in Job 1:9 and in the next verse of Eliphaz's speech (Job 22:6).

Job's 'fear [of God]' is his confidence, and Job's 'blameless (תם) ways', his 'hope' (תקוה) (Job 4:6; cf. 5:16).[119] However here, for Eliphaz, either Job is guilty or this is a test of his loyalty. As Rowley puts it 'if correction is not for piety, then it must be for wickedness, and hence Job's sufferings must prove his sin' (Rowley 1976:154). The interrogation here is in some ways similar to the interrogation from the whirlwind at the end: Eliphaz's questions are not just rhetorical, they are unanswerable because in the context of the dialogue between Job and his friends there is no proof of Job's innocence. These moralising rhetorical questions, however, undermine the entire speech. As Clines points out, 'the question, though expecting the answer No!, is only properly answered with a Yes!' (Clines 2006:554). The friends can only work on the evidence that they have, but only the audience is privy to the knowledge that Job's situation is more complex than their retribution model can account for.

One interesting way of looking at this is through illness narratives. In modern illness narratives people order their experience in terms of what it means to them and to others through narrative. Therefore, narrative provides coherence when it seems there is none, and as a consequence it contributes to the experience of illness. However, there is also a protesting aspect of illness narratives. As Kleinman observes,

> The story of sickness may even function as a political commentary, pointing a finger of condemnation at perceived injustice and the personal experience of oppression. . . . For these reasons, retrospective narratization can readily be shown to distort the actual happenings (the history) of the illness experience, since its raison d'être is not fidelity to historical circumstances but rather significance and validity in the creation of a life story.
>
> (Kleinman 1988:50–51)

This argument aligns well with the speeches of Job. On one level they are absurd, exaggerated, and comical. On another, they betray a serious point, through personal expression, about oppressive and dominant narratives at the time of the play's composition and early performance that interpret reality and create meaning. Through Job's speeches, an alternative set of narratives emerge which are quite possibly uncomfortable for audiences to hear – despite the knowledge from the prologue that Job is not deserving of his situation – if they adhere to ideas about retribution. Through all the hot air and waffling, and all the windy words and moralising, Job's own voice raises its own very serious moral questions about social attitudes towards those who are ill or in pain.[120]

119 Of course, the irony of the use of the word תם here must be noted. This is not the first time the friends have suggested that Job be תם. Refer to note 24 in Chapter 1.

120 Good's argument here is particularly appropriate, given the drama of words in the book and the ultimately unanswered search for meaning:

> when pain is configured as suffering, it evokes intractable, inexhaustible moral and spiritual questions that are worth pursuing to the extent we can better understand human conditions or provide assistance to sufferers. . . . *The moral requirement of engaging people who suffer is to struggle to*

With no small irony, it is his words that function as a de-legitimisation of and resistance to his friends' moralising. As such, in spite of the comedy, Job's words do retain some level of power.

Perhaps part of the reason for this is the focus of the discussion on Job's body. On one level, as observed, the character undermines himself through ridiculous hyperbole, citing a cosmic army attacking his mere tent. He is a satire of wisdom, the wisest fool of all, and audiences might look on and laugh. Yet on another level his words retain a subversive, almost iconoclastic, quality and are difficult to ignore. This is partly because his body is evidence of his case: his is a type of 'wounded storyteller', and as such his narrative is not just any narrative. As Frank explains,

> The figure of the wounded storyteller is ancient: Tiresias, the seer who reveals to Oedipus the true story of whose son he is, has been blinded by the gods. His wound gives his narrative power. The wound that the biblical patriarch Jacob suffers to his hip while wrestling with an angel is part of the story he tells of that event, and it is the price of his story. As Jacob tells his story to those he returns to – and who else could have told it? – his wound is evidence of his story's truth.
>
> (Frank 1995:xi)[121]

Job cries out for help in the most desperate of terms but finds no justice or support. Audiences know the situation was not created by Job, however. Therefore, during the dialogues, the stage itself wherein the friends provide moralising advice becomes a type of microcosm that reflects the cultural norms at the time in terms of responses to pain and illness. The delicious irony here is that any audience members who take the retribution model seriously are forced to watch their own attitudes being undermined by nothing less than Job, a figure of fun who is not particularly cast as one to be taken seriously. Could it be the case that this peculiar misfit, this foreigner from Uz who froths wildly about his

---

> *transcend limited and limiting explanatory models so as to witness, to affirm, their humanity*. For both, there may come a time when, like the grieving author of the ancient 'Lamentations over the Destruction of Sumer and Ur' . . . they need to admit, "There are no words!"
>
> (Good 1992:190 italics not in original)

A key area wherein Job's friends fail is in their stubborn inability to affirm Job's humanity which would mean compromising and perhaps changing their own limiting explanatory models. Their bogus 'advice' is largely what is satirised during the discussions.

121 It is interesting that Frank classifies Job as a story of restitution, stating:

> Restitution stories reassure the listener that however bad things look, a happy ending is possible – Job with his new family and cattle, basking in God's graciousness. Chaos stories are Job taking his wife's advice, cursing God and dying.
>
> (Frank 1995:97)

The restitution story is one way of framing illness narratives and interpreting their function. It is an interesting coincidence, however, that the restitution story framework also matches quite neatly with the comedy U-shape wherein the happy ending is part of the return to reality and harmony (Jackson 2012:17–18).

body in pain and who thinks so highly of himself might actually be right? For his friends, Job's visibly dysfunctional body presents a problem wherein meaning must be found.[122] Job has roared in pain, who will not fear? Job has spoken about his wounded body, who can but moralise? But the audience has been made aware that the whole situation emerged from nothing more serious than a glorified gamble between Yahweh and the Satan.

The image of Job's hope being uprooted like a tree is also interesting. The term תקוה (hope) appears regularly in Job, usually on the lips of the character himself who bemoans his loss of hope (Job 8:8; 14:7, 19; 17:15; 27:8). It does also occur quite early in the dialogues with Zophar's moralising advice to Job that if just were just to put away his 'iniquity' and 'wickedness' (Job 11:14) then he would have 'hope' (Job 11:18, 20). Zophar, so good. But the problems with Zophar's argument are soon uncovered. Here in chapter 19, in contrast with Zophar, Job creates an image of complete lack of agency: his hope is 'uprooted'.[123] In the build-up to the comic anti-climax of the 'tent' Job's speech is poignant and tragic.[124] Indeed, some of the research into illness narratives and expressions of pain focuses on hope as 'the existential and affective counterpart of agency that replaces it where channels for agency are blocked and presence in the world becomes precarious' (Lindquist 2006:4). This may be so for some illness experiences, but for Job, not only is agency absent, so, too, is hope.[125]

122 Although the friends' responses in the context of the entire book of Job are cast as, at best, rather unsympathetic, such responses to pain and illness are not uncommon in many illness narratives. For example, Carel reports:

> Illness and its visible signs may arouse strong emotional responses in healthy onlookers or friends. These emotions may not be consciously experienced and cannot be addressed in a routine exchange. It is difficult to find the right time and words to express these feelings. I witnessed many attempts by people to offer encouragement and support, to express admiration and caring towards ill people. The striking feature of these attempts was how difficult they seemed for the well-intentioned healthy person. They often preface their comments with an apology for being intrusive or speaking out of turn.
> (Carel 2016:76)

The notion of Job as sin visualised creates a type of uncomfortable instability which his friends attempt to address, as Carel's onlookers seek also to do. The irony here is the vast difference between Carel's polite onlookers who 'preface their comments with an apology' and Job's friends. The latter have been gradually but consistently wound up by Job's many complaints to the point that they are so frustrated with him they no longer have patience or sympathy, as Eliphaz's speech betrays.

123 Note the *hiphil* of the verb נסע is used specifically here, adding to the sense of powerless on Job's part.

124 The 'tent' here may well be a metaphor for Job's skin, aligning closely to Greenstein's identification of the metaphor: 'skin is a garment' (Greenstein 2018:44). The term אהל (tent) is a semi-regular metaphor in Job for the body (Job 5:24; 11:14; 18:6, 14, 15; 19:12). Perdue draws out the tragic nature of the 'tent' metaphor at this point, arguing that

> In this world constructed by metaphor, Job's besieged 'tent' refers to both his royal dwelling and his capital city. . . . Like a king who sees the ravaging of his country and the siege of a sinister army set to attack the capital, Job cries out 'violence' . . . a term often designating the bloody slaughter of populations by a ruthless army. . . . But it is also the same term used by P to describe the 'violation' of the earth (Gen. 6.11–12). This 'violation' led to the return of chaos in the Flood.
> (Perdue 1991:173)

125 Much of the literature which focuses on hope in illness accounts examines the nature of chronic illness and the paradox of hope involved and needed to manage conditions. Mattingly, who uses a

Here, just before mention of the violent deity amassing an army against Job, we hit the height of poignant tension. Just as things couldn't get any more tragic there is a sudden shift into comedy as Job's little 'tent' makes its appearance.

'By night he chews at my bones within me': the deity attack metaphor in Job 30

A final part of Job which is particularly focused on the body, again using the metaphor of divine assault, is Job 30. Here there is another extended description of Job's perception of pain and a depiction of the character's feelings about how his identity changes in relation to his body (Job 30:16–19, 27–31). Given that this is an extended description, we will focus on verses 16–19 initially and then move on to 27–31 afterwards.

> And now my soul (נפש)[126] is poured out within[127] me;
> days of affliction (עני)[128] have taken hold of me.
> The night racks (נקר)[129] my bones,

---

narrative phenomenology approach, defines hope in such circumstances as a 'practice'. For Mattingly, hope involves the practice of creating, or trying to create, lives worth living even in the midst of suffering, even with no happy ending in sight . . . This is why we have chosen to speak of hope as a practice, rather than simply an emotion or a cultural attitude.

(Mattingly 2010:6)

We do not know anything about the temporality or not of Job's condition, given that he is only a character in a text, but it is interesting to observe the key role that hope can sometimes play during illness. When contextualised from this angle, the uprooting of hope is deeply poignant. Nevertheless, it should also be pointed out that in many cases people who know their condition is irreversible are happier than those who hope that they may get better: 'in such cases, ironically, hope may be the cornerstone of misery' (Solomon 2013:35).

126 Habel suggests 'my life drains from me'; however, נפש could mean a range of things, from emotions, neck, appetite, to breath, so we do not necessarily need to interpret that the character is close to death at this point, as Habel's translation might suggest (Habel 1985:414). However, a similar description of life poured out which emerges in Lamentations 2:12 might suggest that the character is on the brink of death. Nevertheless, this comparison may also have a material sense, describing the weeping of Jerusalem.

127 The Hebrew here is עלי; an overly literal translation 'upon me' is undesirable (KJV). However, the Old Greek does have this rather literal rendering (καὶ νῦν ἐπ᾽ ἐμὲ ἐκχυθήσεται ἡ ψυχή μου). Gordis suggests 'my soul pours itself out' hence emphasising the *hithpael* form of שפך. Clines suggests that the על is pathetic, so the literal translation is not necessary (Clines 2006:952). For a thorough discussion of the problems related to translating these verses refer to Pinker 2017. Pinker's suggestion that Job 30:17–18 should be understood from the perspective of the contradictory objectives that the ailing Job and his fearful community have is worthy of consideration alongside the detailed exegesis of these verses.

128 The term עני can mean affliction in the sense of illness, for example, barrenness (Gen. 29:32; 1 Sam. 1:11), and 'affliction' sometimes occurs alongside somatic language, perhaps suggesting illness (Job. 30:27; Ps. 25:18). However, in the vast majority of times the term appears it refers to difficulty, misery, and depression more generally, such as is encountered during slavery or poverty, or through being made lowly (Exod. 3:7, 17; Deut. 26:7; 2 Kgs 14:26; Neh. 9:9; CD 19:9).

129 The term נקר means to bore out or pierce. It often refers to the gouging out of eyes (Num. 16:14; Judg. 16:21; 1 Sam. 11:2; Prov. 30:17) or to the digging of a hole or pit (Isa. 51:1). One could be more explicit in translation here and translate 'by night he pierces my bones within me', with the implied subject being El. Ceresko, following Gray, suggests that we emend MT '*niqqar*

and the As above that gnaws me takes no rest.[130]
With violence he seizes[131] my garment;
he grasps[132] me by the collar of my tunic.
He has cast me into the mire,
and I have become like dust and ashes.[133]

(Job 30:16–19)

The images here which describe and depict bodily pain are, again, rather violent. As Lilly argues, the 'ominous assault resembles the medical inundation suffered by Šubši-mešrê-Šakkan' (Lilly 2016:335).[134] Given the graphic corporeal metaphor of El inflicting Job's pain, perhaps as a wild animal with caught prey, it is not particularly surprising that many modern versions (and older translations) sought to restrain the language slightly by making 'disease' the subject (KJV; JPS Tanakh; AKJV; ERV). However, it seems worth pursuing the metaphor of the deity attack directly rather than attempting to sanitise it.

---

to *niqqad* . . . "to burn". This suggestion finds support in two ancient versions. . . . Codex Vaticanus. . . [reads] *sykékauutai* "are inflamed" and the Qumran Targum of Job has *grmy ydwn* "my bones burn"' (Ceresko 1980:76).

130 The NRSV translation here is somewhat different from the Hebrew: וערקי לא ישכבון 'and my ערק do not lie down'. The term ערק only occurs elsewhere at Job 30:3, where it appears to be a verb describing famine and need 'fleeing' into the wilderness. In the context of the sentence we have, the term appears to be a noun. LXX has νεῦρά μου διαλέλυται, 'my sinews are dispersed'. Some translations refer instead to 'veins' on the basis of Targum on Ezekiel 27:19 ערקין דברל 'veins of iron'. The Peshitta paraphrases: 'In the night my bones are in pain and my body has no strength in it. we have put on my garment; and girded up myself with my robe' (*bəlalyō' garmay yəqarû ʿəlay wəgûšmî lō' šərō' bəsûgō'' daḥyolō' 'etlabšet ləbûšî we'tḥazqet bəkûtînî*). Given that the term, whatever its meaning, is in parallelism in Hebrew with 'bones', a body part of some sort is preferable for the translation. It is difficult to be more precise, since there is not sufficient evidence available to ascertain the meaning of the term ערק.

131 MT *hithpael* יִתְחַפֵּשׂ is difficult. The verb חפש usually refers to one's appearance being changed, thus disguise (1 Sam. 28:8; 1 Kgs 20:38). Perhaps audiences are supposed to imagine the metaphor refers to disfigurement? Perhaps the text has been deliberately corrupted on account of Job's blasphemous charges in a manner analogues to a *tiqqun soferim*? The subject here is El but some translations, such as KJV for example, suggest 'by the great force *of my disease*'. Since we can only speculate, the sensible option seems to be emendation. Clines suggests emending in line with the LXX reading (ἐπελάβετό μου 'it has grasped me'), and 11QtgJob (יאחרון 'they seize'), thus יְתַפֵּשׂ "he seizes" (Clines 2006:954). A final suggestion to note is Ceresko's who reads "rifles", arguing 'the usual significance of *ḥpś* in the hithpael "let oneself be searched for = disguise oneself" does not fit the context. An examination of its use in the other intensive conjugation, the piel (e.g., Gen 31:35. . . "he searched carefully"), and the hapax *niphal* in Obad. 6 "pillaged" suggests an English equivalent such as "rifle, ransack, plunder"' (Ceresko 1980:77).

132 Literally "girds" or "encircles".

133 Dust and ashes regularly occur together perhaps functioning like a hendiadys to emphasise human frailty (Gen. 18:27; Job 42:6). They can also appear separately, often as signs of mourning (Ezek. 27:30; Olyan 2004:29–35). Ceresko suggests that Job 30:19 is too brief and therefore supplies "God" as the unexpressed subject. Therefore, he follows a 'slightly different word division and revocalization of *wāʾetmaššēl kĕ* to *wāʾettōm (m)ūšlak* "and we perish, flung (into the slime and ashes)." The result offers a more vigorous image' (Ceresko 1980:79).

134 Lilly's article helpfully explores the metaphor of *Rûaḥ* in Job's depictions of his body in pain (Lilly 2016).

Habel states 'God . . . not only chews on Job's body like a wild beast (cf. 16:9), but as he writes in pain God also ties him up like a prisoner with his own clothes and chokes him with the collar around his neck' (Habel 1985:420). The reference to this happening at night specifically evokes tension and anxiety, as Fohrer remarks 'so kommt ihm der heftige Gliederschmerz vor, der mit fieberhaften Erscheinungen verbunden sein kann und nachts besonders quält' (Fohrer 1963:419). Even in the solitude of what ought to be time to rest, Job's experience of pain remains relentless and intense.

However, as before, the social consequences of the body and pain are just as important. For example, Newsom suggests here that the themes of honour and shame are central, arguing that 'sudden misfortune . . . could be read as divine abandonment or rejection, and as such, an invitation to rejection by the social community. . . . Job explicitly describes God's treatment of him in terms of dishonour and contempt' (Newsom 2009:191; cf. Schmidt 2017). This is clear from verse 19 where the character is cast into the 'mire' or 'clay' (חמר). This may exaggerate the emphasis of the character's current position which seems to dominate this violent description. This is potentially polysemous; it refers to dishonour and abasement given that חמר is one of a few potential terms for 'mud'[135]; however it is regularly used in Job to describe the body (Job 10:9; 13:12; 30:19; 33:6).[136] The latter is dominated by the metaphor of the potter-creator fashioning the human body from the earth (Isa. 29:16; 41:25; 45:9; 64:8; Jer. 18:4, 6). Therefore, interwoven with the theme of rejection and social shame is the idea of the undoing, or reversal, of the body's creation: The creature is returned to dust (עפר Ge. 3:19; Eccl. 3:20; 12:7).[137] Raz makes a similar point here arguing 'the root appears in the sense of making, crafting, or designing. . . . God's hands shift from an artisan's tool to a weapon; their once careful creating touch becoming painful and chaotic' (Raz 2014:90). Job 'dwells in "dust and ashes" and ends up being likened to them' (Lambert 2015:559). His bones are racked with pain and dried up in the wilderness, while the bones of the wicked flow with marrow (Job 21:24; 30:29–30). The image is very much that of an outsider; Job is cast out by the community, not just the deity. This motif of Job as 'outcast' initiated in Job 30:19 is emphatically repeated in 30:28–29. As Newsom suggests,

> Job thinks of his own radical change of status as a displacement, for his thinking is governed by the logic of his symbolic map. He has now become a "brother to jackals, a companion of ostriches" (30:29), animals traditionally associated with the places of desolation (Isa. 13:21–22; 34:13b) and

135 Along with the morphologically and phonologically similar עפר, (dry earth) which is sometimes associated with אפר (ashes).

136 Ironically, in 13:12 Job accuses his friends of giving advice that is like אפר (ashes) and in parallel like חמר (mud) (Job 13:12).

137 This is characteristic of the language in Job. For example, Fishbane and Perdue suggest that Job 3 might be interpreted as a counter cosmic incantation perhaps analogous to an undoing of creation (Fishbane 1971; Perdue 1994, 2007).

> the place of exclusion where Job located the "persons whipped out of the land." Up to this point, although Job has contrasted the "months of old" with his present misery, he has not attended to the dynamics that can apparently so suddenly displace a revered and respected noble from the center [*sic.*] of the social world to exclusion beyond its periphery.
>
> (Newsom 2009:191)[138]

Body shame, constructed through social 'meanings' (usually moralising) associated with illness, especially visible and obvious illness, and isolation are often connected. As Piers and Singer note, 'behind the feeling of shame stands not the fear of hatred but the fear of contempt which, on an even deeper level of the unconscious, spells fear of abandonment, the death by emotional starvation' (Piers and Singer 1953:53). Kohrt and Hruschka make a similar argument, suggesting that '[s]tigma worsens the experience of an illness and often leads to lack of access to care, social isolation and internalized feelings of shame, inferiority and fatalism' (Kohrt and Hruschka 2010:327). Unfortunately, for Job this fear has been realised. His language moves in chapter 30 from a focus on himself in his present social setting to himself and his pain, which is expressed through the deity attack metaphor, and finally to himself and his isolation.[139] The image of pain followed by social exclusion is truly melancholy; the character Job is presented as defeated, pathetic, and helpless. The metaphor about Job being a companion of ostriches and brother of jackals also works powerfully to heighten the pathos and tragedy of the scene. The low, booming howl of the ostrich, mirroring human sobbing, matched with the high-pitched wails of the jackal, mirroring human weeping.

The connection between the body and the social aspects of illness or pain is also concretised through examining the context before, as well as after, the metaphor. Immediately before the extended deity attack metaphor here we have a historical retrospect of Job's former life (Job 29) followed by a comparison with his present circumstances (Job 30:1–11). In this material, the emphatic focus is on Job's social standing and the loss of it. This nostalgic description of the character's fall from grace may be interpreted as the height of the tragic: Job has lost everything, even his bodily integrity, and it is without explanation.

Yet at the same time, this may also be considered so exaggerated that it quickly moves from the deeply tragic to the absurdly comic. Job, the supposedly blameless and upright character, proudly highlights his former status and importance (Job 29:7–25). The scene painted by Job of his former interaction with the councillors is full of self-promoting affectations and hyperbole. However,

138 Using animal imagery in lament to communicate isolation is not uncommon. For example, the psalmist describes himself using various animal metaphors such as 'a pelican of the desert and an owl of the wilderness' and 'a sparrow alone upon the house top' (Ps. 102:6–7; cf. Southwood 2019:236).

139 Greenstein makes an interesting comparison between Job's isolation and Jeremiah's (Greenstein 2004:99–100).

it is also rather confused and illogical, with several mixed metaphors.[140] In Job 29:21–25, the councillors 'listened, they waited, they opened their mouths, he [Job] smiled on them, they did not believe it, they did not disregard his favour, he chose their way, he sat as chief, he dealt as a king' (Clines 2006:993).[141] In these verses, Job speaks to the assembly and they remain silent, his 'wisdom was accepted like an oracle' and his opinions are as welcome and as well-received as spring rain (Rowley 1976:189). Job presided above the community both in status and wealth. He would sit 'enthroned (ישב) . . . as a king' in his blessedness and like a god he would 'tabernacle' (שכן) amongst them (Job 29:25; cf. Exod. 25:8; Jer. 7:3). Thus says the Job, that the light of his face would shine on the councillors and he lists his many gracious deeds (Job 29:24; 29:12, 15–16; cf. Num. 6:25). This is a picture which takes the term 'peculiar' to an entirely new level. As Clines points out, 'no town council in the world ever worked like that' (Clines 2006:993). It is not clear who the strange soliloquy is addressed to or how audiences are supposed to react to the incongruence of the character talking so very proudly about himself with such allusions of grandeur while sitting amongst the ashes. It is hardly surprising that his puffed-up and lordly soliloquy is met with laughter (Job 30:1). What does shine through, however, is Job's high opinion of himself. Indeed, the airs and graces only highlight that Job does not count himself among those vulnerable Others that he lists.[142] The sheer indignity of the sanctimonious Job becoming like one of 'them' is what he grieves about.

140 De Joode notices Job's tendency to mix metaphors, arguing that,

> In his distress the protagonist seems to muddle up a wide variety of metaphors without any apparent care for congruity. It is not uncommon to find a high density of different metaphorical expressions without any particular coherence in the Book of Job.
>
> (de Joode 2014:554)

However, we argue that the mixed metaphors that occur in Job's speeches only add to the comic nature of Job in a way not dissimilar to the characters who talk past one another. As the character becomes increasingly confused and irritated and the friends ever more frustrated, the audience gazes on knowing all along that the entire scenario is tantamount to an elaborate prank.

141 This is analogous, in some ways, with the depiction of Job in the Testament of Job. Here Job celebrates his own musical prowess (perhaps a literal rendering of the well-known English maxim 'blowing of one's own trumpet'). Job says that 'if my maidservants ever began murmuring, I would take up the psaltery and strum as payment in return' (Testament of Job 14:1–5). The depiction of Job's 'prowess' here assumes the maidservants must want to hear his playing of the psaltery. Yet at the same times he describes it as a 'payment', rather suggesting it is their punishment to have to listen. This is reminiscent of the Flanders and Swan 'Ill Wind' lyrics wherein the character's horn playing is so awful that the neighbours steal and hide the French horn.

142 As Olyan lucidly states,

> In this text, [Job 29:12–16] the blind and lame are listed with the poor; the afflicted; the widow; and other categories of persons cast as weak, vulnerable, and dependent, who are helped by a vigorous, autonomous Job before his own calamities incapacitate him. . . . By mentioning the blind and the lame with the poor, the widow, the stranger, and other dependent sufferers, Job 29:12–16 implicitly classifies blind and lame persons with these marginal groups, suggesting that they share the same devalued characteristics (e.g., weakness, dependency). These persons serve as a foil for Job, the ideal man, the paradigm of agency, strength, and autonomy.
>
> (Olyan 2008:6)

One interesting way that research concerning pain and illness narratives is helpful when considering the social exclusion of those who are ill is through the lens of social control and expectations of the 'sick role' (Parsons 1952). Parsons understood illness as a form of deviant behaviour because those who are ill are unable to fulfil their normal social duties and therefore deviate from the norm. Within Parsons's model, patients and healers had certain rights and obligations. One right of the patient was for a *genuine* illness to be understood as beyond the control of the patient and therefore blame should not be assigned. One obligation is for the sick person to seek help and get well as quickly as possible. As a consequence, illnesses that are thought to be 'self-induced' (e.g. because of the assumption of lack of self-control) often carry a negative symbolic meaning signalling deviance.[143] By analogy it is difficult for the character Job to conform to the expected 'sick role' that his friends assign him. This is because the audience has been told that Job is innocent and because the character clearly believes he is blameless.[144] Therefore, he is deviant because he is not following the advice of his friends and therefore it would seem that he is not attempting to re-adjust back to normal social duties. One important aspect of this now rather critiqued[145] model is the role that control plays.[146] Because

---

Perhaps a way to frame this rather egocentric disregard that Job has for those groups of Others who are, in fact, in a similar position to him is through Mazanderani, Locock, and Powell's concept of being 'differently the same' (Mazanderani *et al.* 2012). Mazanderani, Locock, and Powell highlight the epistemic significance of identification, arguing that a tension emerges 'between similarity and difference' when patient experiences are shared (Mazanderani *et al.* 2012:550). For the character Job, this tension is not only between himself and people who are in similar circumstances with whom he does not identify. It is also between his former and his present self.

143 Lupton articulates this argument lucidly:

> Some illnesses or diseases are not considered the 'fault' of the sick person . . . while others are laden with opprobrium which emphasizes the guilt of the victim for bringing the illness or disease upon themselves. Parsons' sick role model cannot be applied to these diseases, because one of his conditions, that the patient is not blamed for his or her illness, is not applicable. Such individuals . . . are still regarded as 'deviant' because they have allowed themselves to fall ill; they have ignored the moral proscriptions of society and are paying the consequences. Illness may thus be designated as originating from either accidental or wilful 'deviance', the sick person categorized as either 'innocent' or 'deserving' of his or her fate.
>
> (Lupton 1994:98)

144 The motif of Job's innocence stands as an organising principle for the entire book. Without the claim to innocence, the entire argument is undermined. Interestingly, however, as we have noted, while Job may be 'blameless' in the prologue, the character is certainly not depicted as flawless in the dialogues.

145 This often-cited model is critiqued by interpretivists. One major early critique, among many other subsequent challenges, was Goffman, who suggested that in 'total institutions' (e.g. asylums, where the institution took over all parts of an individual's life, identity is stripped and replaced with institutionalised identity), doctors have far more power and patients are far more likely to be submissive (Goffman 1961). This is neatly illustrated in the novel (and film) *One Flew Over the Cuckoo's Nest* where the audience knows that Randle is faking a mental illness but he still receives electroshock therapy and later a lobotomy. The power struggles between this character and the nurse are inevitably to be won by the nurse because of the institution.

146 The confrontational reality of chaos when faced with illness is a feature of many illness narratives. For example, Diski upon being diagnosed with terminal cancer reports about feeling embarrassed followed by the realisation that she is not able to control the illness (Diski 2016).

the sick role changes in reaction to the cultural meanings ascribed to illness, illness itself becomes a 'symbol' which 'serves to make moral distinctions in the attempt to control the social disorder it threatens' (Lupton 1994:99). Perceptions of the social and 'natural' order, and anxieties about its potential breakdown leading to chaos, underpin the question of control which emerges in some social reactions to illness. Lupton is, again, helpful here:

> The emergence of a new outbreak or disease becomes an occasion to question the tenets and moral values of everyday life. This is the case because: . . . most of the time . . . our dominant perception is of order. But every now and then chaos erupts . . . epidemics . . . when the symbolic nature of illness is asserted, in attempts to provide explanation, to 'make sense' of threatening events. Morality encroaches when rationality seems not to be espoused.
>
> (Lupton 1994:99)[147]

Therefore, familiar social meaning structures are destabilised and can sometimes completely break down in response to illness. One plausible reason that illness, especially visible and serious illness, evokes feelings of chaos, and in turn anxiety (which is alleviated by the quest for meaning), is because of the inevitability of death.[148] Pain and illness remind us that we are human, 'Sein-zum-Tode', as Heidegger phrased it (Carel 2016:151). The ease of health is a mode of omnipotence until it is taken away or threatened. This argument applies to Job and also, importantly, to his friends. Job directly experiences the chaos that the body's dysfunction and pain bring as his life unravels, and his first response is to curse the day he was born (rather than God) in Job 3, perhaps in an attempt to regain control. The theme of death, then, stubbornly continues throughout the dialogues, like a *basso ostinato*. Indeed, Matthewson suggests that Job is the 'most death-orientated book in the entire Bible' on account of the 'sheer variety and quantity of words used for "death"' and the "strategic narrative placement of depictions of death and conversations about death in

147 Carel makes a similar point, arguing that 'illness [can be experienced] as an unexpected calamity [which] leads to a sense of loss of control' and this 'makes the familiar world suddenly seem inherently unpredictable and uncontrollable'. The result is 'a further heightening of the sense of loss of control' (Carel 2016:42).

148 Otzen's analogy between chaos, death, and the primordial sea is relevant here,

> Otzen claims that common to ancient Israel and its neighbours is the idea that chaos . . . threatens the world of man. . . . The desert may force its way into good arable land and make it uninhabitable by man; death may 'ease his tentacles' into human existence in the forms of illness and sin, which can wreck man's existence; and death itself is the final reality to which every man is subject. Moreover, at any moment the primordial sea, which lies beneath the earth and above the firmament of heaven, may break through and annihilate the cosmos, as in fact happens in the story of the flood.
>
> (Pelham 2012a:139; citing Otzen *et al.* 1980)

the prose and poetic sections"' (Mathewson 2006:4).[149] The theme of death can be interpreted as a metaphor for Job's social exclusion, but it can also be understood literally as a reflection of Job's poor state of health, with 'his bone and flesh' being touched by Hasatan but 'only his life' preserved (Job 2:5–6). Indeed, the latter is how the Testament of Job interpreted the theme, with the entire setting being shortly before the character Job's death. Pelham notes the problematic nature of death for the character Job, arguing he 'is deeply distressed by his mortality. . . . Although in his speeches he sometimes wishes for death as an escape from his suffering, most of the time he sees death as problematic' (Pelham 2012a:115). The deity attack metaphor in this context is powerful because it highlights the chaotic lack of control that human beings are prone to. This is what is particularly confronting for Job's friends, reminding them of the fact that their ordered universe is potentially only ever a moment away from collapsing. After all, death is not merely the fate of the wicked, as Bildad and Eliphaz might like to imagine (Job 4:3–11; 18:13; cf. 9:23; Burns 1987).

Summary

Bearing in mind the hazards and methodological pitfalls associated with using research into expressions of pain and illness narratives, this chapter reflected on the large amount of the book of Job devoted to the character's body, his expressions of pain, and his friends' reactions to him. The examples cited from Job 6, 9, 16, 19, and 30 are some of the most shocking parts of the entire book of Job. This is partly because the responsibility for Job's body in pain is placed squarely at the foot of the deity through what we have labelled the 'deity attack metaphor'. Indeed, the deity is depicted in an anthropomorphic way as a direct prime mover of Job's body in pain.

This was clear in the example of piercing arrows with the playful polysemy of 'anger/poison' and the desire to be crushed in unrelenting pain in Job 6. The character Job sarcastically upended traditional language by imitating piety and mirroring's Eliphaz's language. In doing so a loaded point was made about the shortcomings of the retribution model. However, the strength of Job's argument was undermined by the irate and hyperbolic nature of his speech. This gave way to a turn from tragedy to comedy once we factored in the audience's knowledge of Job's innocence, a classic connection to the superiority theory. There was here, and in the entire dialogues, a double-vision: The perspective of the characters was, we noted, played out between themselves with Job, in the eyes of his friends, falsely putting on airs and graces, exalting in pain while at the same time attempting to maintain his honour. Therefore, from the perspective of the friends, the most logical next step was, we argued, to issue out advice on how Job should cope and seek to rectify his situation. Yet we observed how this perspective was juxtaposed with the perspective of the

149 Matthewson lists 47 different words for death, some of which are euphemisms.

audience, who were made aware that Job is innocent and that the whole setup was based on a frivolous gamble between Yahweh and the Accuser. The irony emerged through the fact that Job's puffed-up protestations about innocence and causation were partially true, thus totally undermining all the moralising advice his friends helpfully provided for him.

In this section we also noticed the significance of the connection between criminalisation and sickness and how Job's protestations of innocence might be understood as a broken norm for any audience members who might have sought to explain the character's position in the way that his friends do. Looking to research concerning illness experiences and expressions of pain, we noted the common tendency to moralise in the face of illness and pain. We also observed the prevalence of negative socially constructed assumptions about illness as a 'deviant' behaviour. Given that the book of Job seemed to resist the arguments of his friends, which align closely with the types of moralising themes emerging in the modern research we surveyed, we suggested the progressive, sophisticated nature of the book of Job in this respect. A final observation was made about speaking and power in terms of the significance of who speaks and for how long. Despite Job's position as a foreigner, fallen from status, and an exile from the world of health, his voice dominates the discussion, with the deity only getting a few chapters in at the very end.

In chapter 9 Job replies with a further deity attack metaphor to Bildad's 'Polyanna theology' concerning the sovereignty of God. Here, Job picks up on Bildad's moralising advice and parodies his example to the extreme in order to undermine it. We noticed the prominence of wind in this deity attack metaphor and for the comedy in general. A great wind רוח is part of the initial calamity in the prologue (Job 1:19), and both the friends and the character Job accuse each other of producing explanations that are windy and, by implication, thus lacking in substance. For example, Job compares Eliphaz's advice to 'wind' (Job 6:26). Bildad then asks Job how long the words of his mouth will be 'like a large wind' (Job 8:2). Eliphaz asks Job why he 'utters windy (רוח) knowledge' and fills his belly with the east wind (קדים Job 15:2). Job accuses his friends of attempting to comfort him with 'puff' and later of being 'ephemeral' (הבל Job 21:34; 27:12). Elihu is perhaps the most insulting here, accusing Job of 'opening his mouth in vain (הבל)' and 'multiplying worlds without knowledge' (Job 35:16), an insult reworked by Yahweh in the whirlwind and sarcastically parroted back at him when Job responds (Job 35:16; cf. 42:3). To some extent the entire discussion is as pointless as 'chasing after the wind', given that none of the characters will budge from their entrenched positions with the result that 'vexation of spirit' is multiplied as all the windbags repeatedly rehearse their views. Unlike Yahweh from the whirlwind (סופה), Job's windy words are likened merely to a storm (שערה). The importance of compassion within the listener during pain was used to analyse this deity attack metaphor. Particularly helpful was Throop's argument concerning pain and ethics wherein confronting suffering compels people to reorient their attention to the other 'as a subject and not an object of experience' (Throop 2010:223). Instead of using narrative and speech as a vehicle through which to emphasise connectedness, the friends focus on meaning in the sense of what is true and false. The effect that this has is to attempt to make Job into a passive victim of pain who needs care and advice. However, Job's resistance to his friends' advice, alongside his insistence on speech, puts him in a position of authority in the dialogue. As Mattingly and Garro argue, during illness 'narrative performance is capable of enacting a new, more empowered position' (Mattingly and Garro 2000:101).

Chapter 16 contained an extended section of the deity attack metaphor. Here God was imagined as a devouring animal searching for prey. The metaphor functioned as an idiom of distress, we argued, and symbolic protest on the part of the main character given the tragedy of his circumstances. The style at that point was, we suggested, highly satirical: A pompous imagined courtroom is portrayed in Job's speech, but his body, like an unhelpful alter ego, betrayed his claim about innocence. The scene was tragic but also ridiculous and comical. Nevertheless, it carried a profound message about the meanings early audiences might have associated with pain and body dysfunction. Job's wish for unrelenting pain back in chapter 6 was, we noted, all but exactly realised in chapter 16. The tension in the conversation between Job and his friends had risen by this point with insult hurled after insult by both sides. Job's friends interpreted him as tearing himself apart in rage and wondered why he assumed they're like dense animals. Perhaps their response here was an appropriately intense response to Job's own puffed-up and extreme deity attack language. However, we suggested that a more sympathetic way of interpreting the character was through recognition of the lack of acknowledgement he received from his friends, who pitted irreducible personal experience against a two-dimensional philosophy of retribution. Instead of compassion and sensitivity, moralising was offered, and the friends' entrenched and unchanging positions were therefore exposed.

It was observed that the presence of irony in modern illness narrative research was helpful for exposing the carnivalesque aspect of suffering wherein tragedy and comedy collide. Also interesting here was the problematic nature of the role of stigma in many illness narratives, requiring those who are ill to cope with a 'second illness' by managing tensions and information. Interestingly, at this point, the research on illness experiences couldn't have been further from what was depicted in the text: Job did not seem to feel any shame or inferiority, but instead seemed determined to annoy his friends, calling them useless quacks for whom it would be better if they were to shut up. Particularly curious here was the comical motif of windy words running through the drama, leading ultimately to the whirlwind. Both Job and the friends suggested the other's words lacked substance, often using the motif of wind and 'puff' (הבל). Before the whirlwind interrogation, Elihu, depicted as a figure of fun, popped up and announced that he was 'full of words, the spirit/wind within constrains [him]'. This playful statement, we suggested, was another example of advice from a pretentious and unsympathetic counsellor, but we also observed that it may be understood as scatological humour, a type of body humour that is a 'stock comic element in other cultures' and which Aristophanic works make much of (Lazarus 2014:218).

The deity attack metaphor continued in chapter 16 with renewed, and rather graphic, attention to the effects the attack had on Job's body. Here the deity, this time referred to as El, was portrayed through military metaphors, and again there was the presence of arrows and archers (similar to chapter 6). The way the attack was described by Job was very violent and shocking. We compared this with modern research concerning idioms of distress wherein the body is used in symbolic protest to communicate about suffering which cannot be articulated in certain socio-political contexts. This comparison seemed helpful through locating Job's body as the source of resistance to his friends' moralising advice. Furthermore, we noticed how the symbolic protest emphasised human suffering on Job's part over attempts to theorise about it by his friends. In addition, the violence of the language was very striking, possibly making it quite difficult for audiences and readers not to pay attention to Job. However, we also noted the double-edged tragic and comic nature of the speech at this point. Job's strange soliloquy-like speech here, 'Oh Earth, do not cover my blood', was, we suggested, in some ways comparable with Lear's mad frothing 'blow winds, and crack your cheeks!' Both characters address no one in particular with dramatic language, possibly raising the tension for audiences. Finally, we noticed the significant role of certainty with regard to agency. We observed the possibility that certainty about pain's causation was undermined by Job's extravagant protestations of pain being inflicted by a violent deity. This was because it removed the age-old 'why me/you' question that often accompanies illness by deflecting agency (and blame) away from Job. However, ironically, this achievement only raised further anxieties because it not only undermined the retribution model, it also undermined the very assumption of the deity's fairness in a just world. Unfortunately for his finger-pointing friends, Job's pain resists moralising and resists the assumption of a neat moral calculus of retribution.

Chapter 19 contained a medley of images concerned with the deity attack metaphor. Ironically, Job's call for help 'violence!' occurred precisely on account of divine violence. As with many sections in Job, traditional language was reworked here, possibly making the audience feel uncomfortable (but with the bonus of getting their attention). Here, occupying the epicentre of the calamity of traditions overthrown is the character Job, whose very presence represents a tragic social inversion: from rich, healthy, and honourable to poor, and unhealthy, having been brought to nothing by the gamble in the story's prologue. Tension mounted throughout the deity attack description until the comical anti-climax of Job's 'tent' – classic relief theory – versus the celestial army. Here the research into illness narratives was helpful, especially with regard to narrative which exposed oppressive and dominant narratives. We suggested that Job's speech here aligned well with this research. Indeed, through all the hot air, and waffling, and through all the windy words and moralising, Job's own voice raises its own serious moral questions about social attitudes towards those who are ill. Job's words here had an iconoclastic quality, partly because they are difficult to ignore: His body was, we suggested, proof of his claims. For his friends, Job's visibly dysfunctional body presents a problem wherein meaning must be found. Job has roared in pain, who will not fear? Job has spoken about his wounded body, who can but moralise? However, we recognised that the audience knows this is not the case because of the prologue. The question confronting audience members and readers who connect physical ill health with the deity's retribution here may have been 'Could it be the case that this peculiar misfit, this foreigner from Uz, who froths wildly about his body in pain and who thinks so highly of himself might actually be right?'

In chapter 30, a further graphic depiction of the deity attack metaphor occurred. Here the polysemous term 'mire' or 'clay' (חמר) was used, a term also regularly deployed to describe Job's body. Therefore, interwoven with the theme of rejection and social shame we noticed the idea of the undoing, or 'uncreation', to borrow Blenkinsopp's term, of the body, Job, which we observed, was returned to clay (Blenkinsopp 2011:21–22, 37–46). The emphasis here on the social exclusion caused by Job's body in pain was particularly tragic. This was highlighted through the selection of animals the character chooses as companions: ostriches, whose booming howls mirror human sobbing, and jackals, whose high-pitched wails mirror human weeping. Nevertheless, even here we saw tragedy tinged with comedy. Immediately before the character slipped over into the deity attack metaphor, the character Job seemed to have a fit of nostalgia (Clines 1998b:792–800). Job proudly highlighted his former status and importance with self-promoting affectation. Job, we are informed, would sit 'enthroned (ישב) . . . as a king' in his blessedness and like a god he would 'tabernacle' (שכן) amongst them (Job 29:25; cf. Exod. 25:8; Jer. 7:3). Thus says Job, the light of his face would shine on the councillors and he listed his many gracious deeds (Job 29:24; 29:12, 15–16; cf. Num. 6:25). We observed that this picture seemed rather peculiar. What was comical about the scene, however, we argued, was the irony of the fact that Job did not count himself among those vulnerable Others that he listed in the chapter: The sheer indignity of the sanctimonious Job becoming like one of 'them' is what he grieved about. Therefore, embedded within his nostalgic self-pity the character experienced, we observed an underlying sense of hubris. Even at his lowest and most tragic, Job still defiantly clings to his former status and power and in doing so emphasises his own incongruence.

We also noted the interpretative possibilities provided by comparing Parson's sick role, wherein one is expected to do all one can to get better once unwell, with Job (noting the critique of Parson's sick role). Job, we suggested, was deviant in the eyes of his friends (and possibly audiences) because he does not follow their advice. Therefore, we suggested, it may seem that he is not attempting to readjust back to normal social duties. We observed the research that described illness as a symbol that makes moral distinctions by attempting to control the social disorder it threatens. The destabilising nature of pain and illness, we suggested, evokes feelings of chaos and anxiety, partly because of the reminder about mortality. Indeed, the theme of death, we suggested, stubbornly continued throughout the dialogues, like a *basso ostinato*.

Bibliography

Aimers, G.J., 2012. "Give the devil his due": The satanic agenda and social justice in the book of Job. *Journal for the Study of the Old Testament*, **37**(1), pp. 57–66.

Aitken, J., 2013. The inevitability of reading Job through lamentations. In: K. Dell and W. Kynes, ed, *Reading Job intertextually*. New York: Bloomsbury, pp. 204–215.

Annus, A. and Lenzi, A., 2010. *Ludlul bēl nēmeqi: The standard Babylonian poem of the righteous sufferer.* Helsinki: Neo-Assyrian Text Corpus Project.

Balentine, S.E., 2015. *Have you considered my servant Job? Understanding the biblical archetype of patience.* Columbia: University of South Carolina Press.

Basson, A., 2008. Just skin and bones: The longing for wholeness of the body in the book of Job. *Vetus Testamentum*, **58**(3), pp. 287–299.

Bastiaens, J.C., 1997. The language of suffering in Job 16–19 and the suffering servant passages of Deutero-Isaiah. In: W. Beuken, J.V.J. Ruiten and M. Vervenne, eds, *Studies in the book of Isaiah: Festschrift Willem A.M. Beuken*. Leuven: Leuven University Press, pp. 421–432.

Berlin, A. and Knorina, L.V., 2008. *The dynamics of biblical parallelism*. Rev. and expanded edn. Grand Rapids, MI; Cambridge; Dearborn, MI: William B. Eerdmans, Dove Booksellers.

Blenkinsopp, J., 2011. *Creation, un-creation, re-creation: A discursive commentary on genesis 1–11*. London; New York: T&T Clark.

Blommerde, A.C.M., 1969. *Northwest semitic grammar and Job*. Rome: Pontifical Biblical Institute.

Blumenthal, D.R., 1993. *Facing the abusing god: A theology of protest*. 1st edn. Louisville, KY: Westminster John Knox Press.

Burnight, J., 2014a. Does Eliphaz really begin "gently"? An intertextual reading of Job 4, 2–11. *Biblica*, **95**(3), pp. 347–370.

Burns, J., 1987. The identity of death's first-born (Job xviii 13). *Vetus Testamentum*, **37**, p. 362.

Carel, H., 2016. *Phenomenology of illness*. 1st edn. Oxford: Oxford University Press.

Carel, H. and Cooper, R.V., 2013. *Health, illness and disease: Philosophical essays.* Durham: Acumen.

Carter, J.A., 2017. *Inside the whirlwind: The book of job through African eyes.* Eugene, OR: Pickwick Publications.

Ceresko, A.R., 1980. *Job 29–31 in the light of Northwest semitic: A translation and philological commentary.* Rome: Biblical Institute Press.

Charon, R., 2006. *Narrative medicine: Honoring the stories of illness.* Oxford; New York: Oxford University Press.

Claassens, L.J., 2015. Tragic laughter: Laughter as resistance in the book of Job. *Interpretation: A Journal of Bible and Theology*, **69**(2), pp. 143–155.

Clifton, G., 2011. Pain without incarnation: Derrida, and the book of Job. *Journal of Beckett Studies*, **20**(2), pp. 149–171.

Clines, D.J.A., 1989. *Job 1–20*. Dallas, TX: Word Books.

Clines, D.J.A., 1998a. *On the way to the postmodern: Old Testament essays, 1968–1998*. Sheffield: Sheffield Academic.

Clines, D.J.A., 1998b. The arguments of Job's three friends. In: D.J.A. Clines, ed, *On the way to the postmodern: Old Testament essays, 1967–1998. Volume II*. Sheffield: Sheffield Academic Press, pp. 719–734.

Clines, D.J.A., 2006. *Job 21–37*. Nashville: Thomas Nelson.

Clow, B., 2001. Who's afraid of Susan Sontag? Or, the myths and metaphors of cancer reconsidered. *Social History of Medicine*, **14**(2), pp. 293–312.

Dahl, E., 2016. Job and the problem of physical pain: A phenomenological reading. *Modern Theology*, **32**(1), pp. 45–59.

Das, V., 1996. Language and body: Transactions in the construction of pain. *Dædalus: Journal of the American Academy of Arts and Sciences*, **125**(1), pp. 67–91.

De Joode, J., 2014. The body and its boundaries: The coherence of conceptual metaphors for Job's distress and lack of control. *Zeitschrift fur die Alttestamentliche Wissenschaft*, **126**(4), pp. 554–569.

Dell, K.J., 2002. *Job.* Oxford: Bible Reading Fellowship.

Dhont, M., 2017. *Style and context of old Greek Job.* Leiden; Boston: Brill.

Diski, J., 2016. *In gratitude.* London: Bloomsbury.

Dolezal, L., 2015. The phenomenology of shame in the clinical encounter. *Medicine, Health Care and Philosophy*, **18**(4), pp. 567–576.

Douglas, M., 1966. *Purity and danger: An analysis of concepts of pollution and taboo.* London: Routledge & Kegan Paul.

Driver, G.R., 1955. Problems in the Hebrew text of Job. *Supplements to Vetus Testamentum*, **3**, p. 72.

Driver, S.R. and Gray, G.B., 1921. *A critical and exegetical commentary on the book of Job: Together with a new translation.* Edinburgh: T&T Clark.

Erickson, A., 2013. "Without my flesh I will see God": Job's rhetoric of the body. *Journal of Biblical Literature*, **132**(2), pp. 295–313.

Evans-Pritchard, E., 1937. *Witchcraft, oracles and magic among the Azande.* Oxford: Clarendon Press.

Ferngren, G.B., 2014. *Medicine and religion: A historical introduction.* Baltimore: Johns Hopkins University Press.

Ferrari, F.M., 2011. *Health and religious rituals in South Asia: Disease, possession, and healing.* London: Routledge.

Fisch, H., 1999. *The biblical presence in Shakespeare, Milton, and Blake: A comparative study.* Oxford: Clarendon Press.

Fishbane, M., 1971. Jeremiah Iv 23–26 and Job Iii 3–13: A recovered use of the creation pattern. *Vetus Testamentum*, **21**(2), pp. 151–167.

Fohrer, G., 1963. *Das Buch Hiob.* 1. Aufl. edn. Gütersloh: Gütersloher Verlagshaus G. Mohn.

Fortes, M. and Horton, R., 1983. *Oedipus and job in West African religion.* Reissued edn. Cambridge: Cambridge University Press.

Fox, M.V., 2011. Reading the tale of Job. In: J.C. Exum, D.J.A. Clines and E.J. Van Wolde, eds, *A critical engagement: Essays on the Hebrew Bible in honour of J. Cheryl Exum.* Sheffield: Sheffield Phoenix Press, pp. 145–162.

Frank, A.W., 1995. *The wounded storyteller: Body, illness, and ethics.* Chicago; London: University of Chicago Press.

Gabe, J. and Monaghan, L.F., 2013. *Key concepts in medical sociology.* 2nd edn. Los Angeles; London: Sage.

Gard, D., 1952. *The exegetical method of the Greek translator of the book of Job.* Philadelphia: Society of Biblical Literature.

Garro, L.C., 1994. Narrative representations of chronic illness experience: Cultural models of illness, mind, and body in stories concerning the temporomandibular joint (TMJ). *Social Science & Medicine*, **38**(6), pp. 775–788.

Goffman, E., 1961. *Asylums: Essays on the social situation of mental patients and other inmates.* London: Penguin Books.

Goffman, E., 1968. *Stigma: Notes on the management of spoiled identity*. Harmondsworth: Penguin.

Good, B., 1994. *Medicine, rationality, and experience*. Cambridge: Cambridge University Press.

Good, M.D., 1992. *Pain as human experience: An anthropological perspective*. Berkeley; London: University of California Press.

Gordis, R., 1978. *The book of Job: Commentary, new translation and special studies*. New York: Jewish Theological Seminary of America.

Grabbe, L.L., 1977. *Comparative philology and the text of job: A study in methodology*. Missoula, MT: Published by Scholars Press for the Society of Biblical Literature.

Greenstein, E.L., 2004. Jeremiah as an inspiration to the poet of Job. In: H. Huffman, J. Kaltner and L. Stulman, eds, *Inspired speech: Prophecy in the ancient Near East. Essays in Honor of Herbert B. Huffmon*. London; New York: T&T Clark, pp. 98–110.

Greenstein, E.L., 2007. On my skin and in my flesh: Personal experience as a source of knowledge in the book of Job. In: K.F. Kravitz and D.M. Sharon, eds, *Bringing the hidden to light: Studies in Honor of Stephen A. Geller*. Winona Lake, IN: Eisenbrauns, pp. 63–77.

Greenstein, E.L., 2014. The invention of language in the poetry of Job. In: J.K. Aitken, J.M.S. Clines and C.M. Maier, eds, *Interested readers: Essays on the Hebrew Bible in honor of David J. A. Clines*. Atlanta, GA: Society of Biblical Literature, pp. 331–346.

Greenstein, E.L., 2018. Metaphors of illness and wellness in Job. In: S.C. Jones and C.R. Roy, eds, *"When the morning stars sang": Essays in honor of Choon Leong Seow on the occasion of his sixty-fifth birthday*. Berlin; Boston: Walter de Gruyter, pp. 39–50.

Guillaume, P., 2008. Dismantling the deconstruction of Job. *Journal of Biblical Literature*, **127**(3), pp. 491–499.

Habel, N.C., 1977. "Only the jackal is my friend": On friends and redeemers in Job. *Interpretation,* **31**(3), p. 227.

Habel, N.C., 1985. *The book of Job: A commentary*. London: SCM.

Hawley, L.R., 2018. *Metaphor competition in the book of Job*. Göttingen: Vandenhoeck & Ruprecht.

Hefferon, K., Grealy, M. and Mutrie, N., 2009. Post-traumatic growth and life threatening physical illness: A systematic review of the qualitative literature. *British Journal of Health Psychology*, **14**(2), pp. 343–378.

Heinen, K., 1979. *Der unverfügbare Gott: Das Buch I Job*. Stuttgart: Verlag Katholisches Bibelwerk.

Henderson, J., 1991. *The maculate muse: Obscene language in attic comedy*. 2nd edn. New York: Oxford University Press.

Hordern, J., 2017. Compassion in primary and community healthcare. In: A. Papanikitas and J. Spicer, eds, *Handbook of primary care ethics*. Boca Raton, FL: CRC Press, pp. 25–34.

Hurwitz, B. and Bates, V., 2016. The roots and ramifications of narrative in modern medicine. In: A. Whitehead, A. Woods, S. Atkinson, J. Macnaughton and J. Richards, eds, *The Edinburgh companion to the critical medical humanities*. Edinburgh: Edinburgh University Press, pp. 559–576.

Hyun, S.W.T., 2013. *Job the unfinalizable: A Bakhtinian reading of Job 1–11*. Leiden: Brill.

Jackson, J.E., 2000. *"Camp pain": Talking with chronic pain patients*. Philadelphia, PA: University of Pennsylvania Press.

Jackson, M.A., 2012. *Comedy and feminist interpretation of the Hebrew Bible: A subversive collaboration*. Oxford: Oxford University Press.

Jarick, J., 2014. Ecclesiastes among the comedians. In: K. Dell and W. Kynes, eds, *Reading Ecclesiastes intertextually*. London: Bloomsbury, T&T Clark, pp. 176–188.

Jones, A., 2010. Justice and biblical interpretation beyond subjectivity and self-determination: A contrapuntal reading on the theme of suffering in the book of Job. *Political Theology*, **11**(3), pp. 431–452.

Jones, S.C., 2013. Corporeal discourse in the book of Job. *Journal of Biblical Literature*, **132**(4), pp. 845–863.

Jurecic, A., 2012. *Illness as narrative.* Pittsburgh, PA: University of Pittsburgh Press.

Kermani, N., 2011. *The terror of God: Attar, Job and the metaphysical revolt.* Cambridge: Polity.

Kirmayer, L.J., 1988. Mind and body as metaphors: Hidden values in biomedicine. *Biomedicine Explained*, **1**, pp. 57–92.

Kleinman, A., 1988. *The illness narratives: Suffering, healing and the human condition.* New York: Basic Books.

Kohrt, B. and Hruschka, D., 2010. Nepali concepts of psychological trauma: The role of idioms of distress, ethnopsychology and ethnophysiology in alleviating suffering and preventing stigma. *Culture, Medicine, and Psychiatry*, **34**(2), pp. 322–352.

Krüger, T., 2007. Did Job repent? In: T. Krüger, M. Oeming, K. Schmid and C. Uehlinger, eds, *Das Buch Hiob und seine Interpretationen: Beiträge zum Hiob-Symposium auf dem Monte Verita vom 14–19 August 2005.* Zürich: Theologischer Verlag Zürich, pp. 217–230.

Kugel, J.L., 1981. *The idea of biblical poetry: Parallelism and its history.* New Haven; London: Yale University Press.

Kutz, I., 2000. Job and his "doctors": Bedside wisdom in the book of Job. *British Medical Journal*, **321**(7276), pp. 1613–1615.

Kynes, W., 2011. Beat your parodies into swords, and your parodied books into spears: A new paradigm for parody in the Hebrew Bible. *Biblical Interpretation*, **19**(3), pp. 276–310.

Lambek, M. and Antze, P., 2004. *Illness and irony: On the ambiguity of suffering in culture.* New York; Oxford: Berghahn Books.

Lambert, D.A., 2015. The book of Job in ritual perspective. *Journal of Biblical Literature*, **134**(3), pp. 557–575.

Lazarus, B.M., 2014. *Humanist comic elements in Aristophanes and the Old Testament.* Piscataway: Gorgias Press.

Lilly, I., 2016. Rûaḥ embodied: Job's internal disease from the perspective of Mesopotamian medicine. In: A. Weissenreider, ed, *Borders: Terms, ideologies, performances.* Tübingen: Mohr Siebeck, pp. 323–336.

Lindquist, G., 2006. *Conjuring hope: Magic and healing in contemporary Russia.* New York; Oxford: Berghahn Books.

Lipshitz, Y., 2015. Biblical Shakespeare: King Lear as Job on the Hebrew stage. *New Theatre Quarterly: NTQ*, **31**(4), pp. 359–371.

Littlewood, R. and Lynch, R., 2016. *Cosmos, Gods and madmen: Frameworks in the anthropologies of medicine.* New York: Berghahn Books.

Lloyd, G.E.R., 2003. *In the grip of disease: Studies in the Greek imagination.* Oxford: Oxford University Press.

Lupton, D., 1994. *Medicine as culture: Illness, disease and the body in Western societies.* London: Sage.

Lupton, D., 2012. *Fat.* Milton Park; Abingdon, Oxon; New York, NY: Routledge.

Lupton, D., 2014. The pedagogy of disgust: The ethical, moral and political implications of using disgust in public health campaigns. *Critical Public Health*, pp. 1–14.

Luther, M. and Bornkamm, H., 1989. *Luthers Vorreden zur Bibel.* 3. Aufl edn. Göttingen: Vandenhoeck & Ruprecht.

Mathewson, D., 2006. *Death and survival in the book of Job: Desymbolization and traumatic experience.* New York: T&T Clark.

Mattingly, C. and Garro, L.C., 2000. *Narrative and the cultural construction of illness and healing.* Berkeley; London: University of California Press.

Mazanderani, F., Locock, L. and Powell, J., 2012. Being differently the same: The mediation of identity tensions in the sharing of illness experiences. *Social Science & Medicine*, **74**(4), pp. 546–553.

McCarthy, C., 1981. *The Tiqqune sopherim and other theological corrections in the Masoretic text of the Old Testament.* Freiburg, Schweiz: Göttingen: Universitätsverlag Vandenhoeck & Ruprecht.

Melcher, S.J., Parsons, M.C. and Yong, A., 2017. *The Bible and disability: A commentary.* Waco, TX: Baylor University Press.

Merleau-Ponty, M. and Smith, C., 2002. *Phenomenology of perception.* London; New York: Routledge.

Merton, R.K., 1976. *Sociological ambivalence and other essays.* New York: Free Press.

Moore, M., 1993. Job's texts of terror. *Catholic Biblical Quarterly*, **55**(4), pp. 662–675.

Moss, C.R., 2012. Christly possession and weakened bodies: Reconsideration of the function of Paul's thorn in the flesh (2 Cor. 12:7–10). *Journal of Religion, Disability & Health*, **16**(4), pp. 319–333.

Nemo, P., 1998. *Job and the excess of evil.* Pittsburgh: Duquesne University Press.

Newsom, C.A., 1999. Job and his friends – a conflict of moral imaginations (An examination of a scriptural model of divine moral answerability). *Interpretation-A Journal of Bible and Theology*, **53**(3), pp. 239–253.

Newsom, C.A., 2003a. *The book of Job: A contest of moral imaginations.* New York; Oxford: Oxford University Press.

Newsom, C.A., 2003b. "The consolations of God": Assessing Job's friends across a cultural abyss. In: J.C. Exum and H.G.M. Williamson, eds, *Reading from right to left: Essays on the Hebrew Bible in honour of David J.A. Clines.* Sheffield: Sheffield Academic Press, pp. 347–358.

Newsom, C.A., 2009. *The book of Job.* Oxford: Oxford University Press.

Nichter, M., 1981. Idioms of distress: Alternatives in the expression of psychosocial distress: A case study from South India. *Culture, Medicine and Psychiatry*, **5**(4), pp. 379–408.

Nichter, M., 2010. Idioms of distress revisited. *Culture, Medicine, and Psychiatry*, **34**(2), pp. 401–416.

Noegel, S.B., 1996. Janus parallelism in Job and its literary significance. *Journal of Biblical Literature*, **115**(2), pp. 313–320.

Nussbaum, M.C., 1998. *Cultivating humanity: A classical defense of reform in liberal education.* Cambridge, MA; London: Harvard University Press.

Ochs, E. and Capps, L., 1996. Narrating the self. *Annual Review of Anthropology*, **25**(1), pp. 19–43.

Olyan, S.M., 2004. *Biblical mourning: Ritual and social dimensions.* Oxford; New York: Oxford University Press.

Olyan, S.M., 2008. *Disability in the Hebrew Bible: Interpreting mental and physical differences.* Cambridge: Cambridge University Press.

Oshima, T., 2014. *Babylonian poems of pious sufferers: Ludlul Bēl Nēmeqi and the Babylonian Theodicy.* Tübingen: Mohr Siebeck.

Otzen, B., Gottlieb, H. and Jeppesen, K., 1980. *Myths in the Old Testament.* London: SCM.

Parsons, T., 1952. *The social system.* London: Tavistock Publications.

Pelham, A., 2010. Job as comedy, revisited. *Journal for the Study of the Old Testament*, **35**(1), pp. 89–112.

Pelham, A., 2012a. *Contested creations in the book of Job: The-world-as-it-ought-and-ought-not-to-be.* Leiden: Brill.

Pelham, A., 2012b. Job's crisis of language: Power and powerlessness in Job's oaths. *Journal for the Study of the Old Testament*, **36**(3), pp. 333–354.

Perdue, L.G., 1991. *Wisdom in revolt: Metaphorical theology in the book of Job.* Sheffield: Almond Press.

Perdue, L.G., 1994. Metaphorical theology in the book of Job: Theological anthropology in the first cycle of Job's speeches (Job 3; 6–7; 9–10). In: W.A.M. Beuken, ed, *The book of Job*. Leuven: Leuven University Press, pp. 129–156.

Perdue, L.G., 2007. Creation in the dialogues between Job and his opponents. In: T. Krüger, M. Oeming, K. Schmid and C. Uehlinger, eds, *Das Buch Hiob und seine Interpretationen: Beiträge zum Hiob-Symposium auf dem Monte Verita vom 14–19 August 2005*. Zürich: Theologischer Verlag Zürich, pp. 197–216.

Piccin, M. and Worthington, M., 2015. Schizophrenia and the problem of suffering in the Ludlul hymn to Marduk. *Revue d'Assyriologie et d'Archeologie Orientale*, **109**(1), pp. 113–124.

Piers, G. and Singer, M.B., 1953. *Shame and guilt; a psychoanalytic and a cultural study.* Springfield, IL: Thomas.

Pinker, A., 2017. Job's enemies in 30,17–18. *Scandinavian Journal of the Old Testament*, **31**(2), pp. 161–184.

Pope, M.H., 1965. *Job*. Garden City, NY: Doubleday.

Raffel, S., 2013. *The method of metaphor.* Bristol; Chicago: Intellect.

Raphael, R., 2004. Things too wonderful: A disabled reading of Job. *Perspectives in Religious Studies*, **4**(31), pp. 399–424.

Raz, Y., 2014. Reading pain in the book of Job. In: L. Batnitzke and I. Pardes, eds, *The book of Job: Aesthetics, ethics, hermeneutics.* Berlin: Walter de Gruyter, pp. 77–98.

Reynolds, E., 2016. Addiction and the duality of the self in a North American Religio-therapeutic community. In: R. Littlewood and R. Lynch, eds, *Cosmos, Gods and madmen: Frameworks in the anthropologies of medicine.* New York: Berghahn Books, pp. 116–132.

Rorty, R., 1989. *Contingency, irony, and solidarity.* Cambridge: Cambridge University Press.

Rowley, H.H., 1976. *Job.* Rev. edn. London: Oliphants.

Sanders, J.A., 2009. The book of Job and the origins of Judaism. *Biblical Theology Bulletin*, **39**(2), pp. 60–70.

Scarry, E., 1985. *The body in pain: The making and unmaking of the world.* New York; Oxford: Oxford University Press.

Schipper, J., 2010. Healing and silence in the epilogue of Job. *Word & World*, **30**(1), pp. 16–22.

Schmidt, U., 2017. Augen war ich für den Blinden. . . (Hi 29,15) Mensch, Körper und Gesellschaft in Hiob 29 und 30. *Vetus Testamentum*, **67**(1), pp. 87–104.

Schroder, E.F., 2015. Reading the Bible positively popular reading of the Bible with people living with HIV/ AIDS in Brazil. *Missionalia: Southern African Journal of Missiology*, **43**(3), pp. 568–582.

Schulze, B. and Angermeyer, M.C., 2003. Subjective experiences of stigma: A focus group study of schizophrenic patients, their relatives and mental health professionals. *Social Science & Medicine*, **56**(2), pp. 299–312.

Seow, C.L., 2011. Orthography, textual criticism, and the poetry of Job. *Journal of Biblical Literature*, **130**(1), pp. 63–85.

Seow, C.L., 2013. *Job 1–21: Interpretation and commentary.* Grand Rapids, MI: William B. Eerdmans.

Solomon, A., 2013. *Far from the tree: Parents, children and the search for identity.* London: Chatto & Windus.

Sontag, S., 1969. *Styles of radical will.* New York: Farrar, Straus and Giroux.

Sontag, S., 1990. *Illness as metaphor and aids and its metaphors.* New York: Picador.

Southwood, K.E., 2018. "You are all quacks; if only you would shut up" (Job 13:4b-5a): Sin and illness in the sacred and the secular, the ancient and the modern. *Theology*, **121**(2), pp. 84–91.

Southwood, K.E., 2019. Metaphor, illness, and identity in Psalms 88 and 102. *Journal for the Study of the Old Testament*, **2**, pp. 228–246.

Southwood, K.E., Forthcoming. The "innards" in the Psalms and job as metaphors for illness. *Horizons in Biblical Literature.*

Strawn, B.A., 2005. *What is stronger than a lion? Leonine image and metaphor in the Hebrew Bible and the ancient Near East.* Fribourg: Göttingen: Academic Press, Vandenhoeck & Ruprecht.

Tham, J., 2013. Communicating with sufferers: Lessons from the book of Job. *Christian Bioethics*, **19**(1), pp. 82–99.

Throop, C.J., 2010. *Suffering and sentiment: Exploring the vicissitudes of experience and pain in yap.* Berkeley, CA; London: University of California Press.

Tilford, N.L., 2016. When people have Gods: Sensory mimicry and divine agency in the book of Job. *Hebrew Bible and Ancient Israel*, **5**(1), pp. 42–58.

Tomlinson, J., 2017. Power, prejudice and professionalism: Fat politics and medical education. In: A. Papanikitas and J. Spicer, eds, *Handbook of primary care ethics.* Boca Raton, FL: CRC Press, pp. 159–168.

Van Hecke, P., 2013. "I melt away and will no longer live": The use of metaphor in Job's self-descriptions. In: A. Labahn, ed, *Conceptual metaphors in poetic texts: Proceedings of the metaphor research group of the European association of biblical studies in Lincoln 2009.* Piscataway: Gorgias Press, pp. 69–90.

Verbin, N., 2010. *Divinely abused: A philosophical perspective on Job and his kin.* London; New York: Continuum.

Von Rad, G., 1970. *Weisheit in Israel.* Neukirchen-Vluyn: Neukirchener Verlag.

Waskul, D.D. and Vannini, P., 2006. *Body/embodiment: Symbolic interaction and the sociology of the body.* Aldershot: Ashgate.

Whedbee, J., 1977. The comedy of Job. *Semeia*, **7**, pp. 1–39.

Williams, H., 2012. *Kant and the end of war: A critique of just war theory.* London: Palgrave Macmillan.

Witte, M., 2007. The Greek book of Job. In: T. Krüger, M. Oeming, K. Schmid and C. Uehlinger, eds, *Das Buch Hiob und seine Interpretationen: Beiträge zum Hiob-Symposium auf dem Monte Verita vom 14–19 August 2005.* Zürich: Theologischer Verlag Zürich, pp. 33–54.

Worsley, P., 1982. Non-Western medical systems. *Annual Review of Anthropology*, **11**, pp. 315–348.

3 The tyranny of tradition

Introduction

Stordalen argues that in the dialogues in Job 'the voice most intensely permeating the monologues in the book, is indeed that of tradition' or 'the implied voice of tradition' (Stordalen 2006:30). While there are not direct quotations from traditional works, that is, material including, but not limited to, Deuteronomy, Proverbs, Psalms, and other texts wherein retribution features, it is nevertheless implicit that Job's friends speak with a high level of confidence. This indicates their reliance on a well-established, authoritative source, which makes their moralising all the worse. Job is expected to be familiar with what they are telling him, and he even protests 'I have intelligence as well as you . . . who does not know such things as these?' (Job 12:3). In response, as we have seen previously, and shall see in the following sections, Job 'attacks the very foundations of the Deuteronomist's worldview, employs polytheistic imagery, baroque anthropomorphisms, and unfiltered mythological motifs' (Aaron 2001:57, n.22). This chapter focuses on the many instances wherein the deity attack metaphor goes hand in hand with the motif of unwanted divine surveillance. This motif is rather prominent in several sections of Job. One well-recognised example of this that we will analyse is Job 7:12–20 with its accusation that the deity is the 'watcher of humanity' and the ironically reworked allusion to Psalm 8. Here, the deity's attack is not quite as violent as the material analysed in the former chapter. Instead misery is inflicted on Job through the means of unwanted visions and dreams and then followed by the surveillance motif. Similarly, in Job 10:14–17, the deity attack metaphor emerges alongside the motif of surveillance: Job is 'watched' and 'afflicted' before being hunted by a lion-like deity. Two further, smaller, instances of watching and attacking occur. These are in Job 13:27–28 and 14:3–6 wherein the former example includes a deity who both hides his face but also watches and restricts Job's movement, and the latter wherein the deity's sight is oppressive to Job. In both examples, Job wishes to be hidden from the accusatory divine gaze, a stark reversal of the traditional psalmist's often-asked questions about the deity's hiding the face from him and request to be hidden in the protective shadow of the deity's wings. Instead of watching over Job with concern, the deity gaze is detached and unemotional, perhaps like the clinical gaze. However, unlike the clinical

DOI: 10.4324/9781003029489-3

gaze, the deity's gaze is dangerous and suddenly gives way to violent attacks on the character Job. Why might the motif of divine scrutiny sometimes be coupled with the more regular metaphor of the deity attack? What is the significance of this recurrent motif, and how does it relate to and rework other aspects of the biblical material? What is the nature of the surveillance? These questions will be addressed in the following sections wherein we shall proceed using the same guiding methodological principles set out in the first chapter. Therefore, we will analyse with close attention to Job's body and communication about pain and his friends' reactions to him.

'Am I Yam?! Or Tannin': creation and the deity surveillance metaphor in Job 7

The allusion to Psalm 8 in Job 7:17–18 is perhaps one of the most popular examples of how Job reworks and reuses traditional material such as Psalms (and Lamentations). However, the material around this allusion is also particularly interesting, especially in terms of how Job communicates about his body. Shortly after the deity attack metaphor which we have explored already in Job 6, we encounter the character towards the beginning of chapter 7 mournfully lamenting his body's demise (Job 7:4–5). Rowley's observations about these verses are interesting, drawing together observations which emphasise the somatic and physical character of the verses.

> Dhorme thinks the meaning here is 'the rambling fancies of the mind', but it is more likely that it refers to the physical restlessness of the sufferer in the night. Despite the uncertainty of detail in the verse, the general sense is clear. Job is describing the ceaseless pain and torture his malady imposes on him, so that neither by night nor by day can he find any relief.
>
> (Rowley 1976:66)

The character goes on to report that his flesh is clothed with worms and dirt and his skin cracks open and festers, and the character communicates about his condition using metaphor, a mode of expression which – as we have demonstrated – dominates his speeches about pain. As Habel notes, the 'description of this physical condition is given in terms of a clothing metaphor rather than in medical language' (Habel 1985:159). Alongside these problems the author also has Job report about nocturnal restlessness, perhaps an allusion to *Ludlul Bēl Nēmequ*, or to Deuteronomy's covenant curses which align closely with retributive justice.[1] Job here is 'sated with sleeplessness', an ironic reversal of the

1 *Ludlul* refers to being unable to relax at night because of the tormentor and of twisted sinews and torn limbs. Similarly, one of Deuteronomy's curses is to dread the night and to be unsure of life (Deut. 28:66–67). Another less widespread but nevertheless rather interesting parallel may be with the *Utukkū Lemnūtu* (*Udug-ḫul*) incantations wherein we have this example,

usual use of the verb שבע, which Raz describes as an 'oxymoron' wherein 'the verb is turned inside out, so as to mean the opposite of its regular referent' (Job 7:4; Raz 2014:85). Later in the same chapter the deity surveillance metaphor appears.

> Am I Yam?! Or Tannin?! That you should set a watch over me? Whenever I say "my couch will comfort me, my bed will bear my complaint" Then you terrify me with dreams and frighten me with visions. So that my throat would choose strangulation, [and choose] death rather than my bones. I reject [life]![2] I would not live for eternity! Leave me! For my days are a wisp (הֶבֶל).[3]
>
> (Job 7:12–16)

There is a peculiar concentration of references to divine surveillance, with an implied deity attack metaphor here, with Job being set up as a target (cf. Job 6; 16). The entire chapter as a whole has an abundance of verbs of sight, as Seow

---

šēdu lemnu ša kīma melê ikattamu
amēlu mutalliku irurūma amēlu šu'āti ittarū
napḫar šerānīšu ilmadūma ašar marṣi irtabṣū
And the evil spirit, who like a tempest envelops,
Have disturbed the restless man and they have turned that man about;

They studied his entire anatomy and have laid down at the place of sickness (III.1–14, Geller and Vacín 2016:62–89).

Later in the same incantations we are informed that a series of evil demons, including Lamaštu and Labāṣu, 'who infect the body . . . approached the restless man' and 'placed Asakka-disease in his body'.

The motif of restlessness aligns well with the term used in Job 7:4 'restlessness' (נְדֻדִים), although we must also note that it is a *hapax*. When the verb related to this term 'to flee, wonder about' (נדד) appears in Rabbinic Hebrew and Aramaic 'sleep is often the subject . . . that is sleep fees of or chased away' (Seow 2013:502). It is interesting to note, however, that the Old Greek and Latin both have terms meaning 'pains' (ὀδυνῶν, *doloribus*). The connection between the Old Greek Job 7:4 and Deut. 28:67 is widely recognised (Dhorme 1967:98–99). Perhaps in light of the connection between these texts, it is possible that the latter part of the verse – 'I am full of pain from evening until morning' – 'serves to emphasize Job's pain by bringing to mind the terrible sufferings listed in Deut. 28:15–68' as Dhont suggests, noting this might be merely an 'assumption about the translator's intentions' (Dhont 2017:268).

2 It is tempting to translate מאס II 'waste away' but this term is not used in the *qal* and therefore perhaps unlikely. Assuming therefore מאס I, 'reject, refuse', the sentence is awkward because we lack an object. The object could be life, if we assume that the allusion to death in the previous verse and the allusion to Job's limited days in the second part of this verse are significant. Note also the connection here with Job's final response to YHWH; if translated 'refuse' there, it adds a final element of absurdity to the picture: After all the talk we have achieved nothing, and Job consoles himself with dust and ashes (Job 42:6; Clines 2011:1204–1224). Refer to Chapter 5.

3 We have discussed the significance of the theme of wind in the previous chapter, hence the decision to translate הֶבֶל as 'wisp'. It is acknowledged that the term הֶבֶל has a wide semantic range and its meaning is difficult to establish fully. Meek explains this well, observing that the 'twentieth and twenty-first centuries have seen an explosion in proposals for how we should read הֶבֶל' (Sneed 2017; Biwul 2017; Meek 2016).

notes (Job 7:7, 8, 19, 20, 21, Seow 2013:507). The deity, addressed directly, is accused of setting a watch over Job, not leaving Job alone, setting his mind on, inspecting, examining, and gazing in a prolonged way at Job. This climaxes with Job addressing the deity with the title 'Watcher of Men' (Job 7:20). The nature of the unwanted, yet relentless, surveillance here seems ominous. This aligns well with other deity surveillance metaphors in Job wherein the deity watches humans and they perish (Job 7:19–20; 40:11–12), and respite is only to be found when he looks away or hides his face (Job 13:24; 14:6); therefore, Job wishes that he could hide in Sheol until God's gaze passes (Job 14:13; Tilford 2016:56).

It is striking that the first occurrence of this surveillance metaphor here occurs with the rhetorical questions 'Am I Yam? Or Tannin? That you set a watch (משמר) over me?'[4] One use of these mythical sea monsters here is to enable Job to compare himself with creatures of primordial power.[5] As Day notes, these references to primordial chaos overlap somewhat with the creation imagery in the epilogue, with mention of the beasts Behemoth and the primeval sea monster Leviathan (Job 3:8; 38:8; 41:1, 31; cf. Ps. 74:12–17; 89:9–13;

4 The significance of these allusions, reflecting a pastiche of mythological traditions, is widely noted, and this has partly informed the decision to transliterate here. For example, some scholars choose to emphasise the link with the Mesopotamian tradition, as Jones observes, 'God has an entire arsenal of weapons that overlap remarkably with those used by Marduk to slay Tiamat in tablet IV of Enüma eliš' including 'bows, arrows, a mace, a net, and the wind' so that 'sympathizing with Tiamat, Job compares his experience to the primeval Sea and Dragon' (Jones 2013; cf., Perdue 1994:136). Janzen also notes this frequently drawn parallel and draws attention also to the Ugaritic references to Yam and Tannin, which he argues 'are not a close parallel; for Yam is typically killed rather than imprisoned' (Janzen 1989:109). Of course, it may be the case that the reference is intentionally multivalent and therefore imprecise, as Diewert suggests (Diewert 1987). Diewert connects the motif of surveillance here closely with surveillance in Job 7:17–20 (Diewert 1987; *pace* Janzen 1989; cf. Job 41:1–34).

5 Pelham argues that the use of these creatures at this point is a device through which to highlight Job's social isolation, suggesting

> whatever cosmic implications may or may not be in these names, what is certain is that the Sea and the Dragon are menacing figures which the boundaries of the town are in place to repulse. Even if Job's question is not directly related to a full-scale combat myth of creation, it is clearly meant to demonstrate his belief that he is being kept out when he should be allowed in. His suffering at the hands of God has made him into an outsider.
>
> (Pelham 2012a:146)

This is an interesting and persuasive argument because it aligns well with the theme of social isolation emerging at other times in Job wherein the character reports, as we shall analyse in the next chapter, that even his family and servant are repulsed by him (Job 19:15–22). It also aligns well with much of the literature regarding illness, especially visible illness, wherein stigma can play a part. As Dolezal argues 'the inherent shame that the vulnerability of the body in illness can provoke . . . is strongly compounded and exacerbated by judgement, cultural stigma and moralising' (Dolezal 2015:573). However, we should note that at this point, and to an extent throughout, Job shows no signs of shame. Indeed, if anything his behaviour is self-righteous: He is adamant that his innocence must be acknowledged by all. This is both irritating (for his friends) and comical for audiences who are aware of his 'innocence'.

104:26; cf. Day 1985). Rather than presenting a very ordered, non-mythological creation narrative such as is found in Genesis, and rather than emphasising the central significance of wisdom's role in creation, Job instead introduces a very different, slightly more chaotic perspective on creation (Gen. 1; Prov. 8; cf. Brown 2014).[6] This aligns well with the play's characteristic undermining of established traditions, and the device the author/s have built in of casting the character Job as a foreigner from Uz enabling this challenge to be aired without being directly threatening to those audience members who may adhere to ordered traditions of creation.

In contrast to these grand mythical beasts, however, Job presents himself as powerless and weak. As Clines notes, 'Job's own evaluation of himself is a "passing wind" (רוח, v 7) or "mere breath" (הבל, v 16), as insubstantial as a cloud (v 9)' (Clines 1989:188). Nevertheless, the supreme irony of even attempting to make the self-aggrandizing comparison, albeit with rhetorical questions, should not be lost on audiences.[7] A man reduced to oozing sores assumes that these mighty symbols of primordial chaos might be distilled and individualised as applying to himself. The parallel between Job and Tannin or Yam is particularly incongruent. As with several of the examples already analysed, this incongruence occupies the ambivalent space between comedy and tragedy. One interesting detail here, however, is perhaps the way the surveillance metaphor is used. Job uses the term מִשְׁמָר here, a term which may be understood as a lookout or protective guard.[8] However, it is possible to interpret this as an example of polysemy, since the term may also be understood as a collective singular, thus indicating a celestial army who 'guards' or 'watches' Job in the sense of imprisonment (Gen. 40:4; 42:17; Lev. 24:12; Num. 15:34).[9]

The metaphor of divine surveillance continues and intensifies as the speech progresses. Job's vision is juxtaposed to that of divine watching as Job goes on to subvert Eliphaz's advice about revelatory dreams and visions (Job 4:12–16),

6 There are some vague similarities, in light of the connection to creation and nature, between the presentation of the play and David Hume's *Dialogues Concerning Natural Religion* wherein four characters, three philosophers and a youth, enter into dialogue about the existence of God (Hume 1779).

7 An alternative way of thinking about the comparison here is offered by Claassens, who argues that 'Job's experience of his disease, and particular his description of physical dismemberment leads him in 7:12 to make a comparison between himself and the primordial monsters' (Claassens 2013:174). It is interesting that the connection between illness experiences and expression is noted by Claassens at this point. However, the assumption that the connection seems to imply here is perhaps that Job is more than a mere pedagogical example or character in a text. In contrast, for reasons already discussed (see Chapter 1), we would wish to avoid the term 'disease'.

8 Compare with 'the protection מִשְׁמָר of [i.e. afforded by] your peace is to rescue my soul' (1QH[a] 9:33 cf., 4Q/Jub[d] 21:20; 4QHod[f] 1:1).

9 This sense is supported by some of the translations. For example, the Greek has ὅτι κατέταξας ἐπ' ἐμὲ φυλακήν (that you set over me a guard). Similarly, the Latin is 'quia circumdedisti me carcere' (that you have enclosed me in a prison). It should be noted that the term is unlikely to mean 'muzzle', as proposed by Dahood, who suggested an identical root in Hebrew by comparing Job 7:12 with Ps. 68:23 (Dahood 1961; *pace* Barr 1973).

a theme which Elihu rather unfortunately insists on recapitulating later on.[10] The effect that these dreams and visions have on Job is communicated in a corporeal way: His neck (נפש) would prefer to be strangled, and his bones (עצם) would prefer death. The style here is either highly poetic and tragic or bordering on pompous as Job talks about himself in the third person, using the terms נפש and עצם which can be used to refer to the self as a way of narrativising his experience of pain.[11] The tension continues to rise in the speech as Job makes exasperated and desperate requests to be free from surveillance, specifically through choosing to reject life and requesting the deity to leave. Clines notes the irony here, observing that what 'any psalmist in distress fears as the worst disaster of all . . . Job craves' (Clines 1989:191). As Newsom expresses lucidly, in Job's mouth

> motifs of psalmic prayer become disarticulated. No longer are they governed by the form of prayer that establishes their meaning. Consequently, Job inflects them with new and disturbing meanings.
>
> (Newsom 1999:247)

The mode of expression here is characteristically double-edged in its distortion of traditional forms. Indeed, adding further incongruity to the expression, Job juxtaposes the wish for death with the statement that he will not live 'for eternity' (לעלם). Although many commentators suggest that this should be translated 'for long', given the supposed context of a character on the brink of death, it is also possible that the term 'eternity' can be read as part of Job's regular use of hyperbole. However, the crowning irony in this small section of expression is the end of verse 16: The Tannin- and Yam-like Job, who may not live for eternity, admits that his days are הֶבֶל. The anti-climax is somewhat comical, making the character Job's wish for death seem overblown and bordering on hypochondria. However, at the same time, this comedy is tinged with darkness and tragedy: The character's level of despondency here is emphasised through the futility and the transitory nature of the image (and by implication of Job's life).

Newsom here notices the prevalence in these few verses of the motif of the 'incessant, invasive presence of God', describing the consequence of Job's experience as 'the disintegration of the self' on account of being deprived 'of the time and space of privacy' (Newsom 1999:244). The level of harassment communicated to audiences through the deity surveillance metaphor here is high. Indeed, as Hyun suggests, 'the invaded, wounded and broken body

10 Despite the fact that Job and Eliphaz have already had this conversation, Elihu takes it upon himself to return to Eliphaz's original argument, claiming that 'in a dream, in a vision of the night . . . he opens men's ears' (Job 33:15).

11 Rowley notes that the mention of bones 'is sometimes taken to imply that Job had wasted away until he was a mere bag of bones' but this isn't necessary (Rowley 1976:68). The terms could instead be interpreted as idiomatic expressions for the self.

represents Job's invaded, wounded, and broken identity' (Hyun 2013:112). This is interesting because the theme of the breaking down of identity is communicated clearly here not only through the focus on Job's body but also through attention to how it affects his entire personhood and character. If, as Schiffrin argues, 'narrative language contributes to the construction and display of our senses of who we are', then Job, at this point in the dialogue, is a character whose identity is deeply fragmented (Schiffrin 1996:168). Although the deity surveillance metaphor here is less immediately shocking than the deity attack metaphors we have explored, it is nevertheless disturbing and sinister. Through communicating in a way which fragments traditional forms with the corporeal internalisation of fragmentation, Job depicts a deity fundamentally at odds with the God of his friends and of the psalmist. Rather than 'hearing from heaven and forgiving', as Solomon's uncontainable God would; or offering a space of vision and provision, Moriah, as Abraham's God is depicted as doing; or even withdrawing his eye from the righteous, as the Elihu's God does, Job's deity instead gazes menacingly and inescapably. Job's deity here might be imagined as a being closer in resemblance to Tolkien's apocalyptic 'Eye of Sauron' than to the God of the psalmist, who is the apple of the deity's eye and protectively hidden in the deity's shadow (Gen 22; 2 Chr. 6; Job 17:8; 36:7; Ps 17:8; Tolkien 1988, 1966a, 1966b).

Before proceeding on to analyse the second section of the deity surveillance metaphor, it is sensible to initially evaluate the metaphor thus far in light of the research into illness metaphors, experiences, and pain. Particularly interesting here in light of the focus on the primordial creatures of chaos, Yam and Tannin, is the role of myth in narrative. These align well with Hawkins's research wherein emphasis is given to the pervasiveness of mythic thinking in situations of extreme distress (Hawkins 1993). Similarly, Steffen discusses the role of myth for that context (Steffen 1997). Steffen's discussion is helpful for our purposes because the focus is specifically on mythical structures wherein experience is narrativised. For Steffen, in the context of illness narratives and ritual myth is an expression of experience wherein 'past events and a fictional representation of culture seems to be intertwined in a generalised kind of story characterised by a certain degree of timelessness' (Steffen 1997:107).[12] One useful element in this definition of myth's role in the expression of narratives about illness is the emphasis on the 'fictional representation of culture'. Job's rhetorical questions are highly socially situated and betray a complex interactive social process between audience/readers and actors/characters in Job. Communication is governed by cultural conventions, but the use of fictional representation enables Job to retain some critical distance from the point being made through

12 Note that Steffen's definition is restricted to the context of exploring the way that rituals and narrative collide in modern Alcoholics Anonymous (AA) meetings. More generalised definitions of myth abound, and a large quantity of literature exists on the subject. Some widely cited publications include Goody 2010; Frazer 1981; Lévi-Strauss 1978.

mythical language, therefore creating a safe space wherein Job's challenge to audiences is not direct. In this case, Job's allusion to Yam and Tannin is important as a device through which the character draws the audience/reader into the drama of his tragic situation. The emphasis here on primordial chaos also betrays the character Job's internal anarchy.[13] Rather like in the cursing sections of Job 3, which may be conceptualised as a type of creation in reverse, the character here positions his corporeal experience in a mythical framework before the creation of the world (Job 3; Jer. 20:14–18; Barbiero 2015; Burnight 2014b; Hays 2012; Langton 2012; Pettys 2002; Perdue 1991:74–112; Fishbane 1971). Such powerful contextualisation not only captures the imagination of audiences, it also communicates to them about a destabilisation of the idea of the deity's agency in ordering the cosmos. This undermining of traditional perspectives of the created world and order yet again hurls the question of responsibility for Job's predicament away from the character himself. Yet again, the idea of retribution is destabilised through Job's language and his body.

The deity surveillance metaphor continues in the next few verses wherein the character Job is depicted as even more irate and the level of tension rises. Here, rhetorical questions tip over into direct and accusatory questions of the deity, which are couched in bitterly satirical language.

> What is man that you make so much of him?
> And that you set your mind upon him?
> Inspecting him every morning?
> Every moment examining him?
> Will you never take your gaze away from me?
> Or leave me alone until I swallow my saliva?
> If I have sinned, then what do I do to you? O Watcher of Men!
> Why have you set me up as your target? Why am I a burden to myself?[14]
> (Job 7:17–20)

13 It is potentially helpful to note here the importance of narrative and metaphor which draws upon rich connotative images to evoke an idea of the world. As Mattingly argues,

> In studies of self-making, narrative offers an avenue for linking personal experience to cultural knowledge, norms, and tenets. . . . Studies highlight how culturally based understandings shape or are reflected in stories about specific, often very personal, experiences with illness.
> (Mattingly and Garro 2000:28)

Although the author/s have Job represent himself as internally fragmented, powerless, and chaotic, the very act of representation is also an act of self-making and identity, even if it is restricted to expression through culturally based understandings and idioms.

14 The Hebrew is עָלָי (preposition על with first-person singular suffix), 'upon / to myself'. BHS notes that this is thought to be a *tiqqun soferim*, or correction of scribes, and therefore many commentaries prefer the suggested translation 'to you' (McCarthy 1981). The justification for the correction is the rejection of the idea that something might be a heavy load for God. A similar, though more widely recognised, euphemistic translation can be found at the beginning of Job, where we find the advice to Job 'curse God and die' being replaced with the idea 'bless God and die' (Job 1:5; 2:9). The choice to retain and not repoint, עָלָי is an attempt to get closer to the original meaning (though, of course, this is ultimately impossible, given the complex textual picture). Refer to note 65 in Chapter 1.

Here we have an explicit parody of traditional prayer (Mettinger 1993; Fishbane 1992; Dell 1991).[15] Gordis goes so far as to make the bold claim here that 'for irony this passage is unsurpassed in world literature' (Gordis 1978:82). Most scholars note the link between these verses and Psalm 8:4–6, although there are also numerous possibilities for making wider connections (Ps, 139:7–8; Kynes 2012; Seow 2013:509; van Leeuwen 2001). The biting satire at this point is so extreme that the text has acquired numerous unflattering titles, such as the widely used label Job's 'bitter parody' or, as Kynes notes, the designations Job's 'anti-psalm' and his 'doxology of sarcasm' (Delitzsch and Bolton 1866:124; Balentine 1988:264; Kynes 2011:305).[16] Although the parody itself is obvious, there is some disagreement about what the object of the satire could be and its

---

Gard, however, argues that this is an example of the Greek translator's preference for anti-anthropomorphism. The Greek reads:

εἰ ἐγὼ ἥμαρτον τί δύναμαί σοι πρᾶξαι ὁ ἐπιστάμενος τὸν νοῦν τῶν ἀνθρώπων διὰ τί ἔθου με κατεντευκτήν σου εἰμὶ δὲ ἐπὶ σοὶ φορτίον

If I have sinned, what am I able to do unto you? You who understands the mind of men? Why have you set me as your accuser? So that I am a burden to you?

For Gard, the translator 'changes the rather unflattering description of God from that of a keeper or warden to that of one who understands the mind of man' (Gard 1952:48). However, as noted formerly, it is difficult to make assumptions about the intentions of translators.

15 Dell suggests that the genre of Job is best understood as parody, but does not go so far as to suggest any element of comedy, instead arguing that the

> attempt to fit Job into the genre of comedy clearly involves reinterpretation of many passages, and the danger of distortion of detail in the service of an overall interpretation can clearly be seen. It involves imposing an artificial overarching unity of genre on the diversity of smaller genres within the book'.
>
> (Dell 1991:97)

It has been acknowledged that the book of Job contains numerous genres and the high level of parody in Job is well-established, partly by Dell (Witte 2013:81; Dell 1991; see Chapter 1). However, the possibility that part of this parody may also contain elements of comedy need not be dismissed so promptly without further analysis.

16 The prevalence of the body in traditional prayers is particularly interesting given the centrality of the main character's body in the book of Job. Newsom suggests that the significance of this rests on the idea of 'God's activity' arguing:

> Traditional ancient Israelite prayers of supplication often referred to the body as a site of God's activity – creating (Pss. 22:10–11; 139:13–16), examining (Pss. 17:3; 26:2; 139:1–5, 23–24), and afflicting (Pss. 6:2–4; 32:3–4; 38:2–9; 39:11–12). But within the rhetoric of lament the broken body was most significantly presented to God as an object for compassion and a motive for deliverance (Pss. 22:15–20; 102:2–12; 109:21–25). As Job struggles to bear witness to his wound, he uses fragmentary motifs from psalmic prayer (e.g., the forgiveness of sin, 7:21a; 10:13–14; cf. Ps 25:7; the ephemerality of human existence, 7:16, 21; cf. Ps 103:15–17; the request that God look away, 7:19; cf. Ps 39:14), including motifs that involve reference to the body (the forming of the body, 10:8–12; the pressure of divine affliction, 7:14–15; divine scrutiny of the inner being, 7:17–18; 10:4–7).
>
> (Newsom 2009:136)

For Newsom, the reuse of these traditional prayers is more fragmentation and a lack of the ability to articulate pain than it is parody. Nevertheless, her identification of the 'body as a site of God's activity' and observation about the prevalence of the body in prayers are helpful and align well with the emphasis on the body in Job.

broader significance. Kynes, for example, understands the satire as 'a weapon to satirize God's behaviour toward him' rather than something designed to subvert the psalm's authority and therefore understands the psalm as a '"reaffirming" parody' (Kynes 2011:306, 2012:137; cf. Frevel 2004). Therefore, for Kynes, Job 'uses the Psalm to . . . plead that the God he is now encountering conform to this paradigm' (Kynes 2012:137). In contrast with this perspective is the idea that the author/s characterise Job as intentionally subverting the psalm. For example, Nicholson argues that,

> Job's purpose in parodying the psalmist's high teaching about humanity as God's noblest creation seems to be to contrast such a status with God's behaviour as a relentless fault-finder in pursuit of Job, whom he apparently treats as a burden rather than as one destined to be crowned with 'glory and honour'. What the author is evidently seeking to do in texts such as these is to voice through his character Job the complaint of many that there is a jarring disjunction between what a text such as Psalm viii declares about human worth and the actual lot of many like Job in God's world.
> (Nicholson 1995:77)

Nicholson's argument here is quite compelling partly because it is supported by much of the rest of the book of Job wherein the idea of divine retribution is undermined and ridiculed. It is also persuasive on account of its depiction of the deity as a 'relentless fault-finder in pursuit of Job', a perspective which is certainly captured in the text itself, wherein the so-called 'bitter parody' is embedded within the deity surveillance metaphor and wherein there are constant inspections and examinations.

The role that language plays to mimic and ridicule here is particularly important. Both Psalm 8 and Job 7 begin with the pious question 'What is man (אנוש מה)?' (cf. Pss. 15:14; 144:3). The psalm goes on to ask, 'what is man that you are mindful' (זכר) of him and that you 'visit/care for' (פקד) him? In this scenario, mere humans are cared for by the deity, whose caring nature goes so far as to pay attention to the details of the lives of humans. In contrast, Job asks 'what is man' that you 'make so much' (*piel* גדל) of him, 'set your mind (לב) upon' him, 'inspect' (פקד) him, and 'examine' (בחן) him? This language directly mimics the psalm yet at the same time its double-edged quality completely undermines it. As Clines observes, '[i]n every respect the language of the Psalm is reapplied ironically by Job' (Clines 1989:192). This occurs through the re-use of terms in a way that emphasises another aspect of their sematic field. For example, פקד 'may be interpreted positively in the sense of "to care for, worry about" . . . or negatively in the sense of "to bring to account, punish"' (Seow 2013:509). It also occurs through polysemy in the introduction of new terms such as the *piel* of גדל which is, as Seow argues, 'intentionally ambiguous, since the Pi. of this root may mean "to exult" . . . "to rear, raise" . . . or "to nurture/care for"' (Seow 2013:509). Likewise, the psalm is belittled through the addition of further terms that exaggerate the deity's attention to detail: The deity sets his heart on man and examines him. The ironic elaboration shifts the meaning of the traditional language of prayer from piety to accusation, turning the depiction of the deity from an interested guardian to an obsessive guard. The psalmist's unassuming sense of wonder provoked by the idea that the deity may even take mankind into consideration is made to look naïve by the author/s of Job through the reuse of language and addition of terms which emphasise the deity surveillance metaphor. The psalmist's logic, which goes from his personal experience of nature to theorising about all humanity, is also mimicked here by Job, whose reasoning moves from the microcosm of his own somatic experience to the cosmos of all humanity. However, instead of reaching the psalmist's conclusion that all humanity is important to the deity, for Job, the outcome of the calculation is 'that everyone else must be, in reality, equally miserable' (Clines 1989:192). On the one hand, we have the expansive and hopeful and, on the other, the defiant and demoralised.

As if exaggeration and parody of the guardian metaphor had not already been taken far enough, the character goes further to hammer home his (already very obvious) counter-metaphor of deity surveillance. Job protests the deity's: unremitting 'gaze' (שעה), unwillingness to let him alone (*hiphil* רפה), and uncompromising surveillance. This reaches a climax with Job's title for him: the 'Watcher of Men'. This verb נצר (to 'watch/guard') is usually positive, expressing God's concern (Deut. 32:10; Ps. 25:21; Prov. 24:12). Here, however, the term appears as a participle and title: 'Watcher' (Isa. 60:21).[17] Rather than being a benevolent guardian, the deity is again a hostile guard who spies on men.[18] What difference should it make if mere Job were to sin for such a magnificent and majestic deity? Perhaps, as Rowley suggests, 'God is too exalted to be affected by Job's actions' (Rowley 1976:69). Clines modifies this suggestion by arguing that Job's position is near to death and emphasising the irony of disproportion: '[c]an the alleged sin of a dying man be so harmful to God that he must bend all his energies to the harassment of that man?' (Clines 1989:194). The menacing watching finally spills over into implied violence, with the character Job reporting having been set up as a target; as Habel observes, '[t]he metaphor shifts from watching to attacking' (Habel 1985:166). Therefore, the deity surveillance and attack metaphors are finally combined. Just as the tension has climaxed Job adds the question 'why am I a burden to myself?'[19] Until now, the ironic parody of piety had been profound and powerful.

17 The Greek translation here is again rather free, rendering the title less dramatically, ὁ ἐπιστάμενος τὸν νοῦν τῶν ἀνθρώπων 'watcher of the mind of man'.

18 Seow notes the widespread nature of the equivalent epithet in Akkadian, *nāṣir napišti amēlūti* (the 'Guardian of the Human Life' Seow 2013:510).

19 Concerning translation refer to note 14. If we accept this translation, then at the end of the speech the character Job seems to slip off of the edge of his own sanity. The powerful language is suddenly interrupted by the character Job, who moves from the complex to the simplistic and two-dimensional by asking himself why he's a burden to himself. The shift is incongruous and bizarre. It has the effect that Job no longer seems like a serious character; instead, the audience can feel superior,

As argued, the sarcasm, achieved through the reworking of traditional pious language and metaphor, is widely recognised here. What is less clear is the reason why the critique of reverence operates at the site of Job's body.[20] The exaggerated deity surveillance metaphor and implied deity attack (through setting Job up as a target) are communicated using explicitly corporeal and violent language. Job's throat might be strangled, and his bones would choose death. Perhaps at least a part of the reason for the somatic nature of the language, coupled with its violence, and its emphasis on startling, overblown depictions of the deity's surveillance, is because traditional piety and the model of retribution were so widespread and dominant at the point of composition and for early audiences. This would seem to align to a pattern in Job's friends' speeches, as Newsom observes:

> The friends, for instance, present their own speech largely as a restatement of what everyone already knows, the rhetoric of common sense. When Eliphaz introduces an argument . . . he situates his remark not only as something he knows to be true but as something that Job and every other person would share as part of a stock of shared knowledge. Rarely, if ever, do the friends actually quote a tradition, yet their speech is thickly populated with the commonplaces of Israelite moral discourse, which, they appear to believe, lend their speech a kind of overwhelming obviousness. By contrast, Job's preferred mode is the explicit subversion of common sense and the language of traditional piety, most brilliantly executed in his parodies of Psalm 8 in ch. 7, and of hymnic and sapiential language in general in ch. 12.
>
> (Newsom 1993:128)

Newsom's observation here is important: The friends certainly seem to be the dominant voice in terms of what audiences might have expected to hear. The friends adhere to what Newsom calls the 'commonplaces of Israelite moral discourse'; a discourse wherein the body's malfunctioning must be a sign that some wrongdoing has taken place. Lest we attribute this 'unsophisticated' moral discourse only to ancient Israel and her neighbours, it is as well to take note of Dolezal's observation that 'human beings have a long history of linking illness and bodily conditions with negative personal attributes and, furthermore,

---

whether or not they agree with Job. The sudden shift is perhaps also a relief from the tension that had been rising on account of the undermining of piety and tradition. By asking himself this question, the power of his parody is also undermined. Job now 'turns his body into a weapon against himself, ultimately turning him into his own enemy' (Hyun 2013:112). However, given that the translation is unclear, it is best to remain cautious about the effect the final line has here.

20 Clements suggests the reason for this is because the 'author's purpose lay not in reaching deep and ultimate conclusions about all human suffering' as is regularly supposed. Instead, the book of Job is 'in a real sense a book about sickness, if only because it singles out this type of human misfortune as one that is especially personal and acute' (Clements 1992:86).

doing so in order to moralize about certain social groups' (Dolezal 2015:572).[21] Nevertheless, it is against this dominant narrative, delivered with complete confidence on the lips of his friends, that Job's own narrative and expression must compete.

In light of his friends' continuous moralising, a default which audiences may also have understood as dominant, is it such a surprise that Job's own language is violent and rebellious and his characterisation is frenzied and enraged? After all, satire and hyperbole are excellent weapons if one intends to destabilise a dominant viewpoint. This is because at the bitingly satirical end of comedy, mockery and ridicule are political. They are weapons used to question 'the establishment its practices, traditions, institutions, and those who are its agents' so that '[p]eople of power and systems of power are overthrown by their underlings', making them the butts of the joke (Jackson 2012:25–26). In this case, it is difficult to pinpoint what establishment might be being ridiculed specifically. Given that we have dated Job roughly to the late exilic or post-exilic period, there is no obvious 'establishment' or institution – such as the Jerusalem temple – for the book to be questioning.[22] Nevertheless, it is still possible that attitudes towards pain were dominated at the time of composition by established traditions. Specifically, the connection between bodily unease and retribution, which dominates much of the Hebrew Bible and many comparable and later

21 Dolezal gives the examples of Victorians for whom 'acne and skin blemishes were considered to be the result of moral failure and frequently associated with sexual deviancy' (Dolezal 2015:572). Similarly, Dolezal argues persuasively that,

> In our cultural context which values autonomy, discipline and self-restraint, illnesses associated with alcoholism, addiction, sexual activity or overeating are strongly stigmatized, and afflicted individuals are made to feel ashamed of their supposed lack of self-control and weak will. . . . What this all points to is an increased tendency in contemporary medicine to moralize about illness and the causes of illness, shifting the onus onto the individual who is responsible for achieving and maintaining his or her own health through (increasingly commercialised) practices involving diet, exercise, digital 'wearables,' and other disciplinary lifestyle choices and practices. (Dolezal 2015:572)

Dolezal's observation here that there is a tendency in present-day medical practice to 'moralize about illness and the causes of illness' illustrates how enduring the idea of retribution can be, especially when the human body is involved. Given this observation, it is notable how sophisticated the book of Job is through departing from the widespread idea of retribution in relation to the body and pain at an early period.

22 Albertz, noting the 'total absence of explicit Israelite nationalism and the prophetic-eschatological horizon of expectations', suggests that the book of Job 'originated with the social crisis experienced by the Jewish community in the early postexilic era. . . . It fell to the sages in this crisis to provide the sufferers with instructive, consoling, and meaningful models of explanation that could open up for them a perspective on the future' (Albertz 1990:260, 250). If this is the case, then failing 'traditions' such as those represented by Job's friends may be the establishment being attacked. Such traditions do not reach Job in his suffering, just as perhaps they do not reach Yahwists during this period.

primary texts,[23] seems dominant enough to be the object of the satire.[24] As Aaron argues,

> Together, the books of Qohelet and Job represent powerful polemics against binary theologies, or perhaps more generally, against the notion that one should have confidence in a specific interpretive strategy. It is certainly a curious fact that the strongest and most clearly sustained arguments in all of Tanakh are those whose goals were to show the flaws in the establishment's principles of meaning. Both of these works argue that despite our greatest efforts, most life decisions and most interpretations of life events involve high degrees of ambiguity in the sense that their meaning, their purpose, remains unknown.
>
> (Aaron 2001:198)

As such, the book, or play, of Job is a satire of the type of moralising discourses which are adopted by those who adhere to the worldview and the traditional piety found in many of the Psalms, Proverbs, and in other traditional material. Comedy is not a weapon against an institution here, but against a set of values and against a mode of interaction wherein the connection between visible pain and illness and the sinfulness of the person are made without pause for thought.

The role of irony in the research on pain and illness narratives is perhaps helpful in answering the aforementioned question about why the critique, through satire, of traditional piety emerges in the play specifically at the site of

23 Refer to note 21 in Chapter 1 for examples of this connection within the Hebrew Bible.

24 However, it should also be noted that Job's attempt to undermine this connection ultimately fails. Even 'during the Persian, Hellenistic, and Roman periods, when diseases were explained by various other means such as the devil or demons, God's own purposes, or fallen angels, and where ideas about the afterlife were emerging, connecting illness and religious transgression was still popular' (Southwood 2019:242). As Hogan notes, the three books of 1 Enoch (Watchers, Similitudes, and the epistle of Enoch) all deal with sin as a cause of illness. Jubilees 10 also deals with the sin of the fallen angels and the sin of mankind as the cause of suffering and illness. The Testaments of the 12 Patriarchs connect sin to the onset of illness (T Reuben; T Gad. 5:11). In the Genesis Apocryphon, three factors bring about the affliction of Pharaoh and his household: his sin in regard to Sarah, the evil spirit who brings about the affliction, and God who is said to have struck the Egyptians with pestilence. Similarly, in the Prayer of Nabonidus at Qumran we may presume by the mention of Nabonidus confessing and being forgiven that sin is responsible for his illness. Likewise, in Ben Sira while justifying the role of physicians and medical remedies, the ill person is encouraged to pray to God first then to acknowledge one's faults and make a generous sacrifice (38:15). In addition, the sins of Geliodorus (2 Macc. 3) and Antiochus IV (4 Macc. 9) bring on their afflictions. Finally, in the New Testament sin is given as a reason for the paralytic's condition (Matt. 9:1–8; Mark 2:1–12; Luke 5:17–26), and in 1 Corinthians a lack of charity leads to the illness of community members. Philo of Alexandria connects illnesses with sin and lack of virtuous living. (*De Sacrificiis* 70–71). Likewise, Josephus attributes the fatal illness of Herod to his wickedness (*Ant.* XVII 168–171), as he does the fatal illness of Catullus to his misdeeds (*J.W.* VII 451–453) (Hogan 1992:145; cf. Southwood 2019:242).

the main character's body. As well as being a weapon through which to ridicule traditions and institutions of power, satire and irony can call meaning into question through focusing on the middle ground between what is said and what is really meant underneath. Certain events, including illness and pain, can cause discrepancies which are usually concealed between what is said and what is meant to be 'thrown into sharp relief' (Lambek and Antze 2004:9). Paradoxically, this means that in some circumstances being ill provides a kind of privileged perspective and voice. Suggesting that illness exposes certain hollow and insincere areas in everyday life, Lambek and Antze cite Woolf, who argues that there is 'let us confess it (and illness is the great confessional), a wildish out-spokenness in illness; things are said, truths blurted out, which the cautious respectability of health conceals' (Lambek and Antze 2004:9).[25] This observation is helpful for analysis of satire in Job. Indeed, one important outcome of situating the entire discussion about suffering specifically at the site of Job's body is that he is able to act in a 'wild' and 'outspoken' way without conforming to any established social niceties and assumed patterns of behaviour. This puts Job in a privileged position wherein his behaviour and his words may be assumed to be a product of his physical condition, but through this the author/s are also given complete freedom to put any words they would wish into the character's mouth. The main character's satirical reworking of traditional piety is a particularly powerful tool here. Epistemologically the repurposing of the psalm invalidates the entire reality it is premised upon: That the deity, who created the heavens, moon, stars, and animals, is also benevolently concerned with humans. Likewise, Job's satirical mimicry of the psalm has an ethical dimension to it: Through resisting simplistic attributions of accountability it is no longer possible to uphold crude advice such as Eliphaz's moralising macarism 'happy is the man (אשרי אנוש) whom Eloah reproves! Do not reject (מאס) the disciplining (מוסר) of Shaddai' (Job 5:17; cf. Deut. 8:5; Ps. 94:12; Prov. 3:11–12).[26] Instead of 'man' (אנוש) being happy, Job asks 'what is man (אנוש)' and goes on to the deity surveillance metaphor. Ethically, the satire no longer allows Eliphaz to condemn Job on account of what Eliphaz understands as the visible 'sinfulness' of his body. For Job's

25 Lambek and Antze also point out the role of irony in illness specifically with regard to social responses, arguing that '[o]ne arena where distinctions of the text and practice, or verbal and situational ironies, are blurred is that of illness and the social responses it generates. . . . Irony comes to the fore in illness' (Lambek and Antze 2004:12). Again, therefore, the use of irony, but also casting Job as one whose body has been struck by the Accuser, creates an excellent device through which to communicate powerfully with audiences.

26 Note the choice of terminology here. Ironically, the verb מאס is exactly what Job ultimately does (Job's response to Yahweh). Similarly, note the significance of the term מוסר. This is stereotypical language associated with traditional wisdom teaching (Prov. 1:2, 3, 7, 8; 3:11; 4:1, 13; 5:12, 23; 6:23; 7:22; 8:10, 33; 10:17; 12:1; 13:1, 18, 24; 15:5, 10, 32, 33; 16:22; 19:20, 27; 22:15; 23:12, 13, 23; 24:32). Finally, Shaddai is here translated παντοκράτωρ as is common for Job (Job 11:7; 15:25; 22:25; 23:16; 27:2, 13; 32:8; 33:4; 34:10, 12; 35:13; 37:22). Dhont notes the omission of the copula in the macarism, perhaps to reflect the same construction of the Hebrew text (Dhont 2017:116).

friends, his body and pain are seen to be a negative and defining feature of his character, and his body bears his moral and ethical failing: It is, to them, some form of divine punishment. But this perspective is eroded through the implications the satire has.

Both for Job and for his friends, a pressing need exists to extract meaning from, and to contextualise, the character's pain or bodily dysfunction. The source of the argument between Job and his friends occurs not on account of Job's body itself, but through the differing conclusions about what his afflicted body must mean. As a consequence, a complex set of social reactions and interactions emerges wherein questions are raised regarding normal assumptions about meaning and also about the nature of the deity and the created order. Schipper highlights this interaction specifically with relation to Job's skin, arguing that

> Bildad connects diseased skin with the wicked when urging Job to admit to his wrongdoing. . . . Bildad describes the wicked as follows: "By disease their skin is consumed, the firstborn of Death consumes their limbs." Bildad implies that Job's diseased skin serves as a sign of his wrongdoing. We find a similar connection made by Zophar earlier in the book. In 10:15, Job complains that even if he remains in the right, he cannot lift his head because of his affliction. In response, Zophar argues that Job appears guilty of wrongdoing and deserves punishment. *Zophar nearly claims to speak for God*. He tells Job, "For you say, 'My conduct is pure, and I am clean in God's sight.' But oh, that God would speak, and open his lips to you".
>
> (Schipper 2010:19, italics not original)

Ironically, in Job 19, Job actually accuses his friends of persecuting him 'like God' (כמו אל), thus refusing to allow his friends the authority of claiming 'to speak for God' (Job 19:22). Of course, as demonstrated throughout, many more examples of this style of moralising exist in Job. A part of the problem is that the friends are so completely convinced of the infallibility of their own argument and cannot possibly entertain the idea that Job might be correct. But a larger problem is their lack of sensitivity and empathy. In a joint article Kleinman and Kleinman argue that during suffering '[m]oral witnessing also must involve a sensitivity to others' unspoken moral and political assumptions' (Kleinman and Kleinman 1996:8).[27] There is not a lot, if anything, left 'unspoken' in the play of Job. However, in terms of moral and political assumptions, far from being sensitive, the friends are totally inflexible in the meanings that they create when faced with Job's body. Nevertheless, before we judge the friends too harshly, it might be prudent to

27 Kleinman and Kleinman do not provide a definition of moral witnessing here. However, a good definition can be found in another article which Kleinman contributes to

> the offer of personal and family support in face of the burdens of illness, bearing witness to the moral experience of suffering, providing suffering with a coherent meaning, and preparing for a socially appropriate death and for religious transcendence are universal features of societal responses to suffering.
>
> (Kleinman *et al.* 1992:13)

remember that the link between morals and the body in pain is not always obvious at a level beyond the individual.[28] As Throop admits, 'I did not go into the field with an explicit interest in exploring the role of morality and virtue in the context of the personal and cultural articulation of lived experiences of pain in Yapese communities'; however, 'while living on the island it did not take long for me to recognize how local understandings of pain were embedded in moral sensibilities' (Throop 2010:22). Throop found that this unexpected connection became central for understanding pain in Yap and also, importantly, for theorising about the articulation of pain meaningfully configured as coherent experience.

Watch and pounce: the deity surveillance and attack metaphor in Job 10

The metaphor of divine surveillance re-appears in Job 10:14–16. Unlike the former example in Job 7, the surveillance metaphor here is accompanied by a direct (rather than implied) attack metaphor. Van Hecke observes the prevalence of the surveillance metaphor and argues that Job 'has the impression of being observed unremittingly and of never even receiving the chance to be on his own' (Job 10:6, 14; 13:27; 14:3; 16:9; 30:20; 31:4; van Hecke 2013:79). We have already noted the deity attack metaphor in chapter 9 being coupled with the metaphor of surveillance and here, yet again, this metaphor emerges in combination with the surveillance metaphor.

> If I sin you watch (שמר)[29] me and will not exonerate me of my guilt
>
> If I am wicked, woe to me! And if I am righteous I cannot lift my head, satiated with shame and sated[30] affliction (עני)[31]

28 At the level of individual experience, the connection between illness or pain and moral meanings is well established. As Lupton argues:

> Moral meanings are frequently ascribed to illness experiences. The advent of a serious illness may cause individuals to question whether there is a connection between the illness and their moral values, or how they live their lives, forcing them to evaluate their lives in moral terms. People may ask themselves whether they 'deserved' the illness.
>
> (Lupton 1994:98)

29 Seow notes that the term 'watch' (שמר) can mean 'to bear ill will' (cf. Lev. 19:89–19; Jer. 3:5; Seow 2013:589). Similarly, Clines notes that this may be rendered 'bear a grudge, keep in mind' (Clines 1989:221).

30 Two synonyms for sated appear here, hence the use of satiated and sated. The first is שָׂבַע 'satiated' and although not regularly used, this is uncomplicated. Ironically, this is a term that is usually a positive, being often used of one who has died at an old age 'satiated with days/years' (Gen. 25:8; 35:29; 1 Chr. 29:28; Job 42:17). In Job, however, the term is used negatively: Job is satiated with shame here and in 14:1 with 'turmoil'. The second term (רְאֵה) is, as Clines suggests, 'a construct of רָאֶה, an orthographic variant of רָוֶה' (cf. Ps. 91:16; Clines 1989:222). Therefore, the translation 'sated' is convincing. This term (רָוֶה) is usually positive, being used as an adjective to refer to well-watered gardens (Isa. 58:11; Jer. 31:12). This idea also emerges in contrast with being parched: 'his parched together with his watered spirit' (1QS 2:14).

31 It is not clear at that point whether we should translate עני as 'affliction' or 'misery' (e.g. Vulgate, *miseria*).

> And I arise.[32] Like a lion you hunt me,[33] and you return to show yourself to be wonderful (פלא) against me.
>
> (Job 10:14–16)

Here we have another example of the verb שמר (watch, guard) being used in a negative sense. The same term is used by the character Job to depict the deity as a guardian, who preserves Job's spirit, or who preserved Job in the days before his affliction (Job 10:12; 29:2). However, here the deity is portrayed as a guard who is waiting for Job to put a foot wrong so that he can be ensnared. In these verses, Job paints a picture of supreme unfairness. Imagining a hypothetical set of circumstances,[34] Job suggests that if he does wrong, there is no forgiveness and if he does right, there is only shame. Clines comments 'the theme of hostile anger, so dominant a leitmotif in this speech, comes to the surface here again', but unfortunately follows this comment by retrospectively diagnosing Job with paranoia (Clines 1989:249).[35] The final line is reminiscent of the royal lion hunts that emerge in Egypt and Mesopotamia with the propagandistic motif of the king as hunter. The final term (פלא) is often used for God's 'wonders' (Exod. 3:20; 34:10; Josh. 3:5; Judg. 6:13; 1 Chr. 16:9, 12, 24; 2 Chr. 26:15; Neh. 9:17; Ps. 71:19; 106:21–22). It is a term used earlier in the dialogue by Eliphaz in a doxology which paints God as a creator of the heavens. However, here it is used satirically to demean and parody this depiction of the deity, whose disproportionate force against Job seems hardly worthy of praise (Job 5:9). As if Job perhaps hasn't already thought of this course of action, Eliphaz

32 The Hebrew lacks a subject for the verb (גאה) here (וְיִגְאֶה). This is the verb to 'grow' (not גֵּאֶה 'proud'). We have assumed the subject is Job (וְאֶגְאֶה) but this is not the only possibility. Indeed, numerous suggestions exist, including the idea that it is the aforementioned 'affliction' that grows (i.e. Job's physical condition worsens) or that we should emend the text. For example, Gordis suggests emending to וְתִגְאֶה 'You are proud to hunt me' (Gordis 1978:114). The versions are somewhat helpful but do not solve the difficulty. The Vulgate has *et propter superviam* 'by reason of pride' i.e. when Job is proud, he gets attacked. Seow suggests that the subject is ראש as mentioned in Job 10:15, thus 'when it [my head] is high' (Seow 2013:576, 590–591).

33 The Old Greek instead has a rather free translation, changing the syntax from the active to the passive, here ἀγρεύομαι γὰρ ὥσπερ λέων ('for I am hunted like a lion').

34 As is clear from the repeated conditional protasis 'if' (אם).

35 Concerning the methodological hazards associated with retrospective diagnosis see Chapter 1. Clines, who is not a medical practitioner, uses a psychiatry textbook to bolster his argument:

> Job is ill, also. Not just his sores but his bruised psyche provokes these words. He speaks with the language of the paranoid, who "brood over grievances, and then project or rationalize their aggression, hatred or longing" . . . *Henderson and Gillespie's Textbook of Psychiatry*, rev. I.
>
> (Batchelor 1969; Clines 1989:249)

We should, nevertheless note that Clines is among a growing number of biblical scholars who have recently sought retrospectively to diagnose the character Job (Dell 2016; Glasby 2017).

suggests to Job a 'new' and 'original' idea: If he were in Job's position he would 'seek God' who 'does great and unsearchable wonders (נפלאות) that cannot be numbered' (Job 5:9).[36] However, the so-called 'wonders' are, for Job, needless displays of strength. The only other place where פלא is used specifically about the body and in a negative sense is in the curses in Deuteronomy, where there is a reference to God making plagues and bad sicknesses which are 'wonderful' and long lasting (Deut. 28:59). As Pope suggests, '[g]od shows his marvellous power and heroism by assaulting a helpless mortal' (Pope 1965:79). Instead of celebrating the God as powerful using the metaphor of the lion,[37] Job uses the metaphor to depict the deity as a wild and dangerous animal.

Job's deeply satirical quotation and then re-use of Eliphaz's pious claims about the wonders of God is, at a surface level, comical. The serious solemnity of the claims about the deity and man's humble place in the world is imitated in such a way as to make said deity nothing but an egotistical bully. Job moves Eliphaz's piety from the sublime, to the 'Riddikulus'; from the fearful and awesome 'wonders' of a creator deity, to a boggart on roller skates (Rowling 1999). Here the comic 'conjures up a separate world, different from the world of ordinary reality, operating by different rules' (Berger 1997:x).[38] But on the other hand, the idea of being satiated with shame is also an expression that is tragic and pointed and which draws attention to Job's lack of support. As other scholars have noted; for example, Lambert describes Job as a 'fable of failed consolation' (Lambert 2015:262). Instead of offering empathy or practical care, Job's friends become 'arch-conservative defenders of the faith' (Perdue 1991:147). Instead of offering non-judgemental help, Job 'accuses his friends of having held on to their own opinions of divine retribution . . .

36 This verse is quoted by Job earlier in his speech, making the sarcastic reworking of the term here all the more powerful (Job 9:10). The term occurs again at the end where Job, also sarcastically, suggests that there were 'things too wonderful (נפלאות) for me' that will not be known to him (Job 42:3). Refer to Chapter 5.

37 Strawn's monograph surveys every mention of lions within the Hebrew Bible and in literary and archaeological evidence. The metaphor of comparing Yahweh to a lion may, Strawn suggests, be linked to violent goddesses. As Strawn argues, 'warlike goddesses like Ishtar and Sekhmet may have been the progenitors or carriers of a tradition that eventually became associated with Yahweh' (Strawn 2005:341).

38 Berger takes a constructivist view of comedy and suggests that 'the experience of the comic is, finally, a promise of redemption. Religious faith is the intuition . . . that the promise will be kept' (Berger 1997:x). This perspective is somewhat helpful, but there are limits to the extent that humour can be healing. In Job, comedy is only redemptive in a two-dimensional way: The U-shape means that the plot does have a 'redemptive' quality, but the ending is very two-dimensional and unrealistic. The idea of Job's new family, for example, simply replacing the old one and the character receiving twice as much as before and living an extended life has a fairy-tale quality about it. However, the serious questions raised by Job, through the focus on his body, about suffering are not directly answered.

without making any attempt to put themselves in *his* position' (Bastiaens 1997:425). Pelham makes a similar point, arguing that 'Job's suffering poses problems for his friends' vision of the world-as-it-ought-to-be' because they 'deny that anything has gone wrong with the world' (Pelham 2012a:45). Eliphaz, with his sense of the well-ordered created world that is full of God's wonders, might just as well be quoting directly from Psalms or Proverbs at Job with his advice.[39] If Job could just "fear the Lord" then he would be "satiated" (שבע), and he would not be "visited" (פקד)[40] with evil (Prov. 19:23). If Job could just have a being (נפש) that could be 'satiated' (שבע), then he would 'loath a honeycomb', but he is instead a 'hungry throat' (נפש רעבה) whose bodily desires and sensations rule over him (Prov. 27:7).[41] If Job could just be satisfied and admit what is obvious, or 'say it like it is' – that the sky is green and that pigs can fly – then all would be well. If Job would just relinquish his foolish worldview, formed perhaps in Νεφελοκοκκυγία, then there would be no problem (Aristophanes *The Birds* 414). But Job's experience of the world does not align, and his key source of information, instead of tradition, is his body. It is specifically the moralising advice communicated through the entrenched, inflexible positions of his friends that the author/s contest and resist through humour and tragedy. In doing so they are able to illustrate the futility of tradition when it is juxtaposed with individual experience. For the friends, the only source of knowledge is tradition, and Job's experience counts for very little. Therefore, in response, 'Job's use of proverbs and other traditional wisdom is nearly the opposite in purpose of his friends' (Greenstein 2007:70). Job's deity is 'wonderful' but only in a comical and tragically negative sense. Through this change that the author/s insert into traditional teaching a paradox is left: The deity is wonderful on account of his miraculous cruelty.

The decision to locate the idea of retribution on the main character's body is particularly helpful in terms of breaking down traditional assumptions. This is because, as discussed,[42] pain and illness regularly give way to the age-old question 'why me?' In other words, illness and pain actively invite moralising.

39 Interestingly, the friends do not actually directly quote at Job, but their positions are so self-assured that they might as well be quoting. The term 'wonder' (פלא), used in a positive sense of the deity's created order, is particularly prevalent in the Psalms (Pss. 9:1; 26:7; 31:21; 40:5; 71:17; 72:18; 75:1; 78:4, 11, 32; 86:10; 96:3; 98:1; 105:2, 5; 106:7, 22; 107:8, 15, 21, 24, 31).

40 Of course, we noted earlier how the character Job sarcastically re-uses the verb פקד: the deity won't keep his distance but instead 'visits' man every morning and watches every moment (Job. 7:18). Refer to section: "Am I Yam?! Or Tannin': Creation and the deity surveillance metaphor in Job 7'.

41 A similar echoing of Proverbs wherein bodily pleasure is rejected occurs in Ecclesiastes wherein if a good name is better than fine oil, then there would be no need for eating, drinking, and merriment. The day of death would be better than the day of birth, if reputation is all that is important (Prov. 22:1; Eccl. 7:1).

42 See Chapter 1.

Likewise, through the focus on the body, individual experience is given a unique status within the dialogues. Job's body becomes 'the centre for him to understand his world', and his body 'determines the power of the other's gaze' (Hyun 2013:110). Given that the play's audience has been made aware from the start[43] that Job is not suffering on account of his own behaviour, the ridiculousness of 'fruitless conversations that attempt to decipher the cause of the suffering' are therefore powerfully exposed (Tham 2013:86). This focus on Job's body allows the extreme absurdity of moralising to be accentuated and highlighted. However, this also enables the author/s to explore and evaluate the underlying cultural assumptions, as well as value structures, that accompany Job's friends' advice. The centrality, therefore, of values and of knowledge is brought to the fore. As Newsom argues,

> The wisdom dialogue thus puts in conversation not simply two different opinions but two quite different moral imaginations. To understand what is at issue and to feel the claims each makes, one needs to examine not just the propositional claims but also the embedded metaphors and other patterns of imagery that direct the argument, the narrative frameworks that implicitly guide the speakers' thoughts, and the cultural discourses that are invoked as the parties grapple with rival structures of meaning.
>
> (Newsom 1999:240)

Newsom's argument here is particularly helpful for drawing attention to the significance of the dialogues with respect to challenging the idea of retribution. What is at stake is not merely an intellectual disagreement between a mythical foreigner and his friends. Instead, the play challenges cultural and epistemological assumptions as well moral values that have become a part of traditional Yahwism at the time of writing or for early audiences and pushes for a more intellectually robust – and more benevolent – way of engaging with fellow Yahwists, and importantly, with fellow foreigners. Therefore, through highlighting the two-dimensional moralising nature of the advice given to Job, the play's audiences are encouraged fervently to reject the simplicity of moralising. As Sanders comments, the effect that this exposure of moralising has is that Job is depicted as having 'cried a loud No to such static views of Scripture and tradition' so that the 'best thing these so-called friends did was to remain silent for seven days' (Sanders 2009:66).[44] In the estimation of Job's friends, his 'physical deterioration is a result of his own moral depravity' (Greenstein 2018:49). However, the challenge the play offers is not to Job to live righteously, but

43 Audience members who arrive late and miss the beginning may risk failing to understand the entire play.

44 Newsom makes a similar point about the attitudes of Job's friends and how audiences are encouraged to react to the moralising, arguing that their words 'seem obtuse at best, hateful at worst' (Newsom 1999:239).

instead for any audience members who adhere to the logic of traditional teachings about suffering that are placed on the lips of Job's friends to reassess their patterns of thought, 'moral imaginations', and entire networks of ideas about how the world operates.

Job's character is particularly confrontational in this respect. Job increases the tension for audiences throughout the play by continually refusing to admit that he has done anything to warrant the deity's treatment of him. This causes Job friends, as well as audiences, to 'see trauma and fear' (Job 6:21). The friends 'have to establish that there is some moral reason for his suffering in order to relieve their own anxiety', Goldingay argues; 'otherwise the framework within which they live their lives and think of God also collapses' (Goldingay 2013:42).[45] So long as Job is 'guilty', then the friends' values, belief systems, and planes of experience are stable. So long as Job is 'sated with shame', then there is a just god who upholds the order of creation. But if such chaos could befall a righteous man, then who is safe? What if the deity is instead monitoring humans unforgivingly and hunting like a lion? To feel secure, the friends must 'place Job on the other side of the morality fence', but Job refuses to be quarantined in the sinners' ward, and, 'by authentically expressing his emotions, he exposes his healers' ineffectiveness' (Kutz 2000:1614). Job's restructuring of his friends' advice, particularly in the reuse of language for metaphors about pain, therefore, decisively interrupts the idea of retribution.

The enduring relevance and importance of the questions raised here are highlighted by analysis using the research concerning pain and illness experiences. Given that illness and pain are always understood through the lens of local cultural orientations, defined as 'the patterned ways that we have learned to think about and act in our life worlds and that replicate the social structure of those worlds', it is not particularly surprising that Job's friends react using the most prevalent systems of knowledge available to them (Kleinman 1988:5). However, pain and illness regularly destabilise said cultural orientations as well as structures of meaning and knowledge. This is because the meaning created in response to serious illness and pain can cause people to be 'shocked out of . . . common-sensical perspectives of the world' with the effect that they enter 'a transitional situation in which [they] must adopt some other perspective on . . . experience' (Kleinman 1988:27). Kleinman goes on to explain that in 'traditional societies, shared moral and religious perspectives on the experience of life crises anchor anxieties in established social institutions of control' (Kleinman 1988:27–28). Though it is not entirely clear what Kleinman means by 'traditional societies' here, the argument concerning shifts in meaning-making in responses to illness and pain is compelling and directly relevant as a lens through which to understand the complex dynamics in the dialogues between

45 A similar line of argument is made by Girard, who suggests that Job's friends 'demand a scapegoat and [project] guilt onto it, whereas Job maintains the truth of his innocence' (Girard and Freccero 1987:145).

Job and his friends. Indeed, the relevance of the play is not entirely ignored in this body of research. As Kirmayer points out,

> Sickness challenges cultural clichés and facile explanations. It poses anew the problem of Job, latent in every life, made personal and immediate by the insistence of bodily suffering. How can meaning and value be sustained when consciousness is constricted, degraded, and defiled by pain?
> (Kirmayer 1992:324; cf. Fortes and Horton 1983)

What is interesting here is Kirmayer's distinction between 'cultural clichés and facile explanations' (which may be understood as a form of moralising) and 'meaning and value'. While Job's friends' limited horizons are exposed through their reliance on 'cultural clichés and facile explanations', the character Job insists on challenging established patterns of 'meaning and value'. The manner in which this is achieved, through biting sarcasm, hyperbole, comedy, and tragedy, does not detract from the underlying power of the challenge. Nevertheless, using metaphors related to pain, in the form of the deity attack and surveillance, are a particularly valuable vehicle through which to posit said challenge. As Throop argues, 'the significance of pain in light of local moral modalities of being provide individual sufferers with a set of inherited cultural tropes', and these tropes may 'help individual sufferers to formulate narratives that give meaning', but in the face of the 'experiences of pain and suffering' they may also 'actively resist such meaningful elaboration' (Throop 2010:160). Whether we use the term 'local moral modalities', 'cultural tropes' 'cultural clichés', or 'facile explanations', the prevalence of the theme of moralising in light of pain and illness is clear. A pattern relevant both to the dialogues within Job, and found in the research concerning illness narratives and pain is that pain does not resist meaning. But it does resist moralising.[46] The relevant question then becomes: What is the distinction between seeking meaning in the face of pain

46 However, it should be noted that the prevalence of moralising is as strong in modern times as it is in the portrayal of the dialogues between the characters of Job and his friends. Kleinman, Brodwin, Good and Good do not accept this argument, claiming that

> What is so impressive about current forms of suffering is the relative weakening in the modern era of moral and religious vocabularies, both in collective representations and the language of experts. In their place we see the proliferation of rational-technical professional argots that express and constitute suffering in physiological, public health, clinical, psychological, and policy terms.
> (Kleinman *et al.* 1992:13)

It is acknowledged that the language around health and the human body has shifted seismically with the emergence of modern biomedicine. However, it is not entirely true that moral and religious vocabularies do not emerge in that language too. Lupton communicates this powerfully, arguing that

> The 'rationality' and 'objectivity' of medicine are assumed to rise above value judgements. Yet the implicit moral evaluation which pervades the biomedical model of disease agents is reflected in everyday rhetoric, such as the basic terms 'poorly', 'bad' and 'better' when speaking about health states; 'as our popular usage suggests, the term "sick" has itself become a powerful metaphor of

in contrast with moralising? Perhaps the answer lies in the attitudes underlying questions about meaning. For meaning-making to be moralising, it is usually judgemental, highlighting personal responsibility and assuming blame.

Shame is another area wherein the research into illness narratives and pain may be helpful for shedding further light on the dialogues within Job. Lazare first pointed out the centrality of shame in the medical encounter (Lazare 1987). Dolezal highlights the connection between shame and perceived responsibility when the body is in pain or illness. Dolezal argues that

> Shame is etymologically and historically connected with the body and nakedness, particularly the desire to conceal one's nakedness. In the biblical story Genesis . . . Adam and Eve become aware of their naked state and cover themselves because they become ashamed of their nudity. In this story, the very origin of humanity is intimately linked with shame about the body. In English, the word 'shame' comes from a pre-Teutonic word meaning 'to cover' where 'covering oneself' is considered the natural expression of shame. In Ancient Greek, *aidoia* (αἰδοῖον), a derivative of *aidōs*, is a standard Greek word for the genitals, again connoting the reaction of wishing to hide or conceal oneself. In addition, the German word for shame, *Scham*, also refers to the genitals as does the Danish word for labia, *skamloeber*, which literally translates to the lips of shame.
>
> (Dolezal 2015:569)

It is interesting that in the heart of a metaphor about deity surveillance and attack, the character Job reports, in parallelism, that he is 'satiated with shame and sated with affliction' (Job 10:15). Given the focus on the body, its 'skin', 'flesh,' 'bones', and 'sinews' in the verses immediately preceding this deity surveillance and attack metaphor, it may be possible to understand the term 'affliction' (עני) as illness, an interpretation that aligns well with the dysfunction of the body and the feeling of shame that often accompanies it (Job 10:11–12).[47] Shame is not something that occurs regularly in Job, only here (קלון)[48] and in Bildad's advice wherein he claims, ironically, that 'God will not cast away a perfect (תם) man', so that if Job would just 'seek God and make supplication to Shaddai' then those that hate Job will be clothed with shame (בשת) (Job 8:5, 20, 22).[49] Far from being ashamed, the character Job usually protests the indignity

---

> moral condemnation' . . . Epidemic disease is particularly potent in inspiring drama, panic, irrationality, stigmatization and attempts to locate the blame.
>
> (Lupton 1994:99)

Of course, Western biomedicine is not directly comparable to Job. The stark difference is mainly that Job is a pedagogical character in a text about whom the audience is aware of innocence. The patterns of moralising exposed and challenged by the character Job are, however, deeply embedded in much the language about illness and pain.

47 Although refer to note 31.

48 Note the link between this term for shame and nakedness (Jer. 13:26; Nah. 3:5; 1QH^{a} 5:21; 20:25).

49 A huge body of material on shame in the Hebrew Bible exists, partly because of the problematic link that many scholars make between 'honour and shame' as if they were balanced opposites. Esler

of his situation and his claim to innocence.[50] Nevertheless, given the marked connection between shame and body, the choice of locating the dialogue about retribution on Job's body is yet again particularly powerful with respect to averting responsibility from Job. The reason the character is satiated with shame is not because of responsibility for his body's dysfunction. It is instead because of the incessant and unnerving gaze of the deity.

'Do you fix your eyes on such a one?': deity surveillance in Job 13 and 14

Several scattered deity surveillance metaphors occur at the end of Job 13 and punctuate Job 14 (Job 13:27–28; 14:3, 6, 16). Given their relative proximity, these will be analysed together in this section. Chapter 13 begins with Job accusing his friends of treating him as an inferior through their moralising advice, suggesting they are 'quacks' for whom it would be best if they learned to 'shut up', and comparing their advice to ashes and mud.[51] Both chapters 12 and 13 begin in this way, as Forti argues, 'the dominant idea is that Job is unwilling to confess (to) a sin he has not committed' (Forti 2015:165). Moreover, as Seow demonstrates, legal terminology is scattered throughout the chapter (Job 13:3, 6 [x2], 8, 10, 15, 18 [x2], 19; Seow 2013:640). The final section wherein our deity surveillance metaphors emerge are part of a larger block of speech, wherein Job addresses the deity (Job 13:20–28). Towards the end of this speech Job paints 'comical scenarios' of the deity as a divine and mighty warrior in whose sincere pursuit is the old, dried-up chaff (Seow 2013:651). The incongruity here certainly adds to the absurdly comical but also rather tragic image. Following this we have the cluster of deity surveillance metaphors.

> You put my feet in stocks (סד)[52] and you watch (שמר) all my paths
> Upon the roots (שרש)[53] of my feet you set for me a boundary (חקה)

---

provides a useful discussion of the criticisms concerned with reifying 'honour' and 'shame', especially if such reification 'entailed homogenised versions of honour and shame substituting for finely focused and discriminating ethnography in particular contexts' (Esler 2012:44–45). Regarding the social dimension of shame, refer also to Bechtel 1991. (cf. Lynch 2010; Lemos 2006).

50 Refer to Chapter 2.

51 Concerning mud and ashes, refer to note 136 in Chapter 2. Also, regarding the translation here, refer to Southwood 2018.

52 The term 'stocks' (סד) does not emerge regularly in the biblical material, only here in Job 33:22, as noted by BHS. The Old Greek has the less literal term 'impediments' (κωλύματι) instead of stocks. Perhaps, in context, given the mention of Job's 'paths' being watched, something akin to 'shackles' or 'impediments' is intended by the term. Without further evidence any judgement will be somewhat tenuous. However we translate, the context seems to suggest a negative restriction of movement of some sort of Job's feet.

53 The noun 'roots' (שרש) can be taken literally or figuratively, the latter meaning the core of a person or lowest stratum of a thing. Here it is unlikely to mean 'soles' of the feet (for which the more regular term would be כף; Deut. 11:24; Josh. 3:13; 4:18; 1 Kgs 5:3; Isa. 60:14; Ezek. 43:7; Mal. 4:3). Instead it is likely to mean the extremities of the feet, thus perhaps their outline, implying with the following verb that the deity limits the movement of Job's feet. Rowley's suggestion is helpful here,

> The one who is like a wineskin (רקב) that is worn out (בלה),[54] like a moth-eaten[55] garment. . . . Nonetheless,[56] on such one you opened your eyes![57]
> Even me,[58] you bring into disputation[59] with you?!
>
> (Job 13:27–28; 14:3)

What is being described here is, again, a contest between unequally matched partners. It is, as Clines suggests, 'not a legally determined punishment, but the kind of oppressive behaviour engaged in by a powerful person against his adversary at law' (Clines 1989:321). However, what stands out in particular is the gaze of this 'oppressive' deity, who is accused of 'watching' (שמר) Job's paths and 'opening [his] eyes' towards Job. The latter expression relates to surveillance, as Seow demonstrates, 'for the expression, see Jer. 32:19, where God is characterized as one who observes the ways of mortals . . . and Zech. 12:4 where God speaks of his observation of Judah' (Seow 2013:684). Habel also observes the prevalence of the deity's aggressive glaring in Job's language, commenting that '[w]ith this cry of anguish Job returns to a favourite theme, that

in that this 'would seem to mean that God draws a ring around Job, out of which he is not allowed to step' (Rowley 1976:102).

54 This translation follows Clines and Seow. It understands הוא 'as if it were relative' (Seow 2013:665). Following Clines, it emends רָקָב to רֹקֶב 'wineskin' (Clines 1989:283). This is persuasive first because it aligns well with the several metaphors that are used in Job to denote the body's boundaries, such as tent and skin (cf. de Joode 2014; Berquist 2002). Second, the Old Greek has ἀσκῷ which is translated 'wineskin' in Mark 2:22. However, as Seow notes, elsewhere the term 'always refers to rotting as in the verb (Isa. 40:20; Prov. 10:7; Sir. 14:19) and the noun. . . (Hos. 5:2; Hab. 3:16; Prov. 12:4; 14:30)' (Seow 2013:666). Perhaps the ambiguity may be read as an implied polysemy?

55 The Old Greek, which 'contains no transliterations, except in reference to popular names', is interesting here, supplying a neologism in translation. . . σητόβρωτος 'moth-eaten' in 13:28, composed of σής and βιβρώσκω (Dhont 2017:147).
The image of the moth in biblical texts 'appears seven times in the biblical texts – three times in Job (4:19, 13:28, 27:18), three times in the Prophets (Isa 50:9, 51:8; Hos. 5:12), once in Psalms (39:12), and once in Sirach (42:13 ms B)' (Forti 2015:162).

56 Literally אף על זה 'also upon this'. The conjunction אף can be translated 'nonetheless', as implied in Lev. 26:44 (אף גם זאת 'nonetheless, in spite of this'; cf. Pss. 44:10; 58:3). Beginning the sentence in this way implies surprise; this is perhaps an exclamation of amazement. Since the first two verses focus on humanity's ephemeral nature, like a flower that withers or a shadow that fades, this exclamation seems to fit the context. As Rowley comments 'Job is astonished that God should scrutinise one so ephemeral as man' (Rowley 1976:103).

57 The Old Greek renders the idiom 'opened your eyes' with the Greek expression λόγον τινὸς ποιεῖσαι as 'to make account of' or 'set a value on'. Seow suggests this translation interprets 'divine intention positively', or that the OG may 'be trying to "improve" the parallelism: "took into account" // "caused to enter judgement"' (Seow 2013:684). This suggestion has some similarities to Gard's theory about theological toning down (Gard 1952). In contrast, Dhont argues that because 'it does not reflect a similar construction in Hebrew', it therefore must be 'a sign of the translator's use of natural Greek idiom' (Dhont 2017:152).

58 As BHS notes, some translations, including the Old Greek, Vulgate, and Syriac, read the third-person, here instead of the first-person, singular here.

59 Literally 'judgement', but given the prevalence of legal terminology scattered throughout the former chapter, translating 'disputation' here seems to fit the context.

of God the oppressor and spy. . . . God's surveillance tactics reflected continued unwarranted harassment of a victim already unjustly afflicted' so that 'the sinister side of God's watching is exposed in all its ugliness' (Habel 1985:232). The image painted here by Job is one of extreme and uncompromising surveillance of a man whose body is already compromised. At this point Job paints a tragic, and rather unflattering, picture of himself as a worn-out old wineskin – quite literally a bag of wind.

Within a few verses, at the end of the first section of poetry in chapter 14, Job returns to the motif of the deity surveillance metaphor, pleading for the deity to 'look away (שעה) and desist (חדל)' (Job 14:6). Likewise, Job ends the second section of poetry in the chapter with the deity surveillance metaphor, turning to his present situation[60] wherein the deity numbers his steps[61] and wishing that the deity would 'not keep watch (שמר) over my sin' (Job 14:16). Job's speech here, about a tree having hope when humans, who quickly die, do not, is an ironic parody of Bildad's moralising musings, which compare the pious to the good, well-watered plant that is able to 'see' (חזה) even in the 'house of stones' (Job 8:17). Likewise, Job's use of the otherwise somewhat odd expression 'roots' of the feet hints back to Bildad's somewhat damming analogy (Job 8:11–19). In twisting Bildad's advice by deliberately missing the point about the well-watered plant, Job moves from the tragic image of a bound-up and exhausted victim who, despite having his movements significantly restricted is under strict guard, to the comic picture of a buffoon pontificating about how much more lucky the little tree is than him.

In the chapters surrounding Job's deity surveillance metaphors, Zophar and Eliphaz attempt to defend themselves against them. Following the deity surveillance and attack metaphor occurring in Job 10:14–17, Zophar responds to Job with an interrogation of rhetorical questions (a tactic also used in the whirlwind speeches at the end). Zophar asks whether 'a multitude of words' should go unanswered and whether one who is 'full of talk' (שפתים; literally a man of 'lips') can be justified as well as whether a boaster (בד)[62] such as Job who mocks (לעג) should not be made to shut up and put to shame (Job 11:2–3). Job's constant, verbose, and overly dramatic language is, for Zophar, a mark of his foolishness (Prov. 10:8, 14, 19). Here, moralising occurs in the rejection of Job's entire speeches. Rather than engaging with them, Zophar 'judges it his moral duty to silence Job . . . for not to accept the rightness of God's punishments is to challenge God's morality, to belittle God' (Clines 1989:259, 260). To engage with Job's arguments would be to let 'the fool [in Zophar's estimation, that is Job] think himself wise' (Prov. 26:5; Seow 2013:598). Thus, Zophar is depicted

60 As signified by the phrase, 'but now' (כי עתה).

61 Bildad's later retort focuses instead on steps, suggesting that 'the wicked' have their steps 'straitened' (Job 18:7). This is in contrast to the psalmist for whom God 'enlarges' their steps in order to prevent them from slipping (Ps. 18:36).

62 The term בד could be translated 'prattle' or 'babble'. Elsewhere it indicates boasting (Isa. 16:6; Jer. 48:30; Clines 1989:260).

as a 'plain orthodox dogmatist' here for whom Job's expressions of pain are too much to engage with (Rowley 1976:87). Following Zophar's retort, Job returns to the deity surveillance metaphors, cited earlier, after which point Eliphaz responds in a similar manner to Zophar. With a series of six rapid rhetorical questions fired at Job in swift succession, Eliphaz answers Job's deity surveillance language. Job had insisted that there was no hope for mortals, and Eliphaz asks, in response, whether he [Job] is the first-born of the humans, created before the hills (with an implied and ironic reference to Wisdom's role in creation; Prov. 8; Job 15:7–8). The sarcasm continues as Eliphaz suggests that perhaps Job has access to God's 'secret council'. Perhaps only Job has access to wisdom (Job 15:8–9)? Despite the fact that it is the case that on the side of the friends is the 'grey haired' and 'elderly', Eliphaz accuses Job of supposing that only he has a monopoly on wisdom.[63] Essentially, while Zophar dismisses Job's perspective entirely on the grounds that it goes against traditional wisdom, or against what Pyper calls 'authoritative readings', and is therefore blasphemous, Eliphaz ridicules Job as a supposed primordial man of wisdom (Pyper 1992:237).

In the latter speeches, bodily experience is contrasted with age, although Job's deity surveillance metaphors are not taken particularly seriously by either of the friends. As Newsom observes, in the dialogue 'hostility and mutual incomprehensibility quickly come to characterize the way Job and his friends perceive each other' (Newsom 2009:184). Amusingly, however, the audience is aware from the start that there is actually some truth in Job's protestations of innocence, despite the character's verbose and overblown language about deity surveillance and attack; therefore, the friends, '"in ridiculing become ridiculous" . . . a fundamental but paradoxical ingredient of comedy' (Whedbee 1977:11). Job's own depiction of himself here, as worn-out, yet heavily guarded, with his feet in the stocks, makes for quite a tragic picture. But it is also a very somatic image. Perhaps this aspect of Job's language of self-representation, coupled with the U-shaped plot wherein Job is restored completely, is what stops this picture from ever fully being tragic. This suggestion better comes into focus if we compare Jackson's description of tragic and comic heroes in classical material.

> In major aspects of form and outlook, comedy and tragedy reflect the opposite in one another. With respect to its main characters, tragedy's stars are powerful and beautiful heroes; comedy's stars are weak and unremarkable antiheroes. In classical manifestations, tragedy was understood to be

63 These rhetorical questions are made all the more insulting by the beginning of the speech wherein, like Zophar, Eliphaz accuses Job of talking too much and suggests that his language is ערום ('crafty'), perhaps pointing to a type of underground knowledge similar to the snake in the Eden story (Gen. 3:1; Job 15:5). This is an accusation that Eliphaz has already made of Job, but in this speech it is more pronounced (Job 5:12).

> inhabited by people of high position, who are portrayed as better than they are; while comedy was inhabited by lowly types, who are portrayed as worse than they are. The tragic character finds dealing "with the burden of human finitude" an embarrassment and a curse; however, the comic character remains unembarrassed "by even the grossest expressions of his creatureliness".
>
> (Jackson 2012:15; quoting from Morreall 1999:34)

Job seems more than willing to express – often at length – the ailments his body seems to be exposed to, or in Morreall's terms his 'creatureliness'. Likewise, we are told that he is innocent and blameless, and Yahweh himself boasts about his servant Job in the prologue, yet in the dialogues he comes across, rather like his friends, as proud, pompous, sarcastic, and sometimes even frenzied. However, we should also recognise that below the comic surface a more serious point is being made about Yahwism at the time of writing, and it is a social point about generosity and humanity in the face of suffering. If Job's question is 'why must I suffer?' then it 'is a lament as well as a question, and the answer to it cannot be argument' (Boss 2007). To provide an answer to a rhetorical question, especially one so loaded – as the friends seek to – betrays a certain level of social insensitivity. This is because, as Balentine argues, 'moralisms can never bandage physical pain' (Balentine 2015:137). Instead, what is often sought through asking the 'why me?' question in the face of pain or illness is what Goffman describes as a 'circle of lament' wherein consolation is found not in an answer, but in respectful companionship (Goffman 1968:20).

Research concerning illness narratives, specifically public health narratives, may be helpful for analysis here. One particularly interesting feature about the material that Job's friends draw on for their advice is its cautionary and conservative nature, which simplistically distinguishes the righteous from the wicked and the wise from the foolish (cf. Job 11.20; 15:20; cf. Ps. 1). For the wicked, it is assumed that they are not following the practical guidelines for flourishing set out in traditional material. Although the friends do not quote them, many of the Proverbs assume this and also link health and wholeness with following the advice that is laid out. For example, if the advice given is taken seriously, it is, for those that find it, 'life . . . and healing (מרפא) to all their flesh' (Prov. 4.22). Whereas, for the wicked, calamity befalls and no healing (מרפא) is available (Prov. 6:15; cf. 12:18; 13:17; 14:30; 15:4; 16:24; 27:1). The assumptions underlying the overarching narratives of such traditional material and ideas focused around retribution align very closely with modern appeals to personal responsibility in public health communication. These narratives are 'intended to be prophylactic – to prevent disease by changing behaviour – by appealing directly to the reader . . . who is situated both as patient and as good citizen' (Belling 2012:157). The purpose of these narratives is threefold: to promote vigilance, to reduce risk-taking behaviours, and to reduce complacency. In such campaigns, health becomes 'an imperative, like a religious or moral code, which dictates specific norms of conduct' (Belling 2012:165). While responsible health behaviours are to be encouraged, the drawback here is the allocation of responsibility which cannot always be matched with agency: Even the most risk-averse person who actively protects their health is subject to illness and pain.[64] It is unavoidable because, as Throop explains,

> Pain is a basic existential fact of our distinctly human way of being-in-the-world. To be human is to be vulnerable to both the possibility and inevitability of suffering pain. Woven into the fabric of our existence, pain is an experience that calls forth questions of meaning, morality, despair, and hope.
>
> (Throop 2010:15)

It is helpful to juxtapose Throop's argument that pain is inevitable and part of being human with Belling's outline of public health narratives and wellness campaigns because ultimately wellness is not governed only by human agency: Sometimes calamity strikes unpredictably.[65] Given that calamity has already happened for Job, the advice being given by his friends is moralising specifically because it emerges from a context assuming health. In Job's case, where this has already been taken, therefore, said advice is redundant. Once health has gone, wellness campaigns are less relevant. Likewise, for Job what is needed is not a static application of what in the past might have helped, but instead a 'life-giving dynamic re-signification of tradition . . . adaptable to the new life in the new situation' (Sanders 2009:69).

Summary

This chapter analysed instances of implied deity attack through unwanted divine surveillance that emerged in Job's speeches and his friends' reactions and their advice. It focused in each section on how traditional works, including but not limited to Deuteronomy, Proverbs, Psalms, and other texts wherein retribution and similar implied authoritative traditions feature, were undermined through parody, comedy, and tragedy, wherein the deity attack metaphor features. It was organised into three sections, the first of which addressed Job's highly sarcastic reworking of Psalm 8 in Job 7:17–18, climaxing in the unflattering title for the deity 'Watcher of Men'. Here a man reduced to oozing sores assumes that mighty symbols of primordial chaos such as Yam or Tannin might be distilled

64 Another, rather ironic, drawback that Belling highlights is hypochondria:

> Despite these good intentions, though, the deliberate provocation of fear about a particular object can easily produce a less coherent anxiety that resists reassurance, an anxiety that can become a public health problem in its own right.
>
> (Belling 2012:162)

65 It is also worth noting that although for the vast majority, pain is inevitable, for a small number of people with congenital insensitivity to pain, it is not inevitable.

and individualised to be contained by his body. The parallel between Job and Tannin or Yam is particularly incongruent. Adding further incongruity, Job juxtaposes his wish for death with the statement that he will not live 'for eternity' (לעלם), a characteristic use of hyperbole and overstatement. However, the crowning irony in this small section of expression is the end of verse 16: The Tannin- and Yam-like Job, who may not live for eternity, admits that his days are הֶבֶל. The sudden anti-climax is somewhat comical, and the character's wish for death, we suggested, was overblown, while the scene as a whole was simultaneously tragic given Job's level of despondency.

Through communicating in a way which fragments traditional forms, with the corporeal internalisation of fragmentation, Job depicts a deity fundamentally at odds with the God of his friends and of the psalmist. Rather than 'hearing from heaven and forgiving, as Solomon's uncontainable God would; or offering a space of vision and provision, Moriah, as Abraham's God is depicted as doing; or even withdrawing his eye from the righteous, as the Elihu's God does, Job's deity instead gazes menacingly and inescapably, like a relentless fault-finder. The use of language here was particularly interesting, with double-edged, direct, and undermining mimicry of traditional material. Likewise, through exaggeration and ironic elaboration, the psalm was belittled to the point where the deity was depicted as an obsessive guard. Interestingly, the psalmist's logic, which goes from his personal experience of nature to theorising about all humanity, is also mimicked here by Job, whose reasoning moves from the microcosm of his own somatic experience to the cosmos of all humanity. We noted comedy's role in overthrowing systems of power and establishments here and reflected on what dominant powers might have been satirised, suggesting that prevailing principles of meaning and interpretations of texts based on retribution might be what was being eroded. Comedy is not a weapon against an institution here, but against a set of values and against a mode of interaction wherein the connection between visible pain, and illness, and the sinfulness of the person are made without pause for thought. The role of irony in the research on pain and illness narratives was helpful here, especially in terms of its function to call meaning into question through focusing on the middle ground between what is said and what is really meant underneath. By situating the discussion about suffering directly on the site of Job's body, the character is cast in a privileged position wherein discrepancies which are usually concealed between what is said and what is meant are 'thrown into sharp relief' (Lambek and Antze 2004:9). We noted here the ethical dimension to Job's satirical mimicry of the psalm in this respect: Through resisting simplistic attributions of accountability, it is no longer possible to uphold crude macarisms about the joys of being disciplined by the almighty. We also noted here the absence of 'moral witnessing' and the significance of embedded moral sensibilities when configuring experience in light of pain.

The second section of this chapter focused on the deity surveillance in Job 10:14–16. This section contained the familiar leitmotif of the hostile and unfair deity who is described using the negative sense of the term שמר wherein the deity is depicted as a 'guard', rather than a 'guardian'. Like the previous section, traditional material was twisted from positive and affirming images of the deity to destructive motifs so that Eliphaz's doxology about God the creator of the heavens with his great, innumerable, and unsearchable 'wonders' (נפלאות) becomes a figure whose 'wonders' are wild and dangerous. The serious solemnity of the claims about the deity and man's humble place in the world was imitated in such a sarcastic way that they ended up producing an unflattering depiction of a deity who was little more than an egotistical bully. Yet again, Job's comical reworking of his friends' moralising advice distorts traditional motifs and ideas to the extent that Job's deity is almost the polar opposite to the one his friends describe. We noted that through using attack and surveillance of Job's body as a vehicle to undermine the traditional ideas that his friends relentlessly repeat to him, underlying cultural assumptions, value structures, and epistemological assumptions that were probably part of traditional Yahwism at the time of writing or for early audiences were also exposed. So long as Job is 'guilty' and his body reflects his inner state, then the friends' values, belief systems, and planes of experience are stable. So long as Job is 'sated with shame', there is a just god who upholds the order of creation. But if such chaos could befall a righteous man, then who is safe? Through refusing to be quarantined to the sinners' ward and placed at the other side of the morality fence, the foreigner Job decisively and irrevocably interrupts a type of outdated Yahwism wherein cultural clichés and facile explanations dominate. We noted that a pattern emerged relevant both to the dialogues within Job and in the research concerning illness narratives and pain: While pain does not resist meaning, it does resist moralising. Finally, we noted the general connection in the research between illness and pain, wherein the body is more exposed, and shame. The character Job did not align to this pattern particularly, despite the claim that he is sated with shame. Perhaps part of the comic aspect of the dialogues was that far from being ashamed, the character Job actively draws attention to his body's role by protesting the indignity of his situation and emphasising that he is innocent.

The final section of the chapter focused on several scattered deity surveillance metaphors that occur in close proximity (Job 13:27–28; 14:3, 6, 16). Chapter 13 is dominated by legal language wherein the implication of the advice given by Job's friends is that he ought to be willing to admit his crime. In response, Job suggests that he is not inferior to his friends (i.e. he feels at most equal and quite possibly superior) and that his friends are 'quacks' that would do best to 'shut up', given that their advice is ashes and mud. The deity surveillance metaphors depicted extreme and uncompromising surveillance of Job whose body was already compromised. We noted that the depiction of Job here was tragic, and rather unflattering, as he deemed himself a worn-out old wineskin – quite literally a bag of wind. We also noted Job's ironic parody of Bildad's advice in Job 14:6. Job distorted this advice through deliberately missing the point about the well-watered plant, thus moving from the tragic picture of an exhausted victim under strict guard, to the comic idea of the buffoon pontificating about how much more lucky the little tree is than him. We noted here the tendency of comic characters to focus on somatic expression of what Morreall termed 'creatureliness'. We also focused on the significance of the 'why me?' question as a rhetorical question but also a lament and the insensitivity of attempting to provide moralisms in answer. Finally, we discussed the significance of Job in light of modern wellness campaigns focusing especially on contested questions of agency and responsibility and on norms in terms of public health communication. For Job what is needed is not a static re-application of a type of Yahwism that in the past might have helped. Instead, the character calls for a reinterpretation, revitalisation, and renewal of Yahwism and for a new type of Yahwism that is able to speak authentically and sincerely to new, and perhaps sometime chaotic, circumstances faced by communities.

Bibliography

Aaron, D.H., 2001. *Biblical ambiguities: Metaphor, semantics and divine imagery.* Leiden: Brill.

Albertz, R., 1990. The Sage and pious wisdom in the book of Job: The friends' perspective. In: J.G. Gammie and L.G. Perdue, eds, *The Sage in Israel and the ancient Near East.* Winona Lake: Eisenbrauns, pp. 243–271.

Balentine, S.E., 1988. "What are human beings, that you make so much of them?" Diving disclosure from the whirlwind: "Look at the behemoth". In: T. Linafelt and T.K. Beal, eds, *God in the fray: A tribute to Walter Brueggemann.* Minneapolis: Fortress Press, pp. 259–278.

Balentine, S.E., 2015. *Have you considered my servant Job? Understanding the biblical archetype of patience.* Columbia: University of South Carolina Press.

Barbiero, G., 2015. The structure of Job 3. *Zeitschrift fur die Alttestamentliche Wissenschaft*, **127**(1), pp. 43–62.

Barr, J., 1973. Ugaritic and hebrew "šbm"? *Journal of Semitic Studies*, **18**(1), pp. 17–39.

Bastiaens, J.C., 1997. The language of suffering in Job 16–19 and the suffering servant passages of Deutero-Isaiah. In: W. Beuken, J.V.J. Ruiten and M. Vervenne, eds, *Studies in the book of Isaiah: Festschrift Willem A.M. Beuken.* Leuven: Leuven University Press, pp. 421–432.

Belling, C.F., 2012. *A condition of doubt: The meanings of hypochondria.* New York; Oxford: Oxford University Press.

Berger, P.L., 1997. *Redeeming laughter: The comic dimension of human experience.* Berlin: Walter de Gruyter.

Berquist, J.L., 2002. *Controlling corporeality: The body and the household in ancient Israel.* New Brunswick, NJ; London: Rutgers University Press.

Biwul, J.K.T., 2017. The use of Hebel in Ecclesiastes: A political and economic reading. *HTS Teologiese Studies/Theological Studies*, **73**(3), pp. e1–e10.

Boss, J., 2007. *Human consciousness of God: A commentary on the book of Job.* Stroud: J. Boss.

Brown, W.P., 2014. *Wisdom's wonder: Character, creation, and crisis in the Bible's wisdom literature.* Grand Rapids, MI: William B. Eerdmans.

Burnight, J., 2014b. Job 5:7 as Eliphaz's response to Job's "Malediction" (3:3–10). *Journal of Biblical Literature*, **133**(1), pp. 77–94.

Claassens, L.J., 2013. Countering stereotypes: Job, disability, and human dignity. *Journal of Religion, Disability & Health*, **17**(2), pp. 169–183.

Clements, R.E., 1992. *Wisdom in theology.* Grand Rapids, MI: Carlisle: William B. Eerdmans, Paternoster Press.

Clines, D.J.A., 1989. *Job 1–20.* Dallas, TX: Word Books.

Clines, D.J.A., 2011. *Job 38–42.* Nashville: Thomas Nelson.

Dahood, M., 1961. Mišmār "Muzzle" in Job 7:12. *Journal of Biblical Literature,* **80**(3), pp. 270–271.

Day, J., 1985. *God's conflict with the dragon and the sea: Echoes of a Canaanite myth in the Old Testament.* Cambridge: Cambridge University Press.

De Joode, J., 2014. The body and its boundaries: The coherence of conceptual metaphors for Job's distress and lack of control. *Zeitschrift fur die Alttestamentliche Wissenschaft,* **126**(4), pp. 554–569.

Delitzsch, F. and Bolton, F., 1866. *Biblical commentary on the book of Job.* Edinburgh: T&T Clark.

Dell, K.J., 1991. *The book of Job as sceptical literature.* Berlin: Walter de Gruyter.

Dell, K.J., 2016. What was Job's malady? *Journal for the Study of the Old Testament,* **41**(1), pp. 61–77.

Dhont, M., 2017. *Style and context of old Greek Job.* Leiden; Boston: Brill.

Dhorme, E., 1967. *A commentary on the book of Job.* London: Nelson.

Diewert, D.A., 1987. Job 7: 12: yām, Tannîn and the surveillance of Job. *Journal of Biblical Literature,* **106**(2), pp. 203–215.

Dolezal, L., 2015. The phenomenology of shame in the clinical encounter. *Medicine, Health Care and Philosophy,* **18**(4), pp. 567–576.

Esler, P.F., 2012. *Sex, wives, and warriors: Reading Old Testament narrative with its ancient audience.* Cambridge: James Clarke & Co.

Fishbane, M., 1971. Jeremiah Iv 23–26 and Job Iii 3–13: A recovered use of the creation pattern. *Vetus Testamentum,* **21**(2), pp. 151–167.

Fishbane, M., 1992. The book of Job and inner-biblical discourse. In: L.G. Perdue and W.C. Gilpin, eds, *The voice from the whirlwind: Interpreting the book of Job.* Nashbille: Abingdon Press, pp. 86–92.

Fortes, M. and Horton, R., 1983. *Oedipus and Job in West African religion.* Reissued edn. Cambridge: Cambridge University Press.

Forti, T., 2015. Human tribulation and transience in Job: The metaphor of the moth. In: S. Yona, E.L. Greenstein, M.I. Gruber, P. Machinist and S.M. Paul, eds, *Marbeh Ḥokmah studies in the Bible and the ancient near East in loving memory of victor Avigdor Hurowitz.* Winona Lake: Eisenbrauns, pp. 161–170.

Frazer, J.G., 1981. *The golden bough.* New York: Gramercy Books.

Frevel, C., 2004. "Eine kleine Theologie der Menschenwürde". Ps 8 und seine Rezeption im Buch Ijob. In: F.-L. Hossfeld, L. Schwienhorst-Schönberger and E. Zenger, eds, *Das Manna fällt auch heute noch. Beiträge zur Geschichte und Theologie des Alten, Ersten Testaments: Festschrift für Erich Zenger, Herders biblische Studien.* Freiburg: Herder, pp. 244–272.

Gard, D., 1952. *The exegetical method of the Greek translator of the book of Job.* Philadelphia: Society of Biblical Literature.

Geller, M.J. and Vacín, L., 2016. *Healing magic and evil demons: Canonical Udug-Hul incantations.* Boston, MA; Berlin: Walter de Gruyter.

Girard, R. and Freccero, Y., 1987. *Job: The victim of his people.* London: Athlone Press.

Glasby, M., 2017. *Wholeness and holiness: Medicine, disease, purity and the Levitical priesthood.* London: Apostolos Publishing.

Goffman, E., 1968. *Stigma: Notes on the management of spoiled identity.* Harmondsworth: Penguin.

Goldingay, J., 2013. *Job for everyone.* London: SPCK.

Goody, J., 2010. *Myth, ritual and the oral.* Cambridge: Cambridge University Press.

Gordis, R., 1978. *The book of Job: Commentary, new translation and special studies.* New York: Jewish Theological Seminary of America.

Greenstein, E.L., 2007. On my skin and in my flesh: Personal experience as a source of knowledge in the book of Job. In: K.F. Kravitz and D.M. Sharon, eds, *Bringing the hidden to light: Studies in honor of Stephen A. Geller.* Winona Lake, IN: Eisenbrauns, pp. 63–77.

Greenstein, E.L., 2018. Metaphors of illness and wellness in Job. In: S.C. Jones and C.R. Roy, eds, *"When the morning stars sang": Essays in honor of Choon Leong Seow on the occasion of his sixty-fifth birthday.* Berlin; Boston: Walter de Gruyter, pp. 39–50.

Habel, N.C., 1985. *The book of Job: A commentary.* London: SCM.

Hawkins, A.H., 1993. *Reconstructing illness: Studies in pathography.* West Lafayette, IN: Purdue University Press.

Hays, C.B., 2012. "My beloved son, come and rest in me": Job's return to his mother's womb (Job 1:21a) in light of Egyptian mythology. *Vetus Testamentum,* **62**(4), pp. 607–621.

Hogan, L.P., 1992. *Healing in the second Temple period.* Freiburg: Universitätsverlag.

Hume, D., 1779. *Dialogues concerning natural religion.* 2nd edn. London.

Hyun, S.W.T., 2013. *Job the unfinalizable: A Bakhtinian reading of Job 1–11.* Leiden: Brill.

Jackson, M.A., 2012. *Comedy and feminist interpretation of the Hebrew Bible: A subversive collaboration.* Oxford: Oxford University Press.

Janzen, J.G., 1989. Another look at God watch over Job (7,12). *Journal of Biblical Literature,* **108**(1), pp. 109–114.

Jones, S.C., 2013. Corporeal discourse in the book of Job. *Journal of Biblical Literature,* **132**(4), pp. 845–863.

Kirmayer, L.J., 1992. The body insistence on meaning: Metaphor as presentation and representation in illness experience. *Medical Anthropology Quarterly,* **6**(4), pp. 323–346.

Kleinman, A., 1988. *The illness narratives: Suffering, healing and the human condition.* New York: Basic Books.

Kleinman, A., Brodwin, P.E., Good, B.J. and Good, M.D., 1992. Pain as human experience: An introduction. In: M.D. Good, ed, *Pain as human experience: An anthropological perspective.* Berkeley; London: University of California Press, pp. 1–28.

Kleinman, A. and Kleinman, J., 1996. The appeal of experience; the dismay of images: Cultural appropriations of suffering in our times. *Daedalus,* **125**(1), pp. 1–23.

Kutz, I., 2000. Job and his "doctors": Bedside wisdom in the book of Job. *British Medical Journal,* **321**(7276), pp. 1613–1615.

Kynes, W.L., 2011. Beat your parodies into swords, and your parodied books into spears: A new paradigm for parody in the Hebrew Bible. *Biblical Interpretation,* **19**(3), pp. 276–310.

Kynes, W.L., 2012. *My Psalm has turned into weeping: Job's dialogue with the Psalms.* Berlin; Boston: Walter de Gruyter.

Lambek, M. and Antze, P., 2004. *Illness and irony: On the ambiguity of suffering in culture.* New York; Oxford: Berghahn Books.

Lambert, D.A., 2015. The book of Job in ritual perspective. *Journal of Biblical Literature,* **134**(3), pp. 557–575.

Langton, K., 2012. Job's attempt to regain control: Traces of a Babylonian birth incantation in Job 3. *Journal for the Study of the Old Testament,* **36**(4), pp. 459–469.

Lazare, A., 1987. Shame and humiliation in the medical encounter. *Archives of Internal Medicine,* **147**(9), pp. 1653–1658.

Lemos, T.M., 2006. Shame and mutilation of enemies in the Hebrew Bible. *Journal of Biblical Literature,* **125**(2), pp. 225–241.

Lévi-Strauss, C., 1978. *Myth and meaning.* London: Routledge & Kegan Paul.

Lupton, D., 1994. *Medicine as culture: Illness, disease and the body in Western societies.* London: Sage.

Lynch, M.J., 2010. Neglected physical dimensions of "shame" terminology in the Hebrew Bible. *Biblica,* **91**(4), pp. 499–517.

Mattingly, C. and Garro, L.C., 2000. *Narrative and the cultural construction of illness and healing.* Berkeley; London: University of California Press.

Meek, R.L., 2016. Twentieth- and twenty-first-century readings of Hebel (לָבָה) in Ecclesiastes. *Currents in Biblical Research,* **14**(3), pp. 279–297.

Mettinger, T.N.D., 1993. Intertextuality: Allusion and vertical context systems in some job passages. In: H.A. McKay and D.J.A. Clines, eds, *Of prophet's vision and the wisdom of Sages.* Sheffield: Sheffield Academic Press, pp. 257–280.

Morreall, J., 1999. *Comedy, tragedy, and religion.* Albany, NY: State University of New York Press.

Newsom, C.A., 1993. Cultural politics and the reading of Job. *Biblical Interpretation,* **1**(2), pp. 119–138.

Newsom, C.A., 1999. Job and his friends – a conflict of moral imaginations (An examination of a scriptural model of divine moral answerability). *Interpretation-A Journal of Bible and Theology,* **53**(3), pp. 239–253.

Newsom, C.A., 2009. *The book of Job.* Oxford University Press.

Nicholson, E.W., 1995. The limits of theodicy as a theme of the book of Job. In: J. Day, R.P. Gordon and H.G.M. Williamson, eds, *Wisdom in ancient Israel: Essays in Honour of J.A. Emerton.* Cambridge: Cambridge University Press, pp. 71–82.

Pelham, A., 2012a. *Contested creations in the book of Job: The-world-as-it-ought-and-ought-not-to-be.* Leiden: Brill.

Perdue, L.G., 1991. *Wisdom in revolt: Metaphorical theology in the book of Job.* Sheffield: Almond Press.

Perdue, L.G., 1994. Metaphorical theology in the book of Job: Theological anthropology in the first cycle of Job's speeches (Job 3; 6–7; 9–10). In: W.A.M. Beuken, ed, *The book of Job.* Leuven: Leuven University Press, pp. 129–156.

Pettys, V.F., 2002. Let there be darkness: Continuity and discontinuity in the "curse" of Job 3. *Journal for the Study of the Old Testament,* **26**(4), pp. 89–104.

Pope, M.H., 1965. *Job.* Garden City, NY: Doubleday.

Pyper, H., 1992. The reader in pain: Job as text and pretext. In: R.P. Carroll and R. Davidson, eds, *Text as pretext: Essays in honour of Robert Davidson.* Sheffield: JSOT Press, pp. 234–255.

Raz, Y., 2014. Reading pain in the book of Job. In: L. Batnitzke and I. Pardes, eds, *The book of Job: Aesthetics, ethics, hermeneutics.* Berlin: Walter de Gruyter, pp. 77–98.

Rowley, H.H., 1976. *Job.* Rev. edn. London: Oliphants.

Rowling, J.K., 1999. *Harry Potter and the prisoner of Azkaban.* London: Bloomsbury.

Sanders, J.A., 2009. The book of Job and the origins of Judaism. *Biblical Theology Bulletin,* **39**(2), pp. 60–70.

Schiffrin, D., 1996. Narrative as self-portrait: Sociolinguistic constructions of identity. *Language in Society,* **25**(2), pp. 167–203.

Schipper, J., 2010. Healing and silence in the epilogue of Job. *Word & World,* **30**(1), pp. 16–22.

Seow, C.L., 2013. *Job 1–21: Interpretation and commentary.* Grand Rapids, MI: William B. Eerdmans.

Sneed, M., 2017. לבה as "Worthless" in Qoheleth: A critique of Michael V. Fox's "Absurd" thesis. *Journal of Biblical Literature,* **136**(4), pp. 879–894.

Southwood, K.E., 2018. "You are all quacks; if only you would shut up" (Job 13:4b-5a): Sin and illness in the sacred and the secular, the ancient and the modern. *Theology*, **121**(2), pp. 84–91.

Southwood, K.E., 2019. Metaphor, illness, and identity in Psalms 88 and 102. *Journal for the Study of the Old Testament*, **2**, pp. 228–246.

Steffen, V., 1997. Life stories and shared experience. *Social Science & Medicine*, **45**(1), pp. 99–111.

Stordalen, T., 2006. Dialogue and dialogism in the book of Job. *Scandinavian Journal of the Old Testament*, **20**(1), pp. 18–37.

Strawn, B.A., 2005. *What is stronger than a lion? Leonine image and metaphor in the Hebrew Bible and the ancient near East*. Fribourg: Göttingen: Academic Press, Vandenhoeck & Ruprecht.

Tham, J., 2013. Communicating with sufferers: Lessons from the book of Job. *Christian Bioethics*, **19**(1), pp. 82–99.

Throop, C.J., 2010. *Suffering and sentiment: Exploring the vicissitudes of experience and pain in Yap*. Berkeley, CA; London: University of California Press.

Tilford, N.L., 2016. When people have Gods: Sensory mimicry and divine agency in the book of Job. *Hebrew Bible and Ancient Israel*, **5**(1), pp. 42–58.

Tolkien, J.R.R., 1966a. *The return of the king: Being the third part of the Lord of the rings*. 2nd edn. London: Allen & Unwin.

Tolkien, J.R.R., 1966b. *The two towers: Being the second part of the Lord of the rings*. 2nd edn. London: Allen & Unwin.

Tolkien, J.R.R., 1988. *The Lord of the rings*. London: Unwin Hyman.

Van Hecke, P., 2013. "I melt away and will no longer live": The use of metaphor in Job's self-descriptions. In: A. Labahn, ed, *Conceptual metaphors in poetic texts: Proceedings of the metaphor research group of the European association of biblical studies in Lincoln 2009*. Piscataway: Gorgias Press, pp. 69–90.

Van Leeuwen, R.C., 2001. Psalm 8.5 and Job 7.17–18: A mistaken scholarly commonplace? In: P.P.M. Daviau, W. Wewers John and M. Weigl, eds, *The world of the Aramaeans. I, Biblical studies in honour of Paul Eugène Dion*. Sheffield: Sheffield Academic Press, pp. 205–215.

Whedbee, J., 1977. The comedy of Job. *Semeia*, **7**, pp. 1–39.

Witte, M., 2013. Job in conversation with the Torah. In: B.U. Schipper and D.A. Teeter, eds, *Wisdom and Torah: The reception of "Torah" in the wisdom literature of the second Temple period*. Leiden: Brill, pp. 81–100.

4 Pride comes before a fool

Job's loss of social status

Introduction

An obvious feature of the way that the character Job uses language concerning his body is the dual focus of both the body and its impact on social status. We have observed this several times in the previous chapters, especially with reference to the research concerning shame and the body. There is an abundance of examples one could choose from the play to analyse the significance of this feature in Job. However, two specific areas for analysis lend themselves well to exploring this feature of Job's language. These include Job 19:13–22 and 21:5–6. These examples have been selected because of their explicit focus on Job's body and the connection between the body and the expression of the loss of social status. We have chosen not to include Job 12:1–4 here given the lack of an explicit focus on the body and given that these verses have already been covered in other sections.

The connection between the body and the social world is particularly important as an approach that this monograph focuses on (as opposed to the problematic analytical perspective of retrospective diagnoses). This focus is flourishing in disability studies generally, and several scholars emphasise the importance of the social world when examining the body in Job. For example, Claassens points out that it is 'Job's experience of a debilitating disease and the accompanying physical, emotional, and social effects of this disease that raises important questions regarding what it means to be human' (Claassens 2013:175). Likewise, in the first commentary which focuses on the Bible and disability, Melcher comments that

> His [Job's] social alienation is deep. Indeed, Job's sense of being abused by God may be related to his experience of being abused by his friends and by society's conventions. In other words, Job's protest is ultimately based in his sense of social alienation, and his only recourse is to cry out to or against God. . . . The speeches of Job's friends are very important because they illustrate the very worldview that the book is challenging.
>
> (Melcher 2017:178–179)

Melcher's point here is helpful for refocusing attention on the significance of the social aspects of the body during illness and pain and, of course, disability, which is the focus of Melcher's and Claassens's approaches. Indeed, a wide

DOI: 10.4324/9781003029489-4

range of scholarship approaching Job using disability studies emphasises the significance of the body and social interaction in Job. Building on this helpful approach, this chapter takes another look at the pivotal role Job's body has for social interaction, and it examines his loss of social status and his reactions to this disruption. It will discuss the body, community, and boundaries in order to identify how the language of deity attack and surveillance might be connected to the loss of social status and prestige.

'My wind is repulsive to my wife': Job 19 and how not to win friends and influence people

In Job 19:13–22, we have a prolonged description of how Job's social circumstances have changed, focusing especially on his body and the types of reactions it elicits even among his family and most intimate friends. The description ends with an explicit focus on Job's body and a call for compassion (Job 19:20–22). It is quite a strange shift from the anticlimactic deity attack metaphor which we explored earlier in Job 19:7–12.[1] The comical anti-climax of siege warfare against a little 'tent' is now followed by a 'crescendo of agony' with details of social alienation, moving tragically from general acquaintances, to kin, and then to intimate friends (Gordis 1978:201). In these verses, there is an undeniable emphasis on the way that the breakdown of Job's body is tightly bound up with a breakdown in his social universe.

> He has put my brothers far away[2] from me,
> And my acquaintances? They have become wholly estranged from me.[3]
> Those who are close to me and known by me have ceased,
> And those who sojourn[4] in my house have forgotten me.[5]
> And my maidservants count me as a stranger,
> I am a foreigner in their eyes.[6]

1 Refer to Chapter 2.

2 If אחי 'brothers' is understood as a collective singular (e.g. 'family') then there is perhaps an argument against emending the text to a plural (הִרְחִיקוּ) as suggested in BHS. Family need not imply blood relations, but could be social or political, given that the idea of relatives through blood has been significantly challenged by Schneider (Schneider 1984). Perhaps relatedness may be a better way of thinking about the concept of 'family' (Carsten 2000; cf. Southwood 2017:61–66).

3 This translation understands אך as the emphatic particle, thus 'wholly estranged'. The Old Greek translation here is rather awkward: ἔγνωσαν ἀλλοτρίους ἢ ἐμέ φίλοι δέ μου ἀνελεήμονες γεγόνασιν ('they acknowledged foreigners, or my friends have become unmerciful').

4 For a recent study of the term גּוּר, refer to Awabdy 2014. The comparison is ironic: Even those temporary resident foreigners/strangers in Job's house forget their absent host (noting, of course, that the idea of 'foreign-ness' is a construct: Southwood 2012:19–36). Nevertheless, note the prevalence of terms in this verse potentially relating to ethnicity (גר; זור; נכרי).

5 This translation follows the suggestion in BHS to place the *athnach* a word later (under the *pual* participle of ידע) and to balance the parallelism of the line, as well as the parallelism of the next verse, by putting the *sof pasuk* after the first two words of verse 15 ('those who sojourn in my house').

6 The Greek translator avoids the anthropomorphic phrase 'in their eyes', simply translating ἀλλογενὴς ἤμην ἐναντίον αὐτῶν ('I became a foreigner to them'). This is a common translation technique (Job 15:15; 18:3; 25:5; 32:1; Dhont 2017:35).

I call out to my servant but there is no answer,
  I implore him with my mouth. . .[7]
My wind (רוח) is repulsive (זור√II)[8] to my wife,
  And I am loathsome (חנן √II)[9] to the sons of my belly.
Even infants despise me,
  I *will* rise up[10] . . . but they speak against me.
All the men of my intimate assembly considered me abominable.[11]
  And those whom I love have turned against me.
My skin and my flesh cling to my bones,[12]
  And I have escaped "by the skin of my teeth".[13]
Pity me! Pity me! *You*, oh my friends.[14]
  For the hand of Eloah has touched (נגע)[15] me.
Why do you pursue me like God?[16]
  Are you not satisfied with my flesh?

(Job 19:13–22)

The emphasis here is on the symbiotic nature of the physical body and the social world that the character Job inhabits. As Seow notes, 'Job is not merely

7 Note the poetic form here בְּמוֹ. The end of the verse seems to trail off somewhat given that there is no parallel for 'but there is no answer'. This is perhaps captured in the translation using the ellipsis to highlight the lack of response. Note the markedly different attitude Job supposes he has towards slaves in Job 31:13–15.

8 The choice in translation to use √II זור is because of the use of זור √I in verse 13. Given that polysemy is not unusual in Job, this may be an example of the poet deliberately using a homonym to develop the thought. Through doing so, this may also make the speech more memorable if we imagine Job as a play.

9 The term חַנּוֹת occurs only here and in Ps. 77:9 and is related to the more widespread term √I חנן ('be gracious' / 'show pity' / 'implore favour'). Using a similar line of reasoning for √II in the translation of זור (refer to note 8), the translation here follows √II ('loathsome') to deliberately contrast with √I חנן which appears twice at a critical point in the speech (Job 21 [x2]) and just above (Job 19:16).

10 The extra effort expressed here on Job's part through the cohortative (אָקוּמָה), which may also introduce a conditional clause, quickly resolves into an anti-climax: He is not listened to regardless of the expressed emphasis on rising up. Through inserting the ellipsis here in translation, it is hoped that the sense of effort, matched only by the result of futility, is captured.

11 Possible translations of the word תִּעֲבוּנִי are 'loathed', 'detested', or 'abhorred'. We have chosen 'considered abominable', which is admittedly rather awkward, but does capture the ritual and ethical senses of the term תעב. The idea here is perhaps more than intense dislike of Job. Instead, perhaps what is being conveyed is not only Job's social distance from his former intimate friends but their perception of him as morally and religiously 'Other'.

12 This rather literal rendering of the Hebrew is deliberate, capturing the graphic somatic image. A translation which aligns more with the English idiom may be 'I am nothing but skin and bones' or, more colloquially, 'I am a bag of bones'.

13 'By the skin of my teeth' is a crux. Despite the phrase having become an idiomatic expression in English for a narrow escape, it is not clear what exactly is meant.

14 The pronoun is emphatic here: אתם רעי ('*You*, oh my friends').

15 נגע can mean 'touched' in the sense of struck with plague when followed by the preposition ב (cf. 1 Sam. 6:9; Ps. 73:14; cf. 4QWays[a]; 4QShir[a] 1[7]). For example, in Isaiah the term occurs in conjunction with 'afflicted' (ענה) (Isaiah 53:4; cf. Lev. 31:2–6).

16 The Greek translator here avoids the simile "like God" instead translating διὰ τί δέ με διώκετε ὥσπερ καὶ ὁ κύριος ("but why do you pursue me, just as the Lord does?"). Many translators seek to tone down Job's unflattering comparison likening God to a hunting animal here (Gordis 1978:203).

describing his physical appearance'; instead, 'the disintegration or distortion of the human body is a metaphor for one's shattered state' (Seow 2013:801). However, it is clear from the beginning of the speech that the one causing Job's social isolation is God: 'he has put my brothers far away' (Job 19:13). Therefore, a direct connection between divine violence and social outcomes for Job is made, perhaps also connecting the two aforementioned seemingly separate, distinctive sections of chapter 19 here.

The series of images conveyed in Job's tragic litany of woes depicts a world that is topsy-turvy and wherein the order of Job's social universe is totally inverted. The servant is the powerful one who can choose to help or ignore the master who explicitly begs for help. The maidservants don't see a master, but a foreigner in Job. The resident stranger in Job's house does not recognise that Job is the host. Here is a figure that has truly lost all social status and recognition in society. However, what is particularly tragic about the speech is the depiction of the loss of affection and acknowledgement from those who one might have expected to be closest to Job: his wife,[17] his siblings, his intimate friends. As Brown argues, 'Job has become the proverbial stranger' here 'castigated by his own household' (Brown 1999:232). Likewise, as Habel notes, 'those who ought to empathise with Job find him repulsive' (Habel 1985:203). Bassons makes a similar argument, suggesting that Job's 'deteriorating body has led to severed social relation[s]' and because of this he 'becomes so repulsive to his fellow kinsmen that they practically push him to the margins of society' (Basson 2008:288). Just as in Job 6, where Job accuses his friends of having seen trauma and feared, so, too, here Job describes how 'even family members look at [his] abject, horrifying appearance and they recoil' (Job 6:21; Greenstein 2018:48). Here Job talks with the heights of hyperbole, to the extent that his speech is full of rather peculiar phrases. For example, the extremely awkward phrase the 'sons of my belly',[18] causes confusion, perhaps evoking a misleading image of Job as a pregnant woman. Likewise the phrase 'my wind (רוח)[19] is repulsive to my wife' may

17 Although note Job's wife's former reactions to him. Perhaps finding Job's windy words odious would not be an entirely surprising response? Especially having been compared to the נבלות ('foolish women') for the crime of suggesting that Job's pious responses to bodily disintegration (Job 1:21) might not be entirely pragmatic (Job 2:9–10).

18 This is a crux of sorts. Given that Job's children are all dead according to the prologue, perhaps this strange phrase refers to Job's brothers (i.e. uterine brothers).

19 Many interpreters understand the term רוח to be indicative of Job's breath. Indeed, some translations reflect this thinking (the Vulgate, for example, as Seow notes has *halitim meum exhorriut uxor mea*, Seow 2013:817). Seow also notes that 'interpreters have even regarded the bad breath to be a symptom of Job's particular illness and, hence, a clue to the precise diagnosis of his malady' (Seow 2013:817). As such, some have even suggested emending the Hebrew to ריחי ('my breath', Clines 1989:429). Given the problems that we have discussed retrospective diagnosis such as this is best avoided (refer to Chapter 1). Indeed, it would particularly problematic, and of course entirely circular in logic, to emend the text simply to reflect more specifically on what Job's condition might be.

If we leave the term רוח as it stands, it is still possible to understand 'breath' as a translation given the wide semantic range of the word. It is also possible to translate 'spirit' here in the sense of 'life' or 'being', suggesting that Job's very existence is odious to his wife. This translation would align with the sense in which the word occurs in the first deity attack metaphor (Job 6:4; refer to Chapter 2).

be another example of hyperbole that is so awkward it verges on misdirection, with 'wind' also evoking flatulence, which would make Job's comment here comparable to Elihu's speech wherein he complains about being distressed by the 'wind in my [his] belly' and thus undermines his entire speech (Job 32:18). Similarly, the use and re-use – in a different guise – of polysemous terms in the speech (זור √I, 'strange' √II; 'repulsive' חנן √I, 'entreat' √II 'loathsome') complicates Job's speech but is also a form of verbal artifice through which the character can emphasise and restate, as if audiences were in any doubt, the socially degrading nature of his situation. Such is the full-blown emphasis on Job's tragic circumstances here that his (quite peculiar) speech crosses from the deeply tragic to the absurd. Job has, yet again, protested too much to be taken seriously. Given the ironic and farcical nature of the entire scenario, as set up in the prologue, the more vehemently Job emphasises the tragedy of his situation through ever more emphatic language, the more he ends up the victim of disparagement, aligning with the classic superiority theory of comedy. Phrased differently, for audiences, Job's melodramatic picture of the height of calamity only serves to emphasise his position in the play as the butt of the joke. With such language, no wonder the author/s have him laughed at (Job 12:4) and mocked (Job 21:3).

The emphasis on the ineffective nature of Job's body in the speech is particularly interesting for concretising the connection between bodily dysfunction and the drop in social status. Job implores his servant, not merely by waving his hand but even 'with my mouth', and there is no response or respect (cf. Ps. 123:2). Job attempts to rise up to speak and be listened to, as he did previously, but instead he is spoken against.[20] The very act of speech is undermined by his body; rather than listening to his arguments and perspectives, the 'wind' his body produces in speech repels his wife away from him. Verse 20 is particularly interesting with its image of emaciation: Job's body lacks physical power. He cannot literally take up space, and this emaciation is matched by his social insignificance. Lack of companionship and emaciation are a common way of expressing distress in laments (e.g. Ps. 105:5; Lam 4:8; cf. Southwood 2019). The image of a lack of substance is also a common one placed on the character Job's lips and one which regularly occurs in the context of the deity attack and surveillance metaphors.[21] Metaphorically, therefore, Job's lack of bodily presence through his leanness reflects his absence of social dignity.

However, the climax of the speech is reached in verses 21 and 22 wherein there is an abrupt shift from a description of Job's circumstances to a direct,

---

The translation 'wind', however, may also be appropriate here, perhaps reflecting Job's pious speech given that the characters in the dialogues regularly refer to each other's speeches as 'windy' words (refer to Chapter 2).

20 As we have discussed, the futility of Job 'rising up' occurs also in the extended deity attack metaphor in Job 30. Refer to Chapter 2.

21 The image of gauntness also occurs in comparable material. For example, the Righteous Sufferer makes a similar complaint, saying
Šīri ištaḫḫa damī izzuba, Eṣettum ussuqat arimat maškī, Šir'ānūya nuppuḫu uriqtum maḫru

and emphatically repeated, plea to his friends for pity because of the 'hand of Eloah' and his sickness-inducing 'touch'. Rather like the call on Job's part for the Almighty to let loose his hand,[22] here again God's body is depicted in a highly unflattering manner which is diametrically opposed to the idea of a 'strong hand' and 'outstretched arm'. In verse 16 Job had 'begged' (חנן) his servant to come, and now he begs his friends for pity (חנן). When this verb is used in the Psalms as an imperative, it is, as Seow notes, 'always addressed to God' (Seow 2013:801). Here in the topsy-turvy world Job now inhabits, however, he is forced to call to friends for mercy given that the attacking deity is the problem. Through the repurposing of conventional language so that it ends up being used in a highly unconventional way, traditional piety is parodied and mocked. The biting irony here is that Job is asking his friends for something he, and the audience, knows he will not get: Thus far, these friends, instructing Job on wisdom, haven't exactly behaved as the fountain of mercy (Prov. 13:14; 14:27). Indeed, Bildad has already 'helpfully' provided Job with moralising advice by suggesting that if he seeks El and begs his pity (חנן) by being upright (ישר) then things will go well.[23] Here, through mimicking traditional language, Job's request for pity is incredibly sarcastic. As a consequence, suddenly the tables are turned at this point of the speech and the 'butt of the joke' becomes Job's friends. Superiority theory helps here: The dramatic irony allows the audience to laugh at Job, as well as his friends, while maintaining a critical distance through being aware of the entire farcical scenario when the characters themselves are not. Job's sarcastic request is made all the more comical by placing it in context: It is entirely out of character with the way he usually addresses his friends. As Clines highlights,

> He has never before asked for their pity. Indeed, having berated them for their treachery (6:15), for their callousness (6:27), their stupidity (12:2–3; 13:2), their worthlessness (13:4), and their attempts to destroy him (19:2), having done everything wrong if he had been trying to win friends and influence people, it is truly amazing that he should suddenly fall into a supplicative mood, and that for only two verses, to be followed shortly be as aggressive an address to the friends as we have heard (vv. 28–29) . . . [Job] does not want their pity so much as their silence.
>
> (Clines 1989:453)

The comical parody of a call for pity in verse 20, however, betrays in the next verse two loaded questions about who has a right to judgement in Job's case. The friends are likened to El, who pursues (רדף) Job (Job 13:25). However,

('[My] flesh has wasted away, my blood drained, [my] bones have become visible, covering my skin, My tissues were inflamed, afflicted with jaundice' [The last term is a hapax, possibly from *arāqu* 'to be green, yellow', hence jaundice])'. (*Ludlul bēl nēmeqi* II.90; Annus and Lenzi 2010).

22 Refer to Chapter 2.

23 Cf. Job 1:1; note the irony of the suggestion.

Job's re-use of traditional language here undermines the seemingly flattering comparison with the deity, since it likens the friends also to the wicked who in the Psalms usually pursue (רדף) the righteous. Job's friends are not 'satisfied' with his 'flesh' but feel the need to 'pursue' him. The language used here reflects the attack of a hungry animal.[24] However, Job applies this metaphor to the incessant, moralising advice he is receiving and his friends' insatiable quest to pursue reasons for his condition. In essence, Job accuses his friends of inducing the 'second illness', stigma, (as discussed earlier)[25] by their moralising.

The connection between the body and community is widely recognised. This connection was explored in detail by Douglas, who, as formerly noted, emphasised the importance of the body's boundaries in several significant publications.[26] For Douglas, the body is a symbolic microcosm of the social, a 'model which can stand for any bounded system' so that 'its boundaries can represent any boundaries which are threatened or precarious' (Douglas 1966:138; cf. Berquist 2002).[27] Berquist follows and extends Douglas's arguments here by emphasising the importance of wholeness. For Berquist in ancient Israel 'the ideal body was the whole body' and 'a body was not complete without its many parts . . . bodies that leak or ooze violate the sense of firm boundaries, and so these bodies are not whole' (Berquist 2002:18, n19). Basson also expands upon Douglas's original theory concerning the connections between the body and social order.

> The abjection of the unclean and improper should be seen a means of maintaining the representation of order. . . . If order is conceived of as an arbitrary arrangement of elements in relative stability and harmony and unwhole [*sic.*] bodies have the potential of disrupting this order, it is not difficult to grasp why Job is treated as an abject figure. . . . The ancient Israelites were interested in the external manifestations of inner states and in these manifestations the body plays a crucial role. . . . Consequently, skin diseases or conditions that affect the integrity of the skin and ultimately the body instilled a particular horror.
>
> (Basson 2008:292)

24 It is not entirely clear what is meant by being satisfied with flesh. It may be an image connected with brute force and animal-like attack, suggesting the literal laceration of flesh. Perhaps, however, a more persuasive way of understanding the phrase is through the idiomatic, metaphoric expression wherein to bite somebody's flesh indicates slander (Ps. 27:2). Note the ironic use of the usually positive verb שבע ('satisfied'), as previously discussed. Refer to Chapter 2.

25 Refer to Chapter 2.

26 Refer to note 45 in Chapter 1.

27 Douglas makes a similar point with respect to what she calls 'leprosy', suggesting that

> The breach of the body's containing walls evidenced by escape of vital fluids and the failure of its skin cover are vulnerable states which go counter to God's creative action when he set up separating boundaries in the beginning.
>
> (Douglas 1999:190)

In this case, what is threatened is not just the social order but even, perhaps, the natural order.

If, therefore, the body functions as a metaphor for society and wholeness is linked strongly to order, harmony, and stability, then by casting the character Job as a person covered 'from head to toe' (i.e. a merismus indicating 'everywhere') in שחין ('boils')'[28] Job's body presents a particular threat to his society. Job, as 'sin visualised' is therefore not only a threat to the social order that his friends imagine and strive to maintain but also to the natural order, as if perhaps reflected in the return to chaos language in Job 3.[29] It is interesting to note here that Job is very seldom referred to as טמא ('unclean'; Job 14:4). Nevertheless, the speech here makes it undeniably clear that he exists at some significant social distance from his friends and society (Job 19:13–22). This, as formerly noted,[30] puts Job in a precarious position of deviance, especially given the connections between sickness and criminality.

Job's social distance from society is not particularly surprising, nor is the connection between illness and deviance confined to the biblical material. Indeed, as Lupton notes, 'illness and disease have long carried the symbolic meanings of loss of control, disorder and chaos and threatened rationality' (Lupton 2012:50). However, it is possible to extend Lupton's point here by suggesting that symbolic meanings associated with sickness regularly incorporate religious, moral, and ethical dimensions. As Littlewood and Lynch argue,

> The social anthropology of sickness and health has always been concerned with religious cosmologies: how societies make sense of such issues as prediction and control of misfortune and fate; the malevolence of others' the benevolence (or otherwise) of the mystical world; how human life may match some overarching ultrahuman principle; all this in terms of local understanding and explanations of the natural and ultra-human worlds – as organized ritual (or other) practice, and as principles of social order and organization.
>
> (Littlewood and Lynch 2016:1)

This argument is particularly helpful for thinking about Job's social status and position in society. Job's body, with its breached boundaries, represents chaos as a threat to the natural, ritual, and social order. But it is also significant that Job's body threatens the entire religious cosmology of the existing social order, perhaps threatening a type of Yahwism that no longer offers compelling resources for thinking about suffering. Phrased differently, if Job can be innocent and nevertheless be visually in pain or ill – through being covered in boils or emaciated – then his protestations are particularly foreboding. This is because they question existing ideas about how the world works and through doing so create anxiety by raising the threat of a world that is not ordered and

28 For a discussion of this term refer to Chapter 1.

29 Refer to note 137 in Chapter 2.

30 Refer to Chapter 2.

not predictable. It is not particularly surprising that Job is cast therefore as a character on the margins of society.

'Look at my body, ye mighty friends, and despair!': the body and powerlessness in Job 21

In Job 21:5–6, the character Job challenges his friends to look at him and to be appalled, a challenge which is made focusing the friends and audiences on his body in a defiant and hubristic way, almost akin to Shelley's Ozymandias. Job's speech here occurs in response to Zophar, who reacted to Job's former speech wherein the section concerning social alienation that we have just discussed occurred (Job 19). In his reaction to Job, Zophar, as we have already discussed, uses the metaphor of hunger and lack of station which the 'Wicked' supposedly experience as a way of emphasising the connection between bodily dysfunction and retribution (Job 20:14–16, 20–25).[31] The speech ends the way it begins, with a direct address to Job's friends. However, at the end Job bluntly accuses his friends that their advice does not have divine origins, as Zophar had suggested, but that their advice is 'puff' (הבל) and 'sinful' (מעל), as Seow notes it is 'idolatrous and hence nefarious' (Seow 2013:866).[32] In this speech Job attempts to undermine the 'idolatrous' form of Yahwism that his friends defend through their moralising advice.

> Face me (imperative פנה) and despair (*hiphil*[33] imperative שמם)!
> Put (imperative שום) your hand upon your mouth!
> When I consider[34] . . . I tremble (בהל)
> And horror (פַּלָּצוּת) grasps my flesh![35]
>
> (Job 21:5–6)

Job's speech to his friends in verse 5 is littered with imperatives urging the friends to face him (cf. Job 6:28). If they were to truly 'face' Job, they would 'despair' (שמם), a term indicating desolation and astonishment.[36] Indeed, Job uses this term to describe God's destruction of him in the extended deity attack

31 Refer to Chapter 2. Concerning the metaphor of digestion in Job and the Psalms refer to Southwood 2019.

32 Seow argues persuasively that the term 'puff' (הבל) has overtones of idolatry on account of being 'commonly associated with idols' finding the 'precise idiom "console with *hebel*"' in Zech. 10:2 wherein the connection is made between idolatry and divination' (Seow 2013:876). The term 'sinful' מעל is usually used to designate a crime against God.

33 BHS suggests that we emend the verb שמם to a *niphal* 'be appalled'.

34 The verb זכר has a rather wide semantic range, including 'remember' but also 'consider', or 'think about' / 'call to mind'. Strangely, here the verb lacks an object – an absence communicated in the translation through the ellipsis. Perhaps the character here considers his physical condition given the plea to the friends in the former verse to face him and despair? Perhaps it is the lack of justice in the world wherein the wicked thrive, as the character goes on to illustrate (Job 21:7ff)?

35 Literally 'my flesh grasps horror', which is awkward.

36 Refer to note 62 in Chapter 2.

metaphor in Job 16.[37] Likewise, he uses the term shortly after said deity attack metaphor in chapter 17, wherein he suggests that the 'upright' would react with 'despair' (שמם) if they considered him (Job 17:8).[38] In the scenario Job paints, 'despair' would be followed with speechlessness, as communicated through the idiom 'put your hand upon your mouth', an idiom which defiantly ends Job's speeches in response to the whirlwind speeches (Job 40:4; cf. 29:9).[39] In verse 6, although the object of 'consider' is missing, the somatic image of Job's flesh 'trembling' as portrayed through the synonyms בהל and פַּלָּצוּת is nevertheless powerful.[40] Here Job's words pick up on, and mock, the motif of astonishment (שמם) that Bildad uses concerning the fate of the wicked (Job 18:20) and of the trembling in Eliphaz's report of his vision (Job 4:14). Instead of the wicked being in 'despair' Job suggests this would be the reaction of his friends if there were to truly 'face' him. Instead of trembling indicating the beginning of a celestial vision, like Eliphaz describes, it is the effect on Job's body of considering either his physical demise or the prosperity of the wicked.[41] Instead of serving the Lord 'with fear' and rejoicing 'with trembling', as the psalmist advises, Job's flesh is grasped by horror (Ps 2:11). However, his friends cannot face the reality that he represents. As Rowley argues, 'God's government of the world is quite other than their vain theorizings have suggested' (Rowley 1976:147). Seow makes a similar but slightly more nuanced case, suggesting that 'Job's brokenness embodies the instability of moral order and the shaking of foundations inasmuch as an innocent man is now in a situation which tradition has taught is the lot of the wicked' (Seow 2013:866). Job's suggestion here is that if his friends were to 'face' him in an authentic way, looking without the rose-tinted lenses of their traditions from wherein their security lies, then the stark reality of the lack of justice in the world, as dramatically embodied by the quivering Job, would be enough to convince them that there is some weight in his arguments. In essence, the challenge Job poses is to suggest that their versions of Yahwism, which Pelham describes as the 'world-as-it-ought-to-be', are shaky and ill-founded because they do not help with Job's reality (Pelham 2012a). Indeed, the character's message goes beyond the metaphorical: Job literally somatises his distress in front of his friends and audiences for emphasis and illustration. Tragically, in the case of his friends, the message is to no avail. But

37 Job 16:7. Refer to Chapter 2.

38 Beuken compares the term שמם followed by the preposition על in Bildad's speech (Job 18:13–18) and Isa. 52:14–15) and draws out the similarities in language between the language of suffering in Job and in the suffering servant passages (Beuken *et al.* 1997).

39 The idiom's meaning is concretised through the fact that it occurs in parallelism with the term חרש ('Silent' / 'speechless') Judg. 18:19; Mic. 7:16.

40 The second term (פַּלָּצוּת) is not widespread, occurring only here and in three other places (Ps. 55:5; Isa 21:4; Ezek 7:18). In Psalm 55 פַּלָּצוּת occurs in parallelism with רעד, another synonym for trembling, and the verse begins with 'fearfulness' (ירע).

41 The object is not clear at the beginning of verse 6. Therefore, both probabilities are included here.

it is interesting to consider how early audiences listening to the drama's central challenge to established Yahwism might react.

These verses and the friends' reactions to Job before and after his speech emphasise the importance of the function of Job's body in the dialogues. As Newsom argues, in Job 'the body plays an important role in Job's struggle against the language of prayer and his search for a possible alternative' (Newsom 1999:246). Balentine also highlights the significance the body has in Job, arguing that 'against the notion that affliction is a metaphor for sin, he insists that the reality, the very physicality of his pain shatters every attempt to give suffering a name that belongs to something else' (Balentine 2015:137). What is exposed in the sight of audiences through Job's insistence that his friends face him is the ineffectiveness of moralising in the face of authentic pain. As Bastiaens argues, their 'lack of understanding goes together with contempt for Job . . . and with a feeling of horror for his suffering, which is apparently well-deserved' (Bastiaens 1997:426–427). The responses that Job elicits, wherein the friends not only moralise but are 'forced to recoil'[42] and 'despair' (שמם) when considering Job illustrate clearly what Lambert designates the 'failure of consolation' represented by the incessant moralising (Lambert 2015:262).

Metaphor and somatisation are key elements in Job's challenge to his friends here. For Job's friends, his body is a metaphor for sinfulness or 'sin visualised'. Job, however, asserts, and draws attention to, the presence of his body as a metaphor expressing the lack of companionship and the absence of the kind of deity that the friends imagine. Rewiring assumptions embedded within the traditional moralising advice of his friends using the body as a metaphor is a particularly powerful strategy. This is because metaphor has the potential to 'define the undefined and nascent identity of a person or group' and is 'strategic; it is a plan for action and performance . . . metaphors are creative and infinitely generative in their allusions and meanings' (Low 1994:143). Low's argument here focuses on *nervos* (nerves) in Brazil, wherein she suggests that nervous attacks occurring have a political meaning; they are 'coded metaphors which are used by the sugarcane workers' in her study to 'express their politically dangerous and therefore unacceptable conditions' (Low 1994:144). Low's argument has some similarities with Nichter's work on 'idioms of distress' (Nichter 1981).[43] For Nichter, 'somatization is . . . an important idiom through which distress is communicated' (Nichter 1981:379). Therefore, bodily symptoms experienced are meaningful also as metaphoric expressions of distress. Somatisation is particularly important in terms of the responses it evokes.[44] This is because the symptoms experi-

42 Job 16:7. Refer to Chapter 2.

43 Although, as noted in Chapter 1, Nichter's theory is not without various critiques. Refer also to Chapter 2.

44 For example, Nichter argues that responses to somatisation enable researchers to make judgements about the reciprocal nature of distress, arguing that

enced 'may also be expressions of types of distress which are symbolically relevant, which accord with the personal and cultural meaning complexes underscoring these symptoms' (Nichter 1981:392). By casting the character of Job as one who emphasises his bodily distress to his friends through commanding them to face him and then by using synonyms for 'trembling', his body becomes a metaphorical expression, or 'idiom', of distress. This is quite a helpful way of framing the emphasis on the body here given the significance of responses. The friends, and Job, have thus far been talking past one another and dismissing each other's arguments as simply wrong. It is becoming clear that dialogue is not working. Therefore, at this interesting juncture in the speech, emphasis is placed on the character Job's plight through casting him as embodying the distress he speaks of. It is entirely fitting that at this point Job directly engages with the perspectives of his friends, 'addressing in turn the arguments of Eliphaz (vv. 8–13; [cf. Job 15]), Bildad (vv. 17–18 [cf. Job 18]), and Zophar (vv. 19–32 [cf. Job 20])', therefore presenting 'a summation of his position' and leaving 'no argument by his adversaries unanswered' (Seow 2013:866). Job is depicted here as a tragic figure who is desperate for a meaningful response from his friends – as he has now given them – or at the very least some recognition of his humanity through simply facing him. This tragic scene heightens tension for audiences, and given the fact that Job has directly answered his friends' arguments, his plea at the beginning of the speech to be faced, and the accusation of idolatrous and false advice at the end of the speech, audience expectations in terms of the response are high.

However, the response Job receives, with more tin-pot theorising advice from Eliphaz, is underwhelming and anticlimactic. Eliphaz demonstrates quite concretely that he has not listened to Job's counterarguments. Instead, ironically, he simply re-emphasises the divine origin of his advice by stating that Job should 'agree with him [God] and be at peace . . . turn to the Almighty and you will be restored' (Job 21:21, 23). The sentiment here in response to Job re-emphasises Eliphaz's earlier argument that the 'consolations of God' are what Job is receiving (Job 15:11). Eliphaz's response to Job aligns well with Zophar's position wherein he claims his advice is tantamount to coming directly from God: 'Oh that God would speak, and open his lips to you' (Job 11:5; Schipper 2010:19). This response is comical to an extent. The anti-climax of realising that the tension created by Job has not been continued aligns with relief theory.

> the response or lack of response (itself a response) of significant others (e.g., household members, practitioners) to an individual's display of distress, and the manner in which feedback (or lack thereof) influenced the experience and expression of distress in a recursive fashion.
>
> (Nichter 2010:404)

In the example Nichter cites of South Kanarese villagers, the reporting of symptoms 'is influenced by notions of ethnophysiology, and etiology' but interestingly, villagers keenly observed which symptoms 'evoke desired responses from different types of practitioners' (Nichter 1981:386). This is not to suggest that symptoms were fabricated, but to emphasise the political and metaphoric importance of bodily expression and the responses it evokes.

Job's own words 'face me and despair' are overblown and exaggerated. His argument is cast in the most dramatic terms possible, so that at this point at the beginning of the speech, it is difficult to take the character entirely seriously.[45] Also moving from the tragic to the comic is the overly flattering comparison that Eliphaz (and Zophar) make: Suggesting their advice to Job is nigh-on equivalent to a direct message from the Almighty is incongruous (and to an extent undermines their entire arguments). As Whedbee argues, through using incongruity which 'stands at the heart of the main course of the dialogues', the author/s create 'a magnificent caricature of the wise counsellor' (Whedbee 1977:7, 10). Nevertheless, despite the entertaining and light-hearted presentation with all its exaggeration and incongruity, the seriousness of Job's charges against his friends at the end of the speech, that their advice is ephemeral, sinful, and therefore idolatrous, endures. Their form of Yahwism is a false form that fails through its lack of benevolence and compassion.

Summary

This section surveyed the connection between Job's social status and his body focusing specifically on Job 19:13–22 and 21:5–6, with examples selected on account of the explicit connection between the body and the character's social world. The first section analysed the prolonged description of changed social circumstances that the character communicates. The incongruence of this rather tragic picture having followed a dramatic, but anti-climactic, deity attack metaphor was recognised (Job 19:7–12). The picture painted in 19:13–22, we argued, was one where the undoing of Job's body was matched symbiotically with the breakdown of his social universe, both of which Job blames the deity for. Job produces a tragic litany of woes in this speech wherein a topsy-turvy world appears with servants more powerful than masters and loss of affection among closest kin and familiar friends. Job's speech is full of rather peculiar phrases such as 'my wind is repulsive to my wife'. The high level of hyperbole in the speech, it was noted, might verge on misdirection. It was also argued that the author/s used polysemy in order to emphasise the socially degrading nature of Job's situation. However, we noted the full-blown emphasis on Job's tragic circumstances. The overly emphatic nature of the speech moved it from being tragic to being absurd. Job's melodramatic picture of the height of calamity only serves to emphasise his position in the play as the butt of the joke. We also recognised the deeply sarcastic nature of Job's plea to his friends for pity at the climax of the speech (Job 19:22). Finally, we recognised the importance of boundaries and of religious cosmologies for the symbolic structuring of ideas about the body and the social order.

45 Although the serious and tragic nature of the speech should not be missed, especially given the direct response that Job gives in response to his friends' arguments and the accusation of adulterous 'puffs' of advice.

The final section examined Job's overblown and defiant, hubristic challenge to his friends to face him. His speech here addressed the concerns of all three friends but ended with the accusation that their advice was ephemeral and sinful, and by extension idolatrous. Job's challenge is followed by the corporeal image of Job's flesh shaking, and it was argued that here the author/s have Job literally somatise his distresses in front of his friends and audiences for emphasis and illustration. Nichter's work on idioms of distress among South Kanarese villagers and Low's work on *nervos* (nerves) in Brazil were used comparatively to suggest that Job's 'trembling' is symbolically and metaphorically relevant. In addition, we noted the comically underwhelming and anti-climactic nature of Eliphaz's tin-pot theorising in response to Job, also noting the relevance of relief theory after Job's accusation of idolatry at the end of his speech. Finally, we recognised the incongruous and overly flattering way that Eliphaz (and Zophar) responds to Job, suggesting that his advice is nigh-on equivalent to a direct message from the Almighty. However, the seriousness of Job's suggestions that his friends' advice is idolatrous endures as a challenge to a type of Yahwism that lacks benevolence and compassion.

Bibliography

Annus, A. and Lenzi, A., 2010. *Ludlul bēl nēmeqi: The standard Babylonian poem of the righteous sufferer.* Helsinki: Neo-Assyrian Text Corpus Project.

Awabdy, M.A., 2014. *Immigrants and innovative law: Deuteronomy's theological and social vision for the [rg].* Asbury Theological Seminary. Tübingen: Mohr Siebeck.

Balentine, S.E., 2015. *Have you considered my servant Job? Understanding the biblical archetype of patience.* Columbia: University of South Carolina Press.

Basson, A., 2008. Just skin and bones: The longing for wholeness of the body in the book of Job. *Vetus Testamentum*, **58**(3), pp. 287–299.

Bastiaens, J.C., 1997. The language of suffering in Job 16–19 and the suffering servant passages of Deutero-Isaiah. In: W. Beuken, J.V.J. Ruiten and M. Vervenne, eds, *Studies in the book of Isaiah: Festschrift Willem A.M. Beuken.* Leuven: Leuven University Press, pp. 421–432.

Berquist, J.L., 2002. *Controlling corporeality: The body and the household in ancient Israel.* New Brunswick, NJ; London: Rutgers University Press.

Beuken, W., Ruiten, J. and Vervenne, M., 1997. *Studies in the book of Isaiah: Festschrift Willem A.M. Beuken.* Leuven; Leuven: Leuven University Press, Uitgeverij Peeters.

Brown, W.P., 1999. Introducing Job – a journey of transformation. *Interpretation*, **53**(3), pp. 228–238.

Carsten, J., 2000. *Cultures of relatedness: New approaches to the study of kinship.* Cambridge: Cambridge University Press.

Claassens, L.J., 2013. Countering stereotypes: Job, disability, and human dignity. *Journal of Religion, Disability & Health*, **17**(2), pp. 169–183.

Clines, D.J.A., 1989. *Job 1–20.* Dallas, TX: Word Books.

Dhont, M., 2017. *Style and context of old Greek Job.* Leiden; Boston: Brill.

Douglas, M., 1966. *Purity and danger: An analysis of concepts of pollution and taboo.* London: Routledge & Kegan Paul.

Douglas, M., 1999. *Leviticus as literature.* Oxford: Oxford University Press.

Gordis, R., 1978. *The book of Job: Commentary, new translation and special studies.* New York: Jewish Theological Seminary of America.

Greenstein, E.L., 2018. Metaphors of illness and wellness in Job. In: S.C. Jones and C.R. Roy, eds, *"When the morning stars sang": Essays in honor of Choon Leong Seow on the occasion of his sixty-fifth birthday.* Berlin; Boston: Walter de Gruyter, pp. 39–50.

Habel, N.C., 1985. *The book of Job: A commentary.* London: SCM.

Lambert, D.A., 2015. The book of Job in ritual perspective. *Journal of Biblical. Literature*, **134**(3), pp. 557–575.

Littlewood, R. and Lynch, R., 2016. *Cosmos, Gods and madmen: Frameworks in the anthropologies of medicine.* New York: Berghahn Books.

Low, S., 1994. Embodied metaphors: Nerves as lived experience. In: T.J. Csordas, ed, *Embodiment and experience: The existential ground of culture and self.* Cambridge: Cambridge University Press, pp. 139–162.

Lupton, D., 2012. *Fat.* Milton Park; Abingdon, Oxon; New York, NY: Routledge.

Melcher, S.J., 2017. Job, proverbs, and ecclesiastes. In: S.J. Melcher, M.C. Parsons and A. Young, eds, *The Bible and disability: A commentary.* Waco, TX: Baylor University Press, pp. 159–187.

Newsom, C.A., 1999. Job and his friends – a conflict of moral imaginations (An examination of a scriptural model of divine moral answerability). *Interpretation-A Journal of Bible and Theology*, **53**(3), pp. 239–253.

Nichter, M., 1981. Idioms of distress: Alternatives in the expression of psychosocial distress: A case study from South India. *Culture, Medicine and Psychiatry*, **5**(4), pp. 379–408.

Nichter, M., 2010. Idioms of distress revisited. *Culture, Medicine, and Psychiatry*, **34**(2), pp. 401–416.

Pelham, A., 2012a. *Contested creations in the book of Job: The-world-as-it-ought-and-ought-not-to-be.* Leiden: Brill.

Rowley, H.H., 1976. *Job.* Rev. edn. London: Oliphants.

Schipper, J., 2010. Healing and silence in the epilogue of Job. *Word & World*, **30**(1), pp. 16–22.

Schneider, D.M., 1984. *A critique of the study of kinship.* Ann Arbor: University of Michigan Press.

Seow, C.L., 2013. *Job 1–21: Interpretation and commentary.* Grand Rapids, MI: William B. Eerdmans.

Southwood, K.E., 2012. *Ethnicity and the mixed marriage crisis in Ezra 9–10: An anthropological approach.* Oxford: Oxford University Press.

Southwood, K.E., 2017. *Marriage by capture in the book of judges: An anthropological approach.* New York: Cambridge University Press.

Southwood, K.E., 2019. Metaphor, illness, and identity in Psalms 88 and 102. *Journal for the Study of the Old Testament*, **2**, pp. 228–246.

Southwood, K.E., Forthcoming. The "innards" in the Psalms and job as metaphors for illness. *Horizons in Biblical Literature.*

Whedbee, J., 1977. The comedy of Job. *Semeia*, **7**, pp. 1–39.

5 Is the answer for Job blowin' in the wind?

Job as a dramatised comedy of advice

This monograph has analysed Job's speeches with a specific focus on the role his body plays for his arguments and for undermining traditional ideas connected with retribution. It has prioritised the speech of Job, although it has also noted the friends' responses and advice. Prioritising Job's speech reflects the text itself: The 'story revolves around his experience', and 'he speaks more than anyone else'; therefore, 'his voice is privileged' (Seow 2013:87). Furthermore, as we shall discuss, Yahweh actually endorses Job at the end, suggesting that he has spoken rightly (Job 42:2). Job's body is particularly important in the speeches, partly because through continual reference to it he introduces a profound juxtaposition between bodily experience and traditional wisdom, which has ethical and epistemological implications for Yahwism at the time of writing and for early audiences.

This monograph has imagined Job as a play wherein tragedy and comedy regularly collide, perhaps with similarities to Aristophanes and the Athenian theatre. The vitality and dynamism of the dialogues in Job emerge more clearly as the characters pontificate about Job's problems. The critical key argument that has been defended is that the moralising[1] and retribution-centred language of Job's friends reflects a type of Yahwism that the author/s seek to destabilise and undermine. This is achieved through casting Job as an upright and blameless character who is nevertheless the subject of bodily dysfunction. This key device creates a double vision for audiences who at once see a world known to the characters but at the same time see how the entire scenario has been set up. Moving through the dialogues, the puffed-up, self-righteous Job becomes ever more frustrated, and his body-centred language adopts key exaggerated and melodramatic metaphors of deity attack and deity surveillance in a symbolic protest against retribution language. In response the friends increase their moralising until, after 30 chapters, the comic character Elihu suddenly emerges

1 Moralising advice and language were defined as judgemental communication, speech emphasising personal responsibility, and incriminating assumptions embedded within advice.

DOI: 10.4324/9781003029489-5

stating that he is 'full of words' and that the 'wind' within 'constrains' him. As all the characters become increasingly vexed, the audience watches the windy discussion elaborate, knowing all along that the entire scenario is the result of a gamble based on Job's supposed blamelessness.

A key contribution of this monograph has been to highlight how the perspective of illness as retribution is powerfully refuted in Job's speeches and, in particular, to show how this is achieved through comedy. Comedy in Job is a powerful weapon used to expose and ridicule the idea of retribution. Rejecting the approach of retrospective diagnosis, this monograph carefully analysed the expression of pain in Job focusing specifically on somatic language used in the deity attack metaphors, in the deity surveillance metaphors, and in the language connected to the body and social status. The analysis relied heavily on research concerning illness narratives and expressions of pain in order to engage critically with these metaphors. The deity attack and surveillance metaphors, as well as the language concerning the social world and Job's body, were analysed in a comparative way using research from medical anthropology and sociology which focuses on illness narratives and expressions of pain.

Why depict a character whose 'bone and flesh' have been attacked and whose expressions of pain are deity attack and surveillance metaphors? It has long been acknowledged that Job is part of a long tradition of theological dissent, but why go to the extremes of casting the deity in such a scandalous and shocking way? Moreover, why do so in a way that dovetails tragedy and comedy? In particular, why use comedy at all? Is doing so unethical? The ethics of humour are, after all, not unproblematic. As Morreall outlines, traditional objections against laughter and humour from an ethical perspective include charges such as 'humor [sic] is hostile . . . diminishes self-control . . . irresponsible . . . insincere . . . fosters anarchy . . . foolish' (Morreall 2008:238–239). Furthermore, Morreall suggests that the Bible is, for the most part, rather negative about comedy and laughter, arguing that,

> When laughter is mentioned in the Bible, it is associated with one of three things. In descending order, they are hostility, foolishness, and joy. In the Bible when someone laughs, it is usually an expression of hostility, contempt, or scorn. Laughter is at a person, and that person's reputation and social standing are diminished by the laughter. . . . The second most common kind of laughter in the Bible is the irresponsible and irrational laugh of the foolish person. . . . Abraham and Sarah's laughter . . . did show two serious shortcomings: the intellectual inability to imagine the maker of heaven and earth performing a simple miracle, and a lack of trust in God. In the Bible, the opposite of the laughing fool is the sad wise person. The Book of Ecclesiastes has this advice: Sorrow is better than laughter, for by sadness of countenance the heart is made glad.
>
> (Morreall 2008:212–213)

Is an argument for the potential presence of comedy alongside tragedy in Job therefore not only ethically inappropriate but also totally out of place in the context of the entire biblical material? Perhaps this would be the case if we were to agree with Morreall's three categories of what laughter is associated with in the Hebrew Bible. However, Morreall fails to consider the widely recognised role of humour, especially in the forms of satire and hyperbole, in the Hebrew Bible (Jackson 2012; Brenner-Idan and Radday 1990; Craig 1995; Lazarus 2014).[2]

If, as has been argued in this monograph, there are elements of both comedy and tragedy within the deity attack and deity surveillance metaphors and in other places wherein Job's body is used as a focal point for the discussion, what possible purpose might it serve? One possibility that we have argued throughout this monograph is that comedy is being used in quite a sophisticated way in order to communicate with audiences. Specifically, we have suggested that comedy is being used as a weapon to undermine a type of Yahwism that existed at the time of writing which was focused on the idea of retribution and on traditional piety and wisdom. Given the shocking ways in which the deity is cast in Job and the high level of theological dissent, it is not unreasonable to suppose that the type of Yahwism being undermined was dominant or somehow powerful at the time of writing and among early audiences: Why else go to such extreme measures to challenge it? This suggestion aligns well with some of the research on comedy. Indeed, Jackson points out that,

> Satire is comedy as weapon. It is 'the literary art of diminishing or derogating a subject by making it ridiculous and evoking toward it attitudes of amusement, contempt, scorn, or indignation'. Satire is very malleable, taking the form that best suits its message.
>
> (Jackson 2012:20; Abrams and Harpham 2005:40)

2 Elements in Esther such as the gallows built for Haman being the height of a six-story building, or the confusion over why Haman is on the couch with Esther, are sometimes considered to be amusing (Jackson 2012:199–220). Likewise, the irony of the fact that Balaam's donkey, rather than Balaam, experiences a vision of the angel of the Lord – and in doing so, in panic, it inadvertently crushes Balaam's foot against the wall – followed by the absurdity of the reversal (the donkey giving Balaam advice) may be read as satire (Num. 22–24). In addition, the book of Jonah – featuring a cantankerous Israelite prophet whose half-hearted warning about the overturning of Nineveh sometime in the distant future prompts one of the most decisive changes of behaviour in the entire Hebrew Bible, and with its the extremes of even the cattle joining the fast, may be considered amusing (Lazarus 2014). Finally, the picture of the half-wit servants waiting for the fatted King Eglon, who has just been murdered, to finish 'covering his feet in his summer chamber', is also sometimes read as a satire of a foreign king which is 'at once shrewd and jubilant' (Alter 1981:39). Finally, Tobit's exaggerated piety might be considered humorous (Lazarus 2014; refer to note 22 in Chapter 1). Perhaps, given the precedent for recognising comedy and humour in the Hebrew Bible, we should entertain the possibility of tragedy and comedy co-existing in Job.

The idea that Job's friends insist on maintaining – that any problem with the body must be the result of retribution – is an easy target for satire in Job. Given the information about causation and responsibility that audiences are privy to in the prologue (classic dramatic irony), the entirety of the friends' advice is ridiculed and scorned, sometimes giving way to humour and sometimes, given the tragic nature of Job's predicament, to indignation. What emerges is a comedy of advice that is played out in front of audiences. However, the use of comedy is quite sophisticated. It creates a safe space for audiences to question the idea of retribution behind which a weight of tradition stands and to think about the possibilities for a renewed form of Yahwism that is able to answer questions about, and engage with, human experience in a more meaningful way. It allows audiences to be at once critically detached but at the same time emotionally involved. As such, dangerous, possibly taboo, topics – such as pain and its meaning, mortality, and suffering – are given space to be explored in earnest because audiences do not have to take the play seriously. Indeed, part of the genius of using comedy to make the argument against retribution is that a deadly serious point can be made in a non-serious, and therefore (to an extent) non-threatening manner. As Berger explains, this is possible because 'the comic conjures up a separate world, different from the world of ordinary reality, operating by different rules' (Berger 1997:x). Furthermore, tragic topics which usually elicit grave and solemn responses can be explored from different perspectives through the device of using comedy to change the mood. Returning to Morreall, one could still argue about ethics here: Is this approach 'irresponsible' or 'insincere'? Does it 'foster anarchy'? (Morreall 2008:238–239). In response, the power dynamics and broader social structures cannot be put aside for answering these questions. Who dictates what counts as irresponsible and insincere? Does using comedy to make a serious point mean that the point is less sincere? If anything, this monograph has argued that comedy is used in a very sincere and responsible way: What was revealed as 'insincere' and 'irresponsible' was the theological cowardice of attempting to defend traditions that no longer effectively answered questions about experience.

The idea that comedy might foster anarchy is particularly interesting in light of the material we have analysed in Job. Of course, while it is possible to make an argument for the presence of comedy alongside tragedy in Job, we must acknowledge that any theorising about why comedy is used will always remain in the realm of conjecture. This is an acknowledged drawback. Nevertheless, the objection that comedy fosters anarchy raises important questions about the connections between the material we have analysed in Job and what broader social structures, power, and controlling narratives existed at the time of its composition or for early audiences. One helpful resource for organising our furniture of thought on this emerges from Douglas's research which attempted to generalise the relationship between joking and the social structure (Douglas 1968). Douglas took a functionalist approach to humour (an approach which interprets it in terms of the social functions it fulfils for a society or social group) and understood joking as a symbolic representation of underlying social arrangements. Douglas argued, therefore, that jokes were anti-rites that subverted the social order, an order regularly validated and maintained by religious rituals. In contrast to this order, jokes assert a lack of control over and against patterns of control (Douglas 1968). Radcliffe-Brown's theory about formalised joking is similar, wherein the choices kin groups face in light of social disjunction were, he argued, extreme respect for social avoidance or, abusive joking which relieved arising hostilities and playfully reflected mutual interests (Radcliffe-Brown 1940). Perhaps something similar may have been in the background for the author/s of Job and for early audiences? Perhaps when confronted with the dominant religious ideas within Yahwism concerning retribution and control it was important to assert the lack of control that human beings have? As Newsom argues, 'the dialogue throws the reader in to very murky moral ground and then removes the help and guidance one normally expects to find in a text' (Newsom 1993:126). Using pain as an example here is quite a good way of emphasising this lack of control and suggesting an alternative moral universe because it is an experience, however widely interpreted, that is unavoidable for most human beings. Furthermore, perhaps through the mechanisms of being indirect (and therefore only subtly challenging) by choosing Job – a foreigner from Uz rather than a Yahwist – and of making the play's setting obscure and distant, 'mutual interests' among Yahwists, both traditionalists and those with an appetite for change, watching the play are attended to.

Finally, it is worth noting that although the functionalist approach that Douglas and Radcliffe-Brown take is helpful, perhaps it is also possible to frame comedy in Job through the theoretical lens of the symbolic interactionist approach to comedy which focuses on the construction of meanings and social relations. According to this approach 'social relations and meanings, and more generally "social reality", are not seen as fixed and given but as constructed and negotiated in the course of social interaction' (Kuipers 2008:373). If we consider this perspective, then whether or not a thing is humorous, or instead serious, is not a given. Rather, it is constructed during the course of the interactions. In this case, the movement from serious to humorous is an act of cooperation which may work or not depending on whether, or not, the parties interacting recognise the freedom to transgress norms. If we consider this perspective on comedy in Job, it is possible that a rather complex interaction between audience and play, or between author and reader, is taking place in the performance or reception of the work. For audience members who are able to laugh when tragedy turns to comedy, the interaction between author and audience has succeeded. Indeed, the interaction has been particularly successful if audience members recognise some of their own views being expressed by Job's friends. This is because it weakens the connection between pain or illness and punishment, often, as we have noted, through satire. Jackson's use of Molière's defence of comedy here is helpful. Molière suggested there is a virtue and a corrective function to comedy, arguing that, 'nothing admonishes the majority of people better than the portrayal of their faults'; therefore, 'to expose vices to the ridicule of all the world is a severe blow to them . . . people do not mind being wicked; but they object to being made ridiculous' (Jackson 2012:26). For those who engage with Job and are persuaded by its comic elements, changes in attitudes to Yahwism at the time have been established. However, for audience members who do not recognise the comedy, the interaction has been unsuccessful. In this case, the lack of success might nevertheless be curtailed by the level of the play's tragedy and by the insistence of the friends' advice. Perhaps such audience members would take the play very seriously by emphasising its tragic aspects and wholeheartedly agreeing with the advice provided. Therefore, while the link between comedy and its uses for original audiences and readers must remain the realm of conjecture, it is nevertheless worth imagining the impact it may have had in terms of the development of ideas within Yahwism. As van Loon states, the real value of the idea of the inner self transcending the dull earthly reality of Job's friends is through the recognition that 'there are [others] whose circumstances may not reflect their moral integrity' (van Loon 2018:210). The ethical implications of such a comedy of 'advice', not just for those who suffer but especially for the community around them, are nowhere more clearly played out than through being dramatised before audiences.

Job's responses to Yahweh

While the main focus of this monograph has been on the dialogues, any monograph on Job would be 'unfinished' without some discussion of its ending. However, Job's responses are not particularly central for the main arguments of this monograph concerning the dialogues being a comedy of moralising advice. Therefore, in keeping with the text itself, we have left off analysis of the ending until this point, specifically after the conclusion. We should acknowledge here the multitudinous scholarship that exists on the whirlwind speeches and their relationship to the dialogues. Likewise, there are countless attempts to translate, interpret, and struggle to make sense of Job's responses. The translation and interpretation provided here unfortunately add to the 'making of many books' and scholarly suggestions on this matter. What follows is an attempt to tread the well-worn path of translating and interpreting Job's responses to Yahweh. But this comes with the full and undivided acknowledgement that it is nigh-on impossible to ever make sense with any level of certainty.

We have already discussed the irony of the fact that although the characters accuse each other of 'windy' words that lack substance and puffed-arguments that don't engage fully or help, Yahweh's answer to Job comes in the form of an interrogation from a 'whirlwind'. It is an interrogation, however, that comes in the form of perhaps *the* most magnificent pieces of poetry in the entire Hebrew Bible. But it does not, for the most part, engage directly with Job's questions about individual experience. Instead the 'answer' blows everybody away, character and audiences, with total surprise. Elihu's speech, it might have seemed, was the last: After no fewer than 30 chapters of advice he, in a rather verbose manner, then adds another 6 chapters which add no progress to the argument already made. Instead of finally ending there, though, the play continues with a new and surprising character: Yahweh. The depiction of Yahweh here is as a God of power and grandeur whose creation is full of joyful and incalculable variety and vitality. Picture cascades upon picture of nature's infinite detail, and the overall impressionistic scene that is painted points to a renewed, almost childlike, sense of wonder. The magnificent (Pleiades, Orion, Behemoth, Leviathan, the soaring eagle, the strong horse) are presented side by side with the eccentric (the harsh mother ostrich, the 'doors' of Leviathan's 'face', the laughing wild ass), but the effect is not comedy. Instead, the scene hints at profound freedom and immeasurability.

Rather, however, than exploring Yahweh's answer to Job, we will stay in keeping with the rest of this monograph by prioritising Job's voice and only then exploring Yahweh's only point of direct engagement with Job and his friends (Job 40:4–5; 42:7–8). As noted, this is also in keeping with the text itself, wherein Job's voice rather than Yahweh's, is what dominates. Therefore, we will focus on Job's response to Yahweh, before considering Yahweh's response to Job and his friends.

Yahweh's majestic, fairly lengthy, and awe-inspiring speech is followed by a clipped and cryptic response from Job. This highlights the incongruity between the speakers who are not matched opponents. Job's response is anti-climactic and underwhelming. As if any reply could hope to be taken seriously after the sublime poetry, not only are Job's replies here clipped, they are also, we will argue, characteristically sarcastic and petulant. Therefore, rather than the anti-climactic capitulation of orthodoxy here, we have a brilliantly double-edged and sardonic response from Job. Even here, at a point in the play wherein to be defiant might well cause audiences irritation and angst – because the character Job is not merely facing Eloah or El but is face to face with Yahweh (referred to by the tetragrammaton, not another name, as in the dialogues) – Job continues to be iconoclastic, irreverent, and shocking.

> Behold, I "*am humble* [*curse*]"! What can I answer you?
> I put my hand to my mouth.
> I have spoken once and will not answer again
> And twice?! But I will not add anything else.
>
> (Job 40:4–5)

Job had claimed that 'the words of Job are complete' (Job 38:40). With such a formal statement, this could potentially have made quite a good ending to the play. Instead, like a work with several endings,[3] the author/s has Job add a few more words. Just as Job and his friends did not, for the most part, directly engage with each other's arguments, here, too, Job does not address Yahweh's speech directly. Indeed, Clines suggests that his response 'makes us wonder whether Job has been listening very carefully to Yahweh' (Clines 2011:1138).

3 For example, 'The French Lieutenant's Woman' (Fowles 1969).

The beginning of the speech opens with the rather ambiguous phrase הן קלתי 'Behold, I *am humble* [*curse*]!' The translation here could possibly be polysemous. The verb קלל which usually means 'of little account', can be understood to indicate 'humility'. At face value, there is an almost innocent and naïve quality to the words similar to the childlike statement 'I'm only little'. However, it is also possible that there is a double-edged, false naivety to Job's words here, given that through drawing attention to his own humble position Job is inadvertently emphasising the difference in status and power between himself and Yahweh. This is not a humble confession of unworthiness: It is more closely akin to the 'meekness' and 'modesty' of Dickens's character Uriah Heep with his insincere (and regular) emphasis on how ever so 'umble' he is. Note also that this is the verb used by Job to 'curse' the day of his birth, perhaps pointing to a covert fury on Job's part that is veiled below a more formal address (Job 3:1). Finally note the context: Job hasn't said at any point in these two verses that he withdraws his lawsuit (ריב). The tone could be sarcastic here, possibly bordering on defiant (hence the translation's use of italics). Why wouldn't Job be angry and defiant? After all he knows he can't win his case. What can he answer? Perhaps this may account for the conscious gesture of self-restraint that follows (cf. Job 21:5; 29:9). As if to emphasise further the need for self-restraint, Job repeats that he will not answer or add anything. But the form of his doing so uses number parallelism or ascending numeration, which is particularly common in what has sometimes been labelled with the contested category 'wisdom literature', perhaps mimicking a wise sage (Prov. 18:21, 29 30:15; Kynes 2019). Is it any wonder that Yahweh is infuriated? His immediate reaction to Job is 'Gird up your loins like a man! I will question you and you shall answer me: will you surely make my judgement void? Will you cause me to be evil just so that you can be right?' Ironically, it seems, this is precisely what Job has been trying to do. Job had hoped for a cosmic bureaucrat or a 'moral bookkeeper' who would assure everybody that he was right all along (van Wolde 1997:3). But instead he got Yahweh. We now turn to Job's second, again very terse, response.

> I *know* that you[4] are able to do everything
> And that no devious scheme can be withheld from you.
> "Who is this that hides counsel by words without knowledge?"
> Therefore[5] I "*declare*" that I did not understand,
> Things too "*wonderful*" for me that I did not know.
> "Hear! And *I* will speak: I will question you! Make it known to me!"
> By the hearing of an ear I have heard you.
> And now, my eyes see you.

4 Note the *qere/ketib*. This translation assumes the *qere*. But if we were to entertain the possibility of not doing so, the reading 'you know that you are able to do everything' would only enhance the irony. The LXX has 'nothing is impossible for you' (ἀδυνατεῖ δέ σοι οὐθέν).

5 This is the beginning of Job's response, as marked by the term לכן ('therefore').

Therefore, I "*submit*!"
And I console myself concerning dust and ashes.

(Job 42:2–6)

Similarly, to the first response, this speech is also very 'tongue in cheek'. As Clines observes, 'it is a crafty and subtle speech that means more than it says. . . . Job's words are both a capitulation and, in a way, a reiteration of his complaint' (Clines 2011:1212–1213). On the one hand Job is following the formal procedure of the lawsuit. But as we will demonstrate, his formality is only lip service: It is decidedly sarcastic. The statement 'I *know*' may be double-edged given that it is in parallelism with the idea that no 'devious scheme' can be withheld from Yahweh. The term מזמה 'devious scheme' usually implies evil and devious scheming and is perhaps a strange choice of words here (Job 21:27; Prov. 12:2; Jer. 11:15). This leads Habel to suggest it is 'a friendly barb' (Habel 1985:581). Similar to the beginning of Job's first response, here we have an admission that Yahweh is more powerful than Job and that this is a case between unmatched opponents (Job 40:5). Through this emphasis, Job is, again, pointing to the fact that the whole scenario is terribly unfair: If imagined as a play the responses might well be acted in a sulky and sarcastic manner.

The next verse is especially sardonic: It parodies Yahweh's question to Job 'who is this that darkens (חשך *hiphil* participle) counsel by words without knowledge?' (Job 38:2).[6] Likewise, Job asks 'who is this that hides (עלם *hiphil* participle) counsel by words without knowledge?' (Job 42:3).[7] Many commentators assume that Job is quoting Yahweh here so that he can answer his question. It is also a possibility, however, that Job is simply parroting Yahweh's words back at him, as seems to be the case in the second half of the verse. The minor change (from 'darkens counsel' to 'hides counsel') in this case may be part of the ridicule: After all, Job has hardly caused counsel to be hidden. All he has received from his three friends, and then from Elihu, throughout the dialogues was 'counsel' in the form of moralising advice. But in response Job did not refrain from letting his thoughts be known. Job proceeds to follow this thought with 'Therefore I "*declare*" (נגד *hiphil*) that I did not understand' (Job 42:3).[8] The verb נגד is regularly found in Job (Job 1:17, 19; 11:6; 12:7; 15:18; 17:5; 21:31; 26:4; 31:37; 33:23; 36:9, 33; 38:4; 38:18). Here, Job's use of the term also parrots Yahweh's challenges to 'declare if you have understanding' (Job 38:4) and 'declare if you know at all' (Job 38:18). However, instead of claiming to have 'understanding' and 'knowledge' Job falls in line with Yahweh's rhetorical

6 Other possibilities are that it is regarded as 'a misplaced variant' (Pope 1965:289) or an editorial gloss (Rowley 1976:265).

7 Clines argues that this is 'a minor change that seems to be without special significance' (Clines 2011:1214).

8 Clines emphasises that this is different from 'uttering' or simply 'speaking', suggesting instead that the term is 'especially used of announcing things not previously known before . . . or things kept secret . . . and is that almost like "reveal"' (Clines 2011:1215).

questions. Nevertheless, his language bears an anthelion of scepticism. This is also made clear in the next statement about 'wonders'. Outside Job, and on the lips of his friends (Job 5:9; 37:5, 14), wonders are positive. However, the term is not always a positive one for Job, as we noted.[9] The double-edged nature of Job's words here may cause audiences to wonder whether this is a confession of ignorance or, more likely, an act of defiance.

Verse 4 may also be parody. It begins with an emphasis on the importance of Job speaking with an imperative 'Hear' an independent personal pronoun followed by the first-person singular prefix 'and *I* will speak'. Here we have a parody of Elihu who, at the end of his long speech tells Job 'shut up! (חרש *hiphil* imperative) And *I* will speak' (Job 33:31, 33). However, the response also parodies Yahweh's demands: 'and I will ask you and you will make it known to me' (Job 38:3; 40:7).

Finally, in verse 5 we have Job's own words without quotations. Here, too, however, they could be sarcastic. Job had hoped to see God (Job 19:26–27). He now has his desired theophany, but it's not enough. He sees and hears Yahweh: This is a most momentous theophany, surely? But, ironically, Job is disappointed. What he really wanted was to be vindicated by Yahweh and in the eyes of his friends. After all, as Rowley notes, 'at the bottom this was not a problem of theodicy, but a problem of fellowship' (Rowley 1976:265). The ceaseless moralising about Job's problems was what he reacted to: By comparison with the frustrated and vehement tone of Job's speeches to his friends, peppered with extreme language of deity attack and deity surveillance, his speech here is, at best, half-hearted.

Surely the crux, however, is verse 6. It is not clear how to translate the verb מאס and, to compound problems, the verb doesn't have a direct object.[10] The most persuasive translation belongs to Clines, who solves the problem of the lack of object by suggesting this is Job's formal response that ends his lawsuit against God: simply 'I submit'. As Clines argues, 'with this one word Job announces the end of his legal claim for justice, while in the rest of the verse he expresses where he now stands in personal and social terms' (Clines 2011:1219). However, it is also possible to suppose that the term might hint at the translation 'reject', possibly implying a rejection of the lawsuit's outcome. This is because most of the time on Job's lips the verb מאס is negative (Job 7:5; 9:21; 10:3; 19:18; 31:1; 31:13). Furthermore, it would seem that one of the antonyms of מאס ('reject') in Job is בחר ('choose') (Job 34:33). Another attractive possibility is Greenstein's rather loose translation: 'this is why I am fed

9 Refer to Chapter 3. Note also that Job does sometimes use the term positively (Job 9:10).

10 As Habel notes, 'the verb *m's* is variously rendered "despise myself" (RSV), "melt" (NEB), "recant" (Pope), "retract" [i.e. retract the "lawsuit"] (JB), "ashamed of" (GNB), "sink down" (Dhorme), "abase myself" (Gordis).' (Habel 1985:576). The translations also seem to show signs of struggling. The LXX gives a double translation of the verb: ἐφαύλισα ἐμαυτὸν καὶ ἐτάκην ('I have held myself cheap and melt'). The Vulgate, similar to RSV, has *ipse me reprehendo*. However, as Pope notes, 'the verb *m's* is not used of self-loathing' (Pope 1965:290). Some also suggest using √II מאס ('to flow / waste away'), suggesting that the verb should be taken in an absolute sense as relating to Job's body (Job 7:5).

up' (Greenstein 2019:185). Is this, therefore, a delicious pun? As Muenchow reflects, 'the suggestion of an originally deliberate polysemy here cannot help but give pause' (Muenchow 1989:598). The author/s do, indeed, have Job submit, but only grudgingly with a backhanded, and not so subtle, dose of rejection and disappointment.

The meaning of the verb נחם is disputed. It regularly means to 'repent' or 'regret'.[11] Here, too, therefore, there is a double-edged quality to Job's words. However, rather than 'repenting upon dust and ashes' (Job 2:8, 12), Job will 'console himself' (assuming the reflexive sense of the *niphal* נחם) 'concerning dust and ashes'. In other words, finding no consolation in the lawsuit, Job plans to try and console himself and grieve about the fact that he has lost his status and is just a mere mortal of 'dust and ashes' (cf. Job 30:19).[12] Of course, 'dust' and 'ashes' might also refer to the advice of his friends.[13]

It is as well to acknowledge Clines's remark here that 'the sentence is almost infinitely ambiguous; it could be straightforwardly submissive . . . or indignant, or sarcastic, or obsequious, or even falsely submissive' (Clines 2011:1214). Given the dominance, however, of retributive theology and the fact that Job is now talking to Yahweh (using the tetragrammaton), it is possible that this polysemy is strategic. After all, if Job were to be unambiguously defiant, that might be understood as blasphemous. Although, as a foreigner from Uz, perhaps this would not be quite as shocking as it would on the lips of a 'good Yahwist'. For audiences who adhere to a type of Yahwism wherein retribution reigns, Job is not an unsuccessful play because such audiences see Job's 'submission' and can interpret it at face value. For other Yahwists seeking a more honest and compassionate type of Yahwism, the response is a pivotal moment of irony: a sardonic nod to orthodoxy. This suggestion is concretised by the fact that in the return to prose narrative, the friends are told that Job 'spoke rightly' or 'honestly' and they did not (42:7–8).[14] This is expressed on the lips of Yahweh using the *niphal* participle of the verb כון which can sometimes mean 'to tell the truth' (Gen. 41:32; Deut. 13:14; Ps. 5:10).[15] This seems a strange way to follow up, especially given the faux 'submission' to orthodoxy: How is it that Job is

11 It can mean to 'change one's mind about something that had intended to do' (Exod. 32:12 14; 2 Sam. 24:16; Jer. 18:8, 10; 26:3, 13, 19). But this is usually used of Yahweh changing his mind rather than of humans doing so.

12 When 'dust' and 'ashes' appear together, they regularly connect with ideas about being mortal (Gen. 18:27; Job 30:19; 42:6; Ezek. 27:30).

13 See Chapter 2.

14 Yahweh addresses Eliphaz only, but the assumption is that this applies to all the friends.

15 Greenstein notes here that

> No mention is made of Job's wife, the Satan, or the curing of Job's disease. One may surmise that his health is restored because he is blessed in every other way and lives a long life.
>
> (Greenstein 2019:186)

Perhaps, however, Job's 'disease' is irrelevant: As we have argued in the preceding chapters, Job's body was only ever an ingenious tool which the author/s use to strengthen the case of experience versus tradition.

'right'? Likewise, as we have seen, Job's speeches were more than a little hostile about the nature of the deity: How is it that Yahweh now seemingly endorses them? Perhaps we have here a final ironic detail: The *niphal* participle of the verb כון means literally 'the established thing'. As we discussed in the previous chapters, throughout the speeches the friends readily claimed to be the guardians of established traditions. Ironically, here it is Job who Yahweh assigns as the one who speaks 'established things'. To add insult to irony, and to punctuate the entire scene with comedy, Yahweh now suggests that Job will 'pray' for his friends. After all the moralising advice they provided, the sanctimonious friends are now to be the subject of Job's prayers: This is surely a comical reversal of roles.

Bibliography

Abrams, M.H. and Harpham, G.G., 2005. *A glossary of literary terms.* 8th edn. Boston, MA: Thomson Wadsworth.

Alter, R., 1981. *The art of biblical narrative.* New York: Basic Books.

Berger, P.L., 1997. *Redeeming laughter: The comic dimension of human experience.* Berlin: Walter de Gruyter.

Brenner-Idan, A. and Radday, Y.T., 1990. *On humour and the comic in the Hebrew Bible.* Sheffield: Almond.

Clines, D.J.A., 2011. *Job 38–42.* Nashville: Thomas Nelson.

Craig, K.M., 1995. *Reading Esther: A case for the literary carnivalesque.* Louisville, KY: Westminster John Knox Press.

Douglas, M., 1968. The social control of cognition: Some factors in joke perception. *Man,* **3**(3), pp. 361–376.

Fowles, J., 1969. *The French lieutenant's woman.* London: Cape.

Greenstein, E.L., 2019. *Job: A new translation.* New Haven; London: Yale University Press.

Habel, N.C., 1985. *The book of Job: A commentary.* London: SCM.

Jackson, M.A., 2012. *Comedy and feminist interpretation of the Hebrew Bible: A subversive collaboration.* Oxford: Oxford University Press.

Kuipers, G., 2008. The sociology of humor. In: V. Raskin, ed, *The primer of humor research.* Berlin; New York: Walter de Gruyter, pp. 361–398.

Kynes, W., 2019. *An obituary for "wisdom literature": The birth, death, and intertextual reintegration of a biblical corpus.* 1st edn. Oxford: Oxford University Press.

Lazarus, B.M., 2014. *Humanist comic elements in Aristophanes and the Old Testament.* Piscataway: Gorgias Press.

Morreall, J., 2008. Philosophy and religion. In: V. Raskin, ed, *The primer of humor.* Berlin; New York: Walter de Gruyter, pp. 211–242.

Muenchow, C., 1989. Dust and dirt in Job 42:6. *Journal of Biblical Literature,* **108**(4), pp. 597–611.

Newsom, C.A., 1993. Cultural politics and the reading of Job. *Biblical Interpretation,* **1**(2), pp. 119–138.

Pope, M.H., 1965. *Job.* Garden City, NY: Doubleday.

Radcliffe-Brown, A., 1940. On joking relationships. *Africa: Journal of the International African Institute,* **13**(3), pp. 195–210.

Rowley, H.H., 1976. *Job.* Rev. edn. London: Oliphants.

Seow, C.L., 2013. *Job 1–21: Interpretation and commentary.* Grand Rapids, MI: William B. Eerdmans.

Van Loon, H., 2018. *Metaphors in the discussion on suffering in Job 3–31: Visions of hope and consolation.* Leiden: Brill.

Van Wolde, E.J., 1997. *Mr and Mrs Job.* London: SCM.

Name index

Aaron, D.H. 6, 8, 111, 124
Antze, P. 76–77, 86, 125, 141
Avalos, H. 5, 23, 33

Balentine, S.E. 30, 81, 119, 139, 158
Basson, A. 79, 151, 154
Bastiaens, J.C. 68–70, 130, 158
Bates, V. 66
Becker, G. 33
Berger, P.L. 14, 22, 129, 166
Blumenthal, D.R. 52, 83
Brown, M.L. 4
Brown, W.P. 11, 115, 151
Bury, M. 25–26, 33

Carel, H. 21, 23–25, 53, 73–74, 91, 98
Claassens, L.J. 5–6, 77, 115, 148–149
Clines, D.J.A. 8, 10, 35, 39, 51, 53, 60–61, 63, 68, 71, 79, 81–82, 86, 88–89, 92–93, 96, 103, 113, 115–116, 120–121, 127–128, 136–137, 151, 153, 169, 171–173
Csordas, T.J. 23

Das, V. 27–28, 33, 51, 74
Day, J. 11, 114–115
Dell, K.J. 2, 9, 18–19, 31, 66, 119, 128
Dolezal, L. 58, 78, 114, 123, 134
Douglas, M. 14, 17–18, 22, 154, 166, 167
Duhm, B. 1, 53

Erickson, A. 51, 68, 70
Eskenazi, T.C. 1
Evans-Pritchard, E. 85–86

Fadiman, A. 20
Ferrari, F.M. 58
Fohrer, G. 19, 94
Forte, M. 86, 133
Frank, A.W. 25, 33, 90

Garro, L.C. 24–26, 28, 59, 66, 85, 101, 118
Geissler, W. 20, 25, 34
Glasby, M. 17–18, 128
Goffman, E. 57, 77, 97, 139
Goldingay, J. 132
Good, B. 22, 25, 57, 59, 90
Gordis, R. 61, 71, 86, 92, 119, 128, 149–150, 172
Gorman, S. 16
Gotto, A. 6–7
Greenstein, E.L. 29–30, 39, 51, 56, 68, 72, 79, 87, 91, 95, 130–131, 151, 172–173
Guillaume, P. 30, 60

Habel, N.C. 52, 54–55, 62, 69, 71, 81, 86, 88, 92–93, 112, 121, 136–37, 151, 171–172
Hawkins, A.H. 117
Hawley, L.R. 37, 62
Horton, R. 86, 133
Houck-Loomis, T. 18
Hruschka, D. 95
Hurwitz, B. 25, 66
Hyun, S.W.T. 53, 72, 83, 116–117, 122, 131

Jackson, J.E., 24, 27–28, 33, 74
Jackson, M.A. 9–11, 14–15, 55, 90, 123, 139, 165, 168
Jones, A. 2, 59
Jones, S.C., 22, 24, 52, 67, 87, 114
Jurecic, A. 20, 26–28, 33, 51, 74–75

Kahn, J.H. 18
Kaplan, D.L. 16
Keller, C. 12
Kirmayer, L.J. 36, 58, 133
Kleinman, A. 21–22, 24–25, 28, 65, 77–78, 89, 126–127, 132–133
Kleinman, J. 126

Kohrt, B. 95
Kynes, W.L. 77, 119–120

Lambek, M. 76–77, 86, 125, 141
Lambert, D.A. 3, 5, 94, 129–130, 158
Lazare, A. 134
Lilly, I. 4, 93
Littlewood, R. 58, 155
Lloyd, G.E.R. 4, 20–21, 23, 56
Low, S. 158
Lupton, D. 25, 58, 75–76, 78–79, 97–98, 127, 133–134, 155
Lynch, R. 58, 135, 155

Magdalene, R.J. 3, 7
Matthewson, D. 98–99
Mattingly, C. 4, 24–26, 28, 59, 66, 85, 91–92, 101, 118
Melcher, S.J. 5, 67, 148
Merleau-Ponty, M. 74
Meshel, N. 8
Morreall, J. 139, 143, 164–166
Moss, C.R. 5, 87
Muenchow, C. 172–173
Müller, U.B. 4, 19
Muramoto, O. 19

Newsom, C.A. 1–2, 4, 18, 30, 32–33, 38, 53, 64, 66, 70–71, 77, 79, 82–83, 85, 94–95, 116, 119, 122, 131, 138, 158, 167
Nicholson, E.W. 120
Nichter, M. 23, 37, 84, 158–159
Nussbaum, M.C. 65–66

Parsons, T. 37, 67, 97
Pelham, A. 15, 31, 54–56, 60, 69–70, 77, 82, 98–99, 114, 130, 157
Piers, G. 95
Pilch, J.J. 3, 22
Pool, R. 20, 25, 34
Pope, M.H. 29–30, 61, 68, 86, 129, 171–172
Pyper, H. 138

Radcliffe-Brown, A. 167
Radday, Y.T. 13, 165
Raphael, R. 5, 8, 19, 30, 55, 73
Raz, Y. 51, 53, 63–64, 68, 94, 113
Rešeph 52–53, 81
Rorty, R. 66
Rowley, H.H. 16, 20, 52–53, 82, 86, 89, 96, 112, 116, 121, 136, 138, 157, 171–172

Sanders, J.A. 55, 131, 140
Scarry, E. 27, 64, 73–74, 83
Schipper, J. 5, 51, 126, 159
Seow, C.L. 30, 51–54, 60–61, 67, 71–72, 82, 86, 113–114, 119–121, 127–128, 135–137, 150–151, 153, 156–157, 159, 163
Seybold, K. 19
Sharp, C.J. 8
Singer, M.B. 95
Solomon, H. 18, 57, 92
Sontag, S. 24, 36, 60, 78–79
Steffen, V. 25, 117

Tham, J. 72, 131
Throop, C.J. 23, 28, 58, 60, 65, 75, 100, 127, 133, 140
Todorov, T. 12–14

Van Hecke, P. 22, 30, 32, 36, 56, 127
Van Loon, H. 37, 168
Venter, P.P. 18
Verbin, N. 52, 83
Von Rad, G. 50–51

Whedbee, J. 9, 11, 14–15, 31, 50, 73, 138, 160
Woods, A. 32
Worsley, P. 56–57

Subject index

absurd 10, 12, 17, 50, 75, 88, 89, 95, 113, 131, 135–137, 152, 160, 165
acknowledgement 28, 33, 51, 72–73, 75, 101, 151, 168: affection and 151; desires and 82–83; of pain 72–75
acute pain 27
affection 82–83, 151
Alcoholics Anonymous 25, 117
anachronism/anachronistic 13–14, 19–20, 33–34
anarchy 118, 164, 166–167
anti-climax 55–56, 60, 72, 87–88, 91, 102, 116, 141, 149, 150, 159
Aramaism 29
archer-like God 52–53
Aristophanes 2, 9, 80, 87, 130, 163
Aristotle 13
Athenian theatre 2, 80, 163
audience 54–55
authority, and power in dialogue 15, 22, 29, 56, 59, 61, 66, 75, 101, 120, 126
autopathography 27, 31

Babylonian sufferer 67
Babylonian Theodicy 4, 5
blameless man 8, 3, 39, 55–57, 61–62, 88, 95, 97, 139, 163–164
body shame 78, 95

capacious category 26
Cartesian dualistic division 53
Cassandra 55
categorisation 30–32
chronic illness 24, 28, 91
city wall in siege 87–88
classic relief theory 88, 102
class structures, social groups and 29
clothing metaphor 112
comedy, and tragedy 7–9, 50, 76–77, 99, 101, 103, 115–116, 130, 133, 138–140, 163–168
comedy of advice 12, 31, 39, 163–168
consolation 10, 18, 53, 129, 139, 158–161, 173
control, lack of 99, 167
crescendo of agony 149
criminal 56–57, 59, 88, 100, 155
cultural competence 20
cultural distance 13–15
cultural humility 20, 34
curse 2, 5, 12, 98, 112, 118, 129, 139, 169–170

death 2, 4–7, 25, 33, 70, 72, 75, 78–79, 81, 86–87, 92, 95, 98–99, 104, 113, 116, 121–122, 126–127, 130, 141
deity attack metaphor: accusation of divine violence 86–87; aggression and brutality 81–82; archer-like God 52–53; attacked body 50–60, 66–80, 86–92, 102, 142, 164; blameless/innocent 3, 8, 11, 39, 55–57, 59, 61–62, 69–70, 73, 76, 84, 87–88, 95, 97, 100, 139, 142, 155, 157, 163–164, 170; bodily distress, human responsibility and 5; bodily pain 1, 15–17; brutality, aggression and 81–82; deity as predator 70–71, 101; divine abuse 83; embodying ambiguity 75–76; forensic metaphor 68–70; God to humanity 64; military metaphor 81–82, 102; personified diseased arrows 53; power 26, 29, 32, 37, 56, 59–61, 66, 84–85, 90, 97, 100, 103, 114, 122–123, 125, 129, 131, 133, 141, 152, 166, 169–170; predator 70–71, 101 Rešeph 52–53, 81; siege 87–88; social responses 55–56, 65, 76, 79, 125; symbolic protest 29, 37–39, 84–85, 101–102, 163; torture 27, 53, 63–65, 112; violence 26, 35, 39, 53, 60–61, 66, 71, 82–87, 91, 93, 102, 121–122, 151; wounds 60–66

deity surveillance metaphor: moral witnessing 126, 141; primordial monsters 114–115, 117–118, 140; public health narratives 139–140; religious faith 129–130; revelatory dreams and visions 115–116; sleeplessness 19, 63, 112–113; social isolation 95, 114, 150–151; watch 11, 90, 111, 113–115, 121, 127–137, 140, 164, 167
depression 5, 19, 92
desolation 69, 94, 156–157
Deuteronomy/Deuteronomic 2, 5, 30, 78
disability as punishment 6–7, 28, 30, 57, 74, 148
disability studies 5–6, 148–149
disease 1–7, 16–22, 24, 30, 36, 38, 52–53, 56, 74, 79, 85, 93, 97–98, 115, 124, 126, 133–134, 139, 148, 154–155, 173
disintegration 27, 68–69, 116–117, 150–151
divine gaze 111–112
double-edged response 169–173
dramatic irony 8, 15, 153, 166
dramatised comedy 2, 8–9, 12–14, 163–168
dreams, and visions 111, 113, 115–116

Edomite 11
El attack 80–83, 85, 93, 102, 153, 169
Eloah 35, 51–54, 63, 71, 81, 125, 150, 153, 169
emaciation 5, 152
embodying ambiguity 75–76
empathy 51, 65–66, 72, 74–75, 126–127, 130
epistemology 56, 73, 131, 142, 163
exclusion 59, 94–97, 99, 103
exemplary sufferer 4–5, 54
exilic period 2, 11, 123

forensic language 68–69
forensic metaphor 68–70
formalised joking 167

genre 2, 4, 12–14, 19, 26, 30–31, 119
groaning 19
guardian metaphor 121
guilt 24, 58–59, 75, 89, 97, 126–127, 132, 142

health 3–5,18, 21, 23, 25, 33, 57–58, 76, 78, 98–100, 103, 123, 125, 133, 139–140, 143, 155, 173
healthy lifestyle and wellness 39, 58
heroic triumph 9
historiography 19–20
Hmong beliefs and behaviour 20
honour 8, 54, 66, 87, 94–95, 99, 120, 134–135
honour and shame 8, 24, 54, 58, 66, 77, 78, 80, 85, 87, 94–95, 99, 101, 103, 114, 120, 128–129, 132, 134–135, 137, 142, 148
hope 10, 24, 54, 71, 87–88, 91–92, 137–140
hyperbole 54, 62, 87, 90, 95, 116, 123, 133, 141, 151, 160, 165
hypochondria 116, 140

identity 13, 22, 25, 29, 33, 36, 55, 68, 77–79, 85, 92–93, 97, 117–118, 158
ideology, values and 23
idioms of distress 37, 83–84, 102, 158–159, 161
illness narratives 16, 24–28, 31–34, 38, 50, 57, 72–73, 76, 79, 89–91, 97, 99, 101–102, 117, 124, 133–134, 139, 141–142, 164; anachronism 13, 19–20, 33–34; capacious category 26; categorisation 30–33; critical engagement 26–27; cultural humility and respect 20, 34; deity attack metaphor 89–91; genre 2, 4, 12–14, 19, 26, 30–31, 119; key 'stories' 25; language and texts 29–30; meaning seeking 24–25; metaphors 35–36; misery memoirs and victim art 26; moral narratives 25; narratability of human experience 32–33; patient experiences 25–26, 97; self and identity 28–29; social groups and class structures 29; social knowledge 34; sublime poetry 32, 169; time theme 33
illness: cultural influence 22–24; curses 2–3; disease and 6, 20–21, 155; divine interest 22; healing 3, 23, 36; juste souffrant 5; moral turpitude 7; and pain 1–2, 21–22, 24, 26, 28–38, 67, 100, 125 130, 132, 134, 140, 142, 148; and responsibility 6–7, 39, 79; as retribution 2, 4, 7, 164; social meanings 21–22; transgression 5, 124
incongruity theory 14
irony and satire 118–120, 123–126; 15, 54, 76–77, 101, 116, 124–126

Janus parallelism 67, 79
Job, and Prometheus 9, 53
judgemental communication 1, 163
juste souffrant 5
justice 25, 30, 56, 79, 85, 86, 88–90, 112, 156–157, 172

lack of control 99, 167
language, and texts 29–30
laughter 14, 61, 76–77, 96, 164–165
legal metaphor 30, 69
legal terminology 135, 136
linguistic sabotage 82
local cultural orientations 132–133
ludicrous absurdity 10
Ludlul Bel Nemequ 4–5, 52, 112

material comedy 13, 124
meaning making 126–127, 132–134
medical anthropology 1, 4, 16, 22–25, 29, 31, 33–34, 36–38, 164; and biblical material 29, 33–34; illness narratives and expressions of pain 24–28; interdisciplinary scholarship 37–38; and sociology 1, 164; *see also* retrospective diagnosis
medical inundation 93–94
medicalization 57
melodramatic metaphors 13, 35, 163
mental health 17–18
metaphor 13, 21–24, 27, 30, 33, 35–39, 50–53, 56, 60–72, 77, 80–86, 92–96, 99–103, 111–140, 149–160, 163–165; anti-deuteronomic theology 30; deity attack (*see* deity attack metaphor); embodied expression 36; illness 35–36; melodramatic 13, 35, 163; for pain 21; somatic 37
methodological hazards 128
military metaphor 36, 81–82, 102
misery memoirs 26
modern illness narratives 26, 32, 36, 72, 76, 89, 101
moral discourse 122–123
moralising 1, 10, 38–39, 55–59, 63, 65–66, 69, 73–75, 78, 80, 83–85, 88–91, 95, 100–102, 111, 123–126, 130–134, 140, 142, 153–154, 158, 163–164, 171–172; advice 1, 13, 39, 54, 61, 63, 65–66, 75, 80, 88, 90–91, 100–102, 135, 137, 142, 153–154, 156, 158, 161, 163, 168, 171, 174; comedy of advice 163–164; about food 58; judgement 57; language 1, 55–57; order 57–59; responses 73; sociocultural categories 58–59
moral meanings 55, 127
moral narratives 25
moral order 57–59, 157
moral turpitude 7
moral witnessing 126, 141
mythic/mythical/mythical thinking 9, 35, 114–115, 117–118, 131

narrative medicine and narrative skills 25, 66
narrative temporality 32–33
narrative time 64
natural order 98, 154–155
Nemo 69
nervous attacks 158
North American religio-therapeutic community 58

Old Comedy 9
Old Greek 30, 51–53, 61, 81, 86, 92, 113, 128, 135–136, 149
Old Testament 6, 8, 57, 63, 79, 80, 83
onomatopoeia 71
ontological stammer 60
Other 11, 66, 79, 150

pain 1–2, 21–26, 28–38, 58–60, 66–67, 71, 90–91, 97–100, 103, 124–125, 130, 132–134, 140–142, 148: acute pain 27; anti-language for 27–28; expressions 15–16, 24, 27–28, 33, 35, 38, 50, 91, 99–100, 138, 164; vs. illness 1–2, 21–26, 28–38, 58–60, 66–67, 71, 90–91, 97–100, 103, 124–125, 130, 132–134, 140–142, 148; language 24–28, 63, 134; narratives 28–38, 67; paradox of language 28; uncontainable 1; *see also* illness
paradox, use of 8
parody 7, 14, 73, 119–122, 129, 137, 140, 142, 153, 172
Parson's sick role 103
pestilence 2–3, 52, 81, 124
phenomenology 23, 73–74
phonological parallelism 82
physical power 152
piety/mercy 7, 10–12, 15, 30, 54, 88–89, 99, 121–122, 124–125, 129, 153–154, 165
polysemous parallelism 67
polysemy 29, 68, 71, 99, 115, 120, 136, 150, 160, 173
primordial creature of chaos 114–115, 117–118
Prometheus, Job and 9, 53
Prometheus Bound (Aeschylus) 9
psychological transformation 18–19
public health narratives 139–140

relief theory 88, 159–160, 159–161
religious cosmology 155–156
religious faith 129–130
response to Yahweh: devious scheme 170–171; double-edged response 169–171; as God of power and grandeur

169; interrogation 168–169; legal claim for justice 172–173; moralising advice 168, 171, 174; retributive theology 173; sardonic response 169, 171–172; submission to orthodoxy 173–174
restitution story 25, 80, 89
resumptive pronoun 53
retribution 2, 4, 7, 13, 15–16, 31, 38–39, 54–57, 59, 69–72, 75–76, 84, 86, 89–90, 99, 101–103, 111, 118, 120, 122–123, 130–132, 135, 139–141, 156, 163–167, 173
retributive justice principle 56, 112
retrospective diagnosis 2, 3, 16–24, 29, 35, 38, 128, 151, 164: cultural influence 22–24; cultural insensitivity 20–21; depression 19; groaning 19; literary figure 19–20; mental health problem 17–18; signs and symptoms of disease 16; symptomatology 18

Sarcasm/Sarcastic 39, 54, 65, 77, 122, 129, 133, 138–140, 142, 153, 160, 169–173
satiation 62–64
satire 2, 12, 14, 90, 118–120, 123–126, 165–167
scatological misfortune 15
sensitivity, and empathy 126–127
Shaddai 8, 50–60
Shakespearean fool 55
shame 24, 58, 77–80, 85, 94–95, 101, 103, 114, 1278–129, 132–135, 137, 142, 148
situation ethics 15
social alienation 148–149, 156
social ambivalence 76
social apologia 25
social duties 97–98, 103–104
social dynamics 1, 22, 37, 79
social exclusion 59, 95–97, 99, 103
social groups, and class structures 29
social interaction 36, 59, 95, 97, 99, 103, 167–168
social inversion 14, 59, 87, 95, 97, 99, 103
social isolation 95, 97, 99, 103, 59, 114, 149–151
social knowledge 34, 59
social order 73, 154–155, 160, 167
social ramifications of suffering 2
social status: affection and acknowledgement 151; affliction 158; body and social order 154–155, 160; consolations of God 159–161; crescendo of agony 149; desolation and astonishment 156–157; emaciation 152; idioms of distress 158–159; justice 156–157; moralising advice 156–161; nervous attacks 158; physical power and 152; relief theory 159–161; religious cosmology 155–156; request for piety/mercy 153–154; social alienation 148–149, 156, 156; social distance from society 155–156; social isolation by God 149–151; tragic litany of woes 151–152, 160
somatic 5, 35, 37–38, 68, 81, 83, 92, 112, 121–122, 138, 141, 143, 150, 157, 164
somatisation 36, 158–159
somatised distress 86–87
Spirit Catches You and You Fall Down, The (Fadiman) 20
status 25, 37, 59, 68–69, 77, 94–96, 100, 103, 120, 131, 148–149, 151–152, 155, 160, 164, 170, 173
stigma 24, 35, 77–78, 101, 114, 154
suffering, social ramifications of 2, 67, 71, 114, 158
superiority theory 14, 99, 152–153
symbolic protest 29, 37–39, 68, 84–85, 101–102, 163

'tehomic' comedy/comedy of creation 12
Testament of Job 12, 31, 96, 99
tetragrammaton 9, 11, 35, 169, 173
texts, language and 29–30
theodicy 5, 57, 73, 79, 172
theological dissent 164–165
Todorov's approach to genre 13–14
torture, language and 63–65
tradition 12, 15–16, 53–54, 83, 84, 111–143, 157, 164, 166, 173; *see also* deity surveillance metaphor
traditional language 52–54, 83, 84, 87, 99, 102, 121, 153–154
traditional prayer 119–121
tragedy 1, 7–9, 50, 53, 76–77, 95, 99, 101, 103, 115–116, 130, 133, 138–140, 152, 163–168
tragic laughter 77
tyranny of tradition 111–143; *see also* deity surveillance metaphor

uncontainable pain 1
U-shaped comic scenarios 10–11, 90, 129

values, and ideology 23
victim art 26
visions, dreams and 111, 113, 115–116

wind 62–63, 80, 89, 100–102, 113, 149–152, 160, 164, 168–169
witches/troublesome spirits 85–86
wonders of God 129–130
wounded body 63–64, 91, 103
wounded storyteller 90

Yahweh *see* response to Yahweh

Biblical index

OLD TESTAMENT

Genesis
1 64n46, 115
2:8 11
3:12 138:63
3:19 94
4:10 84
6:11–12 91n124
12:17 6n20
18:27 93n133, 173n12
19:11 6n20
20:17–18 6n20
22 117
22:12 88
25:8 128n30
29:32 92n128
35:29 128n30
37:33 71n69
40:4 115
41:32 173
42:17 115
42:18 88
44:28 71n69
49:23 81n95
49:27 71n69
Exodus
3:7 92n128
3:17 92n128
3:20 129
5:8 86n108
5:15 86n108
6:1–10 54
7–11 6n20
8:12 86n108
14:10 86n108
14:15 86n108
16:8 63n43
16:12 63n43
17:4 86n108
19:22 82n99
19:24 82n99
21:25 63
22:23 86n108
22:27 86n108
25:8 96, 103
32:12 173n11
32:14 173n11
34:10 129
Leviticus
13:18–23 17
13:20 3n7
13:45–46 17n38
13:49 17n38
19:18–19 127n29
21:20 3n8
22:22 3n8
24:12 115
26:26 63n43
26:31 69n62
26:44 136:56
31:2–6 150n15
Numbers
2:10 17n38
6:25 96, 103
12:9–10 6n20
14:11–12 6n20
14:36–37 6n20
15:34 115
16:14 92n129
17:12–15 6n20
20:14 11n30
22–24 165n2
25:3–9 6n20
25:17–18 6n20
31:16 6n20

Deuteronomy 2n2
2:4–5 11n30
6:11 63n43
7:15 3
8:5 125
8:10 63n43
8:12 63n43
11:15 63n43
11:24 135n53
13:14 173
14:29 63n43
19:10–13 84n105
21:8–9 84n105
24:14 12
26:7 92n128
26:12 63n43
28 5
28:15–68 112–113n1
28:21–22 2–3
28:35 17
28:59 129
28:66–67 112n1
31:19 52
31:20 63n43
32:10 121
32:23 52
32:23–24 53
32:42 52
33:20 71n69
Joshua
3:5 129
3:13 135n53
4:18 135n53
Judges
6:13 129
16:21 92n129
18:19 157:39
19:6 54n19
Ruth 2:14 63n43
1 Samuel
1:11 92n128
5:6 69n62
5:6–6:12 6n20
6:9 150n15
11:2 92n129
12:22 54n19
20:20 81
28:8 93n131
2 Samuel
6:8 82n99
7:29 54n19
14:25 17
15:34 82n97
20:10 82
24:10–15 6n20
24:16 173n11
1 Kings
5:3 135n53
14:10–14 6n20
20:38 93n131
2 Kings
1:16 6n20
5:26–27 6n20
5:27 17n38
6:3 54n19
14:26 92n128
20:7 17n38
25:8 81n95
1 Chronicles 2n2
15:13 82n99
16:9 129
16:12 129
16:24 129
17:27 54n19
21:7–14 6n20
29:28 128n30
2 Chronicles 2n2
6 117
21:14–15 6n20
26:15 129
26:16–20 6n20
31:10 63n43
Ezra
4:10 81n95
9:3–4 69n62
Nehemiah
1:10–14 54
9:9 92n128
9:17 129
9:25 63n43
Job
1:1 8, 11, 56n24, 57, 153n23
1:3 11
1:5 118n14
1:9 62, 88
1:17 171
1:19 62, 62n41, 100, 171
1:21 151n17
2:5–6 99
2:6–7 50
2:7–8 3n7
2:8 173
2:9 118h14
2:9–10 151n17
2:12 173
2:13 77n86

3:1 170
3:8 114
3: 19, 94n137, 98, 118
3:23 86n110
3:27 31
4:3–11 99
4:6 54, 89
4:7 8n24, 56n23
4:8–9 54
4:9 62n41
4:12–16 115
4:14 157
4:15 62, 62n41
4:19 54, 136n55
4:21 22n45
5:2 52
5:9 129, 171
5:12 138:63
5:16 89
5:17 56n23, 88, 125
5:18 5, 52
5:24 22n45, 91n124
6 99, 101, 102
6:1–10 51
6:3 52
6:4 38, 51, 62n41, 63, 81
6:9–10 53
6:10 71, 81n94
6:14–16 56
6:15 153
6:21 56, 132, 151
6:26 62, 62n41, 100
6:27 153
7 122, 127
7:4 63, 113
7:4–5 112
7:5 51n1, 68, 172, 172n10l
7:7 62n41, 114
7:8 114
7:11 62n41
7:12 115:9, 115n7
7:12–16 113
7:12–20 111
7:14 18
7:14–15 119n16
7:16 119n16
7:17–18 112, 119n16, 140
7:17–20 39, 114n4, 118
7:18 130n40
7:19 114, 119n16
7:19–20 114
7:20 52, 114
7:21 114, 119n16
7:39 39
8:2 62, 62n41, 80, 100
8:5 134
8:5–6 56n24
8:6 8n24
8:8 91
8:11–19 137
8:17 137
8:20 8n24, 134
8:21 61
8:22 22n45, 134
9 100
9–10 38
9:10 129n36, 172n9
9:17 62n41
9:17–19 38, 51, 61
9:18 61, 62n41
9:20 61
9:20–21 70n65
9:21 61, 172
9:22 61
9:23 99
9:30–31 62
10:3 172
10:4–7 119n16
10:6 127
10:8–12 119n16
10:9 94
10:11 51n1
10:11–12 134
10:12 62n41, 128
10:13–14 119n16
10:14 127
10:14–16 39, 127–128, 141
10:14–17 111, 137
10:15 62, 128n32, 134
11:2–3 137
11:4 8n24
11:5 159
11:6 171
11:7 125n26
11:13 8n24
11:14 22n45, 91, 91n124
11:18 91
11:20 91, 139
12 122
12:1–4 148
12:2–3 153
12:3 79, 111
12:4 152
12:6 22n45
12:7 171
12:10 62n41

12:14 52n9
13 135
13:2 79
13:3 135
13:4–5 79
13:6 86n109, 135
13:8 135
13:10 135
13:12 80, 94, 94n136
13:15 135
13:18 88, 135
13:18–23 88
13:19 135
13:20–28 135
13:24 114
13:25 153
13:27 127
13:27–28 39, 111, 135–136, 142
13:28 136n55
14 135
14:3 39, 88, 127, 135–136, 142
14:3–6 111
14:4 155
14:6 39, 114, 135, 137, 142
14:7 91
14:13 114
14:16 39, 135, 137, 142
14:19 91
14:36–37 88
15 159
15:2 62, 62n41, 80, 100
15:2–6 88
15:5 138:63
15:6 72n74
15:7–8 138
15:8–9 138
15:11 159
15:13 61n35, 62n41
15:15 149n6
15:18 171
15:20 57n27, 82, 139
15:25 125n26
15:26 82
15:30 62n41
15:34 22n45
16 83, 99, 101, 102, 157
16:2 80
16:3 62n41, 80
16:6–17 51
16:7 157n37
16:7–9 38, 66, 67, 158:42
16:8 67, 68
16:9 72, 93, 127
16:10–11 71n72
16:12–13 52
16:12–14 38, 80, 84
16:13 81n94
16:14 87
16:17 69
16:18 84
16:19–21 85n107
17:157
17:1 62n41
17:5 171
17:8 117, 157
17:15 91
18 159
18:3 149n6
18:3–4 71
18:4 72
18:6 22n45, 91n124
18:7 137n61
18:11–13 72
18:13 73, 99
18:13–18 157n38
18:14 91n124
18:14–15 22n45
18:15 91n124
18:20 157
19 99, 102–103, 156
19: 13–22 148
19:2 22n45, 153
19:7–12 38, 51, 87, 149, 160
19:12 91n124
19:13–20 73
19:13–22 39, 149–150, 151, 155, 160
19:14–19 69
19:15–22 114n5
19:16 150n9
19:17 62n41
19:18 172
19:20 51n1
19:20–22 148
19:22 63, 80, 126, 160
19:26 51n1
19:26–27 33n72, 172
19:28–29 153
20 159
20:3 62n41
20:14–16 72, 156
20:20–25 72, 156
20:26 22n45
21:3 152
21:4 62n41
21:5 170
21:5–6 39, 148, 156, 160

21:7ff 156n34
21:18 62n41
21:21 159
21:23 159
21:24 94
21:27 171
21:28 22n45
21:31 171
21:34 62, 80, 100
22:6 88n118
22:16 67
22:23 22n45
22:25 125n26
23:16 125n26
25:5 149n6
26:13 62n41
26:44 171
27:2 125n26
27:3 62n41
27:8 91
27:12 62, 100
27:13 125n26
27:14 63
27:18 136n55
27:21 62n41
28:25 62n41
29 95
29:2 128
29:4 22n45
29:7–25 95
29:9 157, 170
29:12 96, 103
29:12–16 96
29:15–16 96, 103
29:16 86n109
29:21–25 96
29:24 96, 103
29:25 96, 103
29–37 31
30 92, 99, 103, 152n20
30:1 96
30:1–11 95
30:1a 77n85
30:3 93n130
30:8a 77n85
30:9 77n85
30:12 87n111
30:15 62n41
30:16 54
30:16–19 38, 92–93
30:16–20 51
30:17–18 92n127
30:19 93n133, 94, 173, 173n12
30:20 127
30:22 62n41
30:27 92n128
30:27–31 92
30:28–29 94
30:29–30 94
30:30 51n1
31:1 22n45, 172
31:4 127
31:13 12, 86n109, 150n8, 172
31:13–15 150n7
31:31 63
31:35 86n109
31:37 171
32:1 149n6
32:6 80
32:8 62n41, 125n26
32:18 62n41, 80, 152
33:4 62n41, 125n26
33:6 94
33:15 116n10
33:22 135n52
33:23 171
33:31 172
33:33 172
34:10 125n26
34:12 125n26
34:14 62n41
34:33 172
35:13 125n26
35:16 62, 100
36:7 117
36:9 171
36:33 171
37:5 171
37:9 62n41
37:14 171
37:21 62n41
37:22 125n26
38:1 62n41, 80
38:2 171
38:3 172
38:4 171
38:8 114
38:18 171
38:27 63
40:4 157
40:4–5 169
40:6 62n41
40:7 172
40:11–12 114
41:1 114
41:1–34 114n4

41:16 62n41
41:31 114
42:2–6 39, 163, 170
42:3 62, 100, 129n36, 171
42:5 33n72
42:6 39, 93n133, 113n2, 173n12
42:7–8 169, 173
42:17 128n30
Psalms 2n2, 112
1 139
1:3–4 33
2:11 157
3:4 52n8
5:10 173
6:2 52n8
6:2–4 119n16
7:1 70
7:2 71n69
7:9 61
7:11 52n8
7:13 52
8 111, 122, 140
8:4–6 119
8:6 87
9:1 130n39
9:10 52n8
11:2 52n8
11:5 61
15:4 88n117
15:14 120
17:3 119n16
17:12 70, 71n69
18:3 52n8
18:15 81n95
18:36 137n61
22:10–11 119n16
22:12 70
22:13 71n69
22:15–20 119n16
22:23 88
22:25 88
25:7 119n16
25:12 88n117
25:14 88n117
25:18 92n128
25:21 121
26:2 119n16
26:7 130n39
27:2 154n24
27:3 52n8
28:7 52n8
28:8 52n8
31:3–5 52n8
31:19 88n117
31:20 81n95
31:21 130n39
31:22 52n8
32:3–4 119n16
33:18 88n117
33:20 52n8
34:7 88n117
34:21 61
35:2 52n8
35:16 71n70
37:12 71n70
37:14 52n8
37:21 61
37:32 61
38:1–2 52n8
38:2 52
38:3 6n20, 52n8
38:5 6n20
39:2–9 119n16
39:11–12 119n16
39:12 136n55
39:14 119n16
40:5 130n39
44:10 136n56
48:7 53n17
51:7 62
55:5 157:40
58:3 136:56
60:4 88n117
61:5 88n117
64:7 52
65:4 63
66:16 88n117
68:23 115n9
71:17 130n39
71:19 129
72:18 130n39
73:14 150n15
74:12–17 114
75:1 130n39
77:9 150n9
78:4 130n39
78:11 130n39
78:12 63n43
78:32 130n39
81:16 63n43
85:9 88n117
86:10 130n39
88 63n44
88:1 63n44
89:9–13 114
91:5–6 53

91:16 63, 128n30
94:5 53n14
94:12 125
96:3 130n39
98:1 130n39
102:2–12 119n16
102:6–7 95n138
103:11 88n117
103:13 88n117
103:15–17 119n16
103:17 88n117
104:16 63
104:26 115
105:2 130n39
105:5 130n39, 152
105:40 63n43
106:7 130n39
106:21–22 129
106:22 130n39
107:8 130n39
107:15 130n39
107:21 130n39
107:24 130n39
107:31 130n39
109:21–25 119n16
109:24 68
111:5 88n117
112:10 71n70
115:11 88n117
115:13 88n117
118:4 88n117
119:74 88n117
119:79 88n117
123:2 152
128:1 88n117
128:4 88n117
135:20 88n117
139:1–5 119n16
139:7–8 119
139:13–16 119n16
139:23–24 119n16
144:3 120
145:19 88n117
147:11 88n117

Proverbs 2n2
1:2 125n26
1:3 125n26
1:7 125n26
1:8 125n26
1:13 63n43
3:11–12 125, 125n26
4:1 125n26
4:13 125n26
4:22 139
5:12 125n26
5:23 125n26
6:15 139
6:23 125n26
7:22 125n26
8 115, 138
8:10 125n26
8:33 125n26
10:7 136n54
10:8–12 137
10:14 137
10:17 125n26
10:19 137
11:8 61
11:10 61
11:31 61
12:1 125n26
12:2 171
12:4 136n54
12:7 61
12:11 63n43
12:18 139
13:1 125n26
13:5 61
13:14 153
13:17 139
13:18 125n26
13:24 125n26
14:19 61
14:27 153
14:30 136n54, 139
15:4 139
15:5 125n26
15:10 125n26
15:32 125n26
15:33 125n26
16:22 125n26
16:24 139
18:21 170
18:29 170
19:20 125n26
19:23 130
19:27 125n26
20:14 63n43
21:18 61
22:12 130n41
22:15–20 125n26
23:12 125n26
23:13 125n26
23:23 125n26
23:29 63
24:12 121

24:32 125n26
25:16 63n43
25:26 61
26:5 137
26:27 69n64
27:1 139
27:7 130
28:19 63n43
30:15 170
30:17 92n129
30:22 63n43
Ecclesiastes
1:14 63n42
2:11 63n42
2:17 63n42
2:26 63n42
3:20 94
4:4 63n42
4:6 63n42
6:9 63n42
7:1 130n41
9:21 62
12:7 94
Isaiah
3:15 53n14
13:8 53n17
13:21–22 94
16:6 137n62
21:4 157:40
24:19 82n97
26:21 84n105
29:16 94
34:13b 94
38:12 53n15
38:20 54n19
38:21 17n38
40:20 136n54
41:25 94
45:9 94
50:9 136n55
51:1 92n129
51:8 136n55
52:14–15 157n38
53:4 150n15
58:11 128n30
60:14 135n53
60:21 121
64:8 94
Jeremiah 2n2
3:5 127n29
6:24 53n17
7:3 96, 103
11:15 171
12:5 67
13:26 134n48
17:14 52n9
18:4 94
18:6 94
18:8 173n11
18:10 173n11
20:8 86n109
20:14–18 118
21:6 2n5
22:23 53n17
23:29 82n98
26:3 173n11
26:13 173n11
26:19 173n11
31:12 128n30
32:19 136
48:30 137n62
50:20 81n95
50:43 53n17
Lamentations 2n2
1:1 81n95
2:3 52
2:11 82
2:12 92n126
2:16 71n70
3:1–20 70–71n68
3:12 52, 81, 82n98
3:13 82
3:15 63n44
3:21 70–71n68
3:22–24 70–71n68
3:25–30 70–71n68
3:30 63n44
3:31–39 70–71n68
3:34 54n20
4:7 62n40
4:8 152
4:21 11n30
Ezekiel
3:15 69n62
7:18 157:40
19:3 71n69
19:6 71n69
22:25 71n69
22:27 71n69
24:7–8 84n105
27:19 93n130
27:30 93n133, 173n12
30:12 69n62
30:14 69n62
43:7 135n53
Daniel 2:14 81n95

Hosea
4:10 63n43
5:12 136n55
5:14 71n69
5:24 136n54
13:14 2n5
Joel 2:19 63n43
Amos 1:11 11n30, 72
Obadiah
1:10–14 11n30
6 93n131
Jonah
4:3 7n22
4:8 7n22
Micah
4:9 53n17
5:8 71n69
6:14 63n43
7:16 157:39
Nahum
1:3 61n34
2:12 71n69
3:5 134n48
Habakkuk
1:2 86n109, 87
3:16 136n54
Zechariah 2n2
12:4 136
Malachi 4:3 135n53

NEW TESTAMENT

Matthew 9:1–9 124n24
Mark
2:1–12 124n24
2:22 136n54
Luke 5:17–26 124n24
John 9:2 6n20
1 Corinthians 124n24
James 5:11 54n21

APOCRYPHAL WRITINGS

Enoch 124n24
Jubilees 10 124n24
Sirach (Ben Sira)
14:9 136n54
38:15 124n24
42:13 136n55
Testament of Job 31n67
13:1–6 12
14:1–5 96
20:9 12
Tobit
2:7 16
2:7–10 15
2:13–14 15
3:6 7n22
2 Maccabees 3 124n24
4 Maccabees 9 124n24